What senior leaders have to say working with Dr Richard Ford

"I actively encouraged my senior managers to avail themselves of the support of a great executive coach like Richard Ford, if they really want to be a stand-out performer".

- Ian Paterson, President and CEO, Bayer Polymers

"I have known Richard for over 10 years. He has worked closely with my senior executives to enhance their leadership capability, assess their potential, identify their strengths and development areas. He has a creative and expert, out-of-the-box, approach which is refreshing".

- John Wrighthouse, Chief People and Communications Officer, First Utility

"Working with Richard was revealing in that I was forced to think deeply about the impression I wished to create. I recommend Richard to anyone who is willing to face reality".

- Sean Lance, Chairman and Chief Executive, Chiron Corporation

"Since the coaching with Richard, I have been promoted twice in three years. We were able to 'think out loud' and work through the alternatives".

- Joe Martin, Senior VP and General Manager, Bayer Diagnostics Division

"Richard's value to the business was his objective perspective and his ability question our attitudes so that it wasn't so much a case of 'this is the way it is' but 'how can it be different ?'"

- Alex Smith, Chairman, TK Maxx

"I would highly recommend Dr Richard Ford as an outstanding executive coach and business psychologist who has helped Nationwide develop over 30 senior executives in the last 3 years to increase the quality of leadership within the business".

- Helen Busby, Senior Manager,
Nationwide Building Society

"Richard has helped me to break barriers within a business hierarchy, and overcome difficult, personal issues which need to be tied into the business life. In short, Richard is an excellent coach, who has helped me a lot".

- Rainer Gebbe, CEO Germany, JP Morgan

"Richard has outstanding credentials that enable him to work with individuals on a broad range of issues. One of his great strengths is his ability to connect with the client in a pragmatic way that really helps them focus on the key business challenges they face which has resulted in significant bottom-line performance improvement".

- Jeff Jones, Head of Executive Development,
NatWest Group

"Richard's coaching made me focus on those areas of personal performance where I needed to be more proactive, and helped me be seen within the company as a 'big picture' player, shaping the agenda and driving change".

- Mike Higgins, Group Human Resource Director,
Bayer Group

"I invited Richard to work with myself and eleven other members of my team and we chose Richard because of his expertise and credibility coupled with a strong intellectual background. The process was challenging and it was not a comfortable experience for some but Richard proved to be a valuable catalyst for personal growth in several members of the team".

- Ian Jenkins, Managing Director, Credit Suisse

"I've known Richard professionally since 1986, and Richard has proven highly credible, having the experience and intellectual clout to challenge and stimulate senior players. Richard's impact was to help established managers generate more alternatives and options to the problems they faced, and consequently raise the quality of analysis and decision making which in turn led to greater collaboration, better business judgements and improved business performance".

- Brian Lewis, Group Human Resources Director, Premier Farnell Plc

"I've used other coaches before, but none has been as effective for me as Richard Ford. I have found Richard Ford's widespread experience with other executives to be of enormous value in enriching my understanding of how good leaders can maximise their personal impact every day!"

- Neil Patrick, Chief Operating Officer, Firstplus

This book is dedicated to my wife Ann with love and thanks for all her help and support, and to all those leaders and potential leaders who want to get even better.

HOW LEADERSHIP REPUTATIONS ARE WON AND LOST

How to Build a Successful Reputation and Create a Personal Brand to Fast-Track Career Success

Dr Richard G Ford

First published in 2020 by Libri Publishing

Copyright © Dr Richard G Ford

The right of Dr Richard G Ford to be identified as the author of this work has been asserted in accordance with the Copyright, Designs and Patents Act, 1988.

ISBN: 978-1-911450-62-7

All rights reserved. No part of this publication may be reproduced, stored in any retrieval system or transmitted in any form or by any means, electronic, mechanical, photocopying, recording or otherwise, without the prior written permission of the copyright holder for which application should be addressed in the first instance to the publishers. No liability shall be attached to the author, the copyright holder or the publishers for loss or damage of any nature suffered as a result of reliance on the reproduction of any of the contents of this publication or any errors or omissions in its contents.

A CIP catalogue record for this book is available from The British Library

Cover and book design by Carnegie Publishing

Libri Publishing
Brunel House
Volunteer Way
Faringdon
Oxfordshire
SN7 7YR

Tel: +44 (0)845 873 3837

www.libripublishing.co.uk

Contents

About the Author   x
Acknowledgements   xii
Foreword   xiii
Introduction   1

PART 1: Reputation – Rhetoric versus Reality   15
Chapter 1: What is Reputation?   16
  1.1: What is Reputation?   16
  1.2: Strangers to Ourselves   22
  1.3: Reputation and Self-delusion   26
  1.4: Memory and Self-deception   30
  1.5: Reputation and Unreliable Observations   33
  1.6: Reputation and the False-Confidence Phenomenon   34

Chapter 2: The Importance of Reputation   37
  2.1: The Importance of Reputation   37
  2.2: How our Behaviour Impacts our Reputation   40
  2.3: How our Reputation is Assessed and Evaluated   42
  2.4: The Career Paradox: How the Rules of the Game Change   43

Chapter 3: Reputation, Bias and Prejudice   46
  3.1: Reputation and Personal Bias   46
  3.2: Reputations and Potential Sources of Error   48
  3.3: Reputation and Memory Distortion   52
  3.4: Cognitive Dissonance and the Failure to Process Information Logically   53
  3.5: Attribution Errors in Describing Reputations   56
  3.6: Personal Construct Theory of Reputation   57
  3.7: Misunderstandings   59
  3.8: Judgement Errors that Distort Reputations   60
  3.9: Ten Common Cognitive Biases   61
  3.10: Subliminal Impact on Reputation – Eight Subliminal Conditioning Effects   64
  3.11: Distorted Perceptions and the Impact on Reputational Value   66

PART 2: How Reputations are Won and Lost — 71

Chapter 4: Reputation Perceived from Outside-in and Inside-out — 72
- 4.1: Outside-in and Inside-out Perspectives — 73
- 4.2: The Fundamental Five Outside-in Reputation Winners — 78
- 4.3: The Fundamental Four Inside-out Reputation Winners — 82

Chapter 5: The Fundamental Five Outside-in Reputation Winners — 85
- 5.1: How to Win a Reputation for Building Strong Cultures — 86
- 5.2: How to Win a Reputation for Strategic Thinking — 93
- 5.3: How to Win a Reputation for Delivery and Execution — 98
- 5.4: How to Win a Reputation for Outstanding Team Leadership — 105
- 5.5: How to Win a Reputation for Outstanding Organisational Influence — 112

Chapter 6: The Fundamental Four Inside-out Reputation Winners — 125
- 6.1: How to Win a Reputation for Self-Awareness — 126
- 6.2: How to Win a Reputation for Likeability — 139
- 6.3: How to Win a Reputation for Making Wise Judgements — 154
- 6.4: How to Win a Reputation for Perceptiveness — 162

Chapter 7: Reputation Leakage and the Fundamental Five Reputation Losers — 176
- 7.1: Reputation Derailers — 176
- 7.2: Reputation Leakage and Reputation Derailment — 178
- 7.3: The Three Reputation Leakage Behaviour Patterns — 179
- 7.4: The Fundamental Five Reputation Losers — 185
- 7.5: Reputation Loser 1 – Untrustworthiness — 185
- 7.6: Reputation Loser 2 – Narcissism — 189
- 7.7: Reputation Loser 3 – Myopia — 193
- 7.8: Reputation Loser 4 – Dogmatism — 195
- 7.9: Reputation Loser 5 – Emotional Detachment — 197

Chapter 8: Taking the First Steps to Manage One's Reputation — 203
- 8.1: Building a Stronger Reputation — 203
- 8.2: Cultivating Self-Awareness — 204

CONTENTS

PART 3: Building and Maintaining a Personal Brand   217
Chapter 9: Developing a Personal Brand   218
    9.1: Creating a Personal Brand   219
    9.2: The Value Proposition   222
    9.3: Planning to Manage your Personal Brand   223
    9.4: Eight Key Steps to Building a Personal Brand   224

Chapter 10: Managing Expectations   242
    10.1: The Importance of Managing Upwards   242
    10.2: The First 100 Days Plan   245
    10.3: Understanding What your Boss Thinks of You   250
    10.4: How to Improve the Relationship and Communication with your Boss   256
    10.5: Attitude Change towards your Boss   259
    10.6: How to Manage Different Boss Profiles   263
    10.7: Career Management Strategies   267

Chapter 11: Networks and Reputation   272
    11.1: The Importance of Investing in Relationships   272
    11.2: Key Principles of Building Successful Network Relationships   276
    11.3: Understanding Networking Rapport   278
    11.4: A Purposeful Networking Model – Who Should be Included?   279
    11.5: Networking Discussion Topics – So What do we Talk About?   280

Chapter 12: A Final Thought – Working with a Coach to Enhance Reputation and Personal Brand   284
    12.1: Working with a Coach for Marginal Gains   285
    12.2: Six Different Benefits of Working with a Coach   287
    12.3: The Five Key Ingredients of a Successful Coaching Engagement   289

Chapter Notes   292
Further Reading References   295
Appendix: Sixty Ways to Build Reputation Capital   297

About the Author

Dr Richard Ford is one of the pioneers of corporate psychology in the UK as he was a founding partner of the corporate psychology consultancy Psychological Consultancy Services Ltd (PCS) in 1983, when there were barely 10 private practices of corporate psychologists in the UK. For over 30 years, Richard has worked primarily at senior executive levels advising senior and potential leaders on a range of issues relating to how to get the best out of themselves and the people who work for them. As one of the UK's leading leadership coaching psychologists and senior executive assessment specialists, Richard has helped hundreds of senior leaders to develop successful careers. As a corporate psychologist working predominantly in the finance, investment banking and retail sectors, Richard has worked with several hundred senior executives based around the world in over 20 countries. Richard has also further broadened his experience in roles as a non-executive chairman of a manufacturing company and as a non-executive director in medical, recruitment and training consultancies.

By way of background in helping to understand the ideas shared in this book, Richard has had a particular interest for the last 30 years in the concept of reputation. In particular, Richard has been fascinated by how reputations are won and lost, and with identifying which specific behaviours are most significant in enhancing or diminishing a person's reputation. In addition, Richard has researched into how personal brands can constructively be developed with authenticity and integrity to shape future career directions.

As further personal detail, Richard graduated with an MA Honours degree in Psychology from the University of Edinburgh, an MSc in Applied Psychology and a PhD in Occupational Psychology from the University of Wales. Richard is also a Chartered Occupational Psychologist, an Associate Fellow of the

ABOUT THE AUTHOR

British Psychological Society, a Principal Member of the Association of Business Psychologists, Member of the Association for Coaching, and a Member of the International Society for Coaching Psychology. Richard can be contacted at richard.ford@psych-pcs.co.uk.

Acknowledgements

In essence, this book is the product of working with many hundreds of clients who have engaged me as a leadership coach in an exploration of their leadership challenges and opportunities, so the biggest thanks must go to those many talented clients who have shared their experiences and insights about leadership.

I also wish to give my heartfelt thanks to my friend and professional colleague, Malcolm Hatfield, who has spent many hours reviewing the book and offering great wisdom and insights on how it should be structured, and who displayed such thoughtfulness in his care and interest in the messages that the book is designed to share. I don't know anyone else who would have been prepared to invest the time and who has the capability to review the book in such a thoughtful, informed and value-added way.

And finally my love and gratitude to my wife, Ann, who has provided me with great support and understanding, and tolerated with patience, kindness and understanding the many hours spent at my study desk wedded to my keyboard.

Foreword

Malcolm Hatfield

Consultant Business Psychologist
Former Senior Partner,
Hatfield Jefferies Occupational Psychologists

One of the main statements made early on in this book is "Reputation is what people say about you when you are not in the room *and no other tangible or intangible asset is worth as much as your reputation or will have such a positive or detrimental impact on your career.*" This made such an immediate impact that I immediately noted, "You're so right and no-one else has dared to say this quite so clearly before!" As someone who, like Richard, has spent most of my working life helping organisations make the most of their people and helping the people make the most of themselves, this was the first of so much of this book that resonated with my experience and, crucially, seemed not to have been written before. What is more, it is all fully backed up and given a clear psychological explanation by a well-respected professional.

So how do you, the prospective reader, react to this? If the statement reflects the reality of your experience then you should gain a lot from this book. If you don't agree with the statement then it is almost certain that you really should read this book, as you are likely to be heading for disappointment: the book contains a reality you ignore at your peril!

Richard's book makes us think about what he calls the "leadership paradox" in that, when we are asked how we are doing at work, we are inclined to talk about what we have done and what we have achieved. After all, it's all about results, isn't it? However, next door, someone talking to our boss or our colleagues about how we are doing at work will immediately switch from hard outcomes and use adjectives to describe ***how*** we behave and **how** we think and **how** we have got things done. As Richard says, our real legacy is the memories we leave about how we have behaved towards others, how we are as a person, how we think about issues and how we follow a personal code of values.

So what we have achieved becomes history very rapidly. Maybe only at weddings and funerals do others try to get a glimpse of the real essence of a person and consider their reputation. Otherwise, for most of our lives we are in the dark, not really knowing what people say about us when we are not in the room. Most definitely there is a secret vocabulary used at work and many of the phrases used to describe someone's reputation will not appear in the traditional performance-review documentation. In effect, what you have achieved is *necessary* to be successful but that is assumed; after all, if you have not achieved results you will know all about it! But it most assuredly is not *sufficient*, so you had better work out what else you have to do in order to build your reputation.

If you think this is simply a prescription for flannelling your way up the career ladder, what is inside this book will soon dispel that view. You may also feel that if your organisation does not look at you objectively, or follow their published formal procedures strictly, then this is the worse for them and maybe you should look elsewhere. But this would be a mistake on your part. This book shows the underlying reality of the psychological reasons why reputation is so crucial in all organisational settings, and indeed why you are part of this process too.

This is not a book that presents a quick-fix formula for success. Despite what some may hope and despite the many claims, theories and beliefs about the inherent qualities of so-called leadership, there is no magic bullet to be found. To do well requires both understanding and effort on your part. So Richard does not present a new theory or plan derived from his extensive experience – he presents descriptions of how reputations are created and possibly lost, then shows how you can work via this understanding to improve. It is not necessarily easy, but there are numerous options that you can take. Furthermore, the reader can

FOREWORD

rely on the fact that what is written here is derived from a very rare blend of huge experience and sound, empirically based psychological research.

Amongst the number of things making this book special is that Richard Ford is a lifelong practitioner. He is not an academic riding along the wave of a new idea or piece of research; he is always grounded in the reality of working with and for his client. What comes across is that he is erudite about his subject, wise and someone worth listening to. He has a great deal of information to share that will be of immense value to everyone whether they are an inexperienced junior manager or a long-in-the-tooth senior executive.

In this book Richard chooses not to use case studies. I see this as a reflection of his client-focused approach: case studies may make a colourful point but they suffer from a real psychological weakness in that it is easy for the individual to sidestep their implications. "Interesting, sad for them but my boss isn't really like that" or "well my situation/company is different". This is correct: your situation is unique to you and in this book you can learn how to make your own individual best way forward, not on the basis of some generalised principle.

From all this it might appear that the book is only for those involved in or embarking on an organisational career. However, it is also a book for the budding psychologist or HR practitioner as, despite everything that you will have learned, inside this book is the reality you will face and information on how you can develop genuine client focus.

The book has been designed to be used in different ways, which Richard describes early on. It has a clear structure in that in Part 1 you can learn and think more deeply about the psychological theories and insights that explain how reputations are formed. In Part 2, Richard outlines his proposition on what are the fundamental five factors that others need to see as outside evidence if you are to develop a good reputation. Then he outlines the fundamental four factors or characteristics that need to be part of your behaviour if you are going to develop a good reputation. Finally, Richard outlines the fundamental five factors that will lead to the *loss* of a good reputation. In Part 2 there is extensive advice and tips on what these qualities look like and how you can develop a higher level of ability in these areas. In Part 3, you are taken through the process of building a narrative about yourself to 'sell your future' by way of shaping your personal brand. There is also much useful information about how to manage your boss and how to work your network in a way that has integrity and authenticity.

Dr Richard Ford is one of the UK's leading leadership coaching and assessment psychologists. He has helped hundreds of senior leaders and potential leaders to develop successful careers. Here, he shares 35 years of learning about what really happens to help you achieve career success. So much of this book reflects my own experiences in the same field of work. I can guarantee that you will learn something new about yourself and how your organisation really makes people decisions, so that you can then develop new skills to make your career more successful and more satisfying.

Introduction

Why the Book was Written

The motivation for this book emerged from the promptings of my clients as so many of my client conversations have touched on a person's reputation in terms of how they impact on others and what others say about them. As a consequence, many clients have asked for further reading references in which they can find out more about the concept of reputation, but unfortunately I have had to tell them that there is little written on the subject of personal reputation – and thus the idea of this book was born. Therefore, my purpose for writing this book is to share what I have learned to offer some support for those who may benefit from some help to manage their existing reputation, and to create and market their future-oriented personal brand with integrity and authenticity.

I have been interested in the ideas around the concept of reputation since I started working as a corporate psychologist, and many of the ideas in this book have taken shape over the last 30 years. This book is an attempt to scale up my work with my individual clients, and make many interesting concepts and strategies accessible to a wider audience. Many of my clients have also unwittingly contributed to this book as they have offered many great insights into how reputations are formed and how reputations can be managed, changed, maintained and damaged.

What the Book is About

This book has been a long time in the writing because it has taken a long time to establish what I really think about reputation and what I want to say about it. My challenge has been to bring together a number of different principles and concepts which are both simple and complex in a way that helps to make better sense of what reputation is, how it is formed, and the consequences in terms of reputational gain and reputational damage. In addition, I also wanted to focus on what we can do to create our own future-oriented personal brand to help guide the impressions formed about us in a way that is proactive, influential, authentic and appropriate.

The book offers insights on almost everything you need to know to progress your career and build your reputation and career legacy. And in order to provide some early signposting on what to expect in the book, the key arguments and threads of the book are as follows:

1. Reputation is what other people think of us and the widespread beliefs that other people may have about our characteristics based on what we say and what we do.
2. Our reputation cannot be understood as 'factual' in any straightforward sense as our reputation is a set of perceptions, beliefs and memories that exist in other people's minds, so a single event can be perceived and described in many different ways and, consequently, there can be several different perceptions about a person's reputation.
3. In essence, there is a reputation paradox in that, contrary to what most people think, our reputation and career success is based not on **what** we have done or achieved but **how** we have behaved and the way that we have done it, and this is a crucial principle in understanding how our reputation and career legacy is shaped. What we have done becomes history very quickly but how we behaved remains in the memory of others, and this is what leaves an enduring impression and constitutes our personal legacy.
4. Of course, you already have a reputation, both positive and negative, and your reputation is based on how you are perceived to behave, and what you actually 'achieve' only confirms whether your reputation is deserved or not.
5. To make reputation management more complicated, many of your managers at work have a hidden secret agenda in terms of not sharing what they really believe

INTRODUCTION

about you and your reputation in order not to risk demotivating you.

6. Therefore, an understanding of our own reputation is elusive as we tend not to have access to good-quality feedback data on how we are perceived, and we tend not to see ourselves as others see us as our capacity for self-assessment and self-understanding of our reputation is generally poor.
7. Our challenge is to get better at understanding how our reputation has evolved in order to provide ourselves with more opportunities to influence the process.
8. Our understanding of how people cognitively construct their world is fundamental to our understanding of how another person's reputation is formed. We all process information differently, we all have cognitive biases that help us to filter information, and these filters are used to take shortcuts to form a view about someone else's reputation.
9. This book describes how reputations are formed from an outside-in perspective based on the observable outcomes and impact of one's behaviour, and an inside-out perspective based on intention and personal characteristics.
10. The behaviours that lead to short-term reputation loss and the behaviours that lead to long-term reputation damage, which may in turn lead to long-term career derailment, are also discussed.
11. Part 1 of the book starts by looking backwards at how our current reputation has been formed and how perceptual biases and filters can both enhance and distort our reputation. Part 2 looks at the key behaviours for winning an outstanding reputation and looks at the key behaviours that can lose you your reputation in the short-term and in the long-term. In addition, many practical suggestions and tips are offered on how you can develop your reputation in the key areas discussed. Finally, Part 3 of the book looks forward to how you can

create a personal brand narrative to influence your future in a way that is authentic and appropriate, and presents many practical tools and strategies to facilitate this process.

The Leadership Reputation Paradox – Why Getting a Good Result is not as Relevant as How You Did It

There is a paradox in the way that reputations are formed. It is not so much what you have done but the way in which you did it that is crucial for your reputation. For example, in the course of my work it has often struck me that when you ask an individual about their performance at work, they will typically describe what they have done, and usually refer to tangible task achievements, outcomes and results. However, when you ask bosses, colleagues or senior executives about an individual's performance at work, they use a different language and vocabulary: they speak with more passion and emotion, and they refer to the person by using about five or six adjectives or soundbites to describe **how** the person has behaved, what they are like as a person and how they achieved certain results.

So it seems that there are two parallel career currencies in play – one language used by the individual about themselves to describe their performance, and another language, which is often hidden or undisclosed, which is used by colleagues and bosses to describe that individual's performance. Management is concerned about how you are likely to perform in the future, much less about what you have achieved to date. What has taken place here is that the boss, senior manager or colleague has analysed, often implicitly, what has been achieved or not achieved, and they have formed conclusions about what behaviours, skills and personal characteristics have led to these positive or negative outcomes. In the natural course of events, 'what' has been achieved becomes history very quickly but 'how' it was achieved is more important and more likely to be the lasting legacy that will shape and influence a person's reputation and future career direction. In other words, our legacy is not what has happened on the pitch or field of play; our reputational legacy is the memories we leave behind, and how we are remembered according to how we have behaved in order to achieve certain successes.

What You Have Achieved Only Confirms Whether or not Your Reputation is Deserved

To use a golfing metaphor, the golf swing (the how) is a better predictor of golf proficiency than the outcome (the what) of a few good golf shots. And so it is with leadership that if someone appears to behave in the right way and they build a good reputation then we have more confidence that they will be able to deliver effectively in the future in a bigger or different job. How people communicate, how they think, how they behave, how their attitudes and values are expressed, and how their personality impacts on their relationships with others are more important than the technical, knowledge and functional assets that an individual brings to the organisation. This is not to say that outcomes and results are not important but they will be forgotten, or taken as a given, in a few months, and the only legacy will be a perception that the individual knew how to act, think, behave and relate to others to get the job done. It is often the apparently well-qualified and experienced candidate who is rejected in favour of someone less qualified who seems to portray the 'right kind of behaviours' (the 'how') – although the rejected candidate often fails to see why.

Hidden Agenda

We also do not have access to our reputation in the feedback provided by management as part of annual performance review meetings. Management often has a hidden agenda concerning what they believe about you that is not often shared because of the risk of demotivating you, and as a consequence, many individuals have a limited understanding and appreciation of their reputation in the workplace. There is a high amount of miscommunication between senior managers and individual direct reports because the organisation wants to maintain morale, keep individuals happy, contented and focused on the job without telling them how they are valued or if they have limited prospects to develop or progress their career. As a consequence, individuals are told that they are 'doing fine' or 'doing great' but there is typically a dishonesty here, in that they are not told how well they might be doing in relation to their aspirations to be promoted, to do some different role or to earn more money!

Of course, many bosses like to say in public that it is only the results that matter; whereas in reality there is a shelf-life to any results or tasks achieved or any success in a role, and your personal or career legacy is more about how you behave in executing a particular job as the job achievements will become history in the space of a few months.

For many people, reputations are the secret language of organisational life – the unspoken elephant in the room – that can make or break careers. There is an entire hidden language of phrases and descriptions that are commonly used to describe us that rarely appear in performance review documentation. I have identified over 60 terms (see Appendix) frequently used to describe an individual's performance that rarely, if ever, appear in performance review documentation, and which can destroy or plateau a career despite rarely being shared with the individual concerned. Consequently, many senior executives are unaware of their reputation and so tend to do nothing to change these perceptions.

Our Challenge is to Get Better at Understanding Our Reputation

Everyone, of course, already has a reputation with both positive and negative elements. Our colleagues already have a view about what is helpful or unhelpful about our behaviour at work, and the higher we go in an organisation, the more myths and stories develop. The situation is also more complicated because each of us will have different reputations with different stakeholder groups with whom we interact. Our senior managers, our colleagues and peers, and our direct reports all have different needs and expectations, and each group will value different attributes to a greater or lesser extent.

Our task is thus to get better at understanding how our reputation has evolved, which will give us some possibility of influencing the process. It also follows that in order to be in more control of managing and shaping our career, we need to get better at understanding how our reputation has evolved and the impact it has had on our career, and so we need regular access to a good quality database on how we are perceived.

Our Capacity for Accurate Self-Assessment is Generally Poor

Research suggests that we are generally poor at assessing our own reputations. There is a very low correlation between how we see ourselves and how others see us. The correlation between people's ratings of their own personal attributes and the ratings of these by other people tends to be rather low (although the extent of the correlation can depend on the personality trait in question).

It is almost always the case that most individuals have limited self-awareness and understanding of their blindspots. Most individuals, as a consequence, have a limited understanding of their reputation and are very poor at understanding how they compare to others or what others might expect from them in their current role. This book should help you address these crucial issues.

So What Soundbites Are Used about You When You're not in the Room?

It only takes a few adjectives or soundbites to describe a person's reputation. Are you thought of as bright, strategic or creative? Or are you thought of as uninspiring, boring or stubborn? Are you trusted and easy to work with? Are you likeable? How good are you at building relationships? Are you self-serving or do you put the interests of others first? Are you humble or overly keen to promote and talk about yourself? How well do you use questions to reach out and engage with others? How well do you ask questions to convey interest and find out what other people think and feel? Do you show sufficient interest in others? How much confidence do colleagues have in your judgements? To what extent do colleagues seek you out to include you in discussions so as to capture your opinions and perspectives? To what extent are you able to see different points of view? Are you adaptable or set in your ways and reluctant to change? To what extent are you a black-and-white thinker who tends to polarise issues? Are you more dogmatic than consensual? Are you more ego-driven or collaborative? How well do you let other people know that you can see other points of view?

So given that we all have a reputation inside our employing organisation, what five or six adjectives would colleagues use about you? However, whatever list of adjectives you consider, you will almost certainly have over-estimated your personal worth or value, as research shows that when it comes down to an assessment of our personal attributes, we do have a tendency to be immodest and unrealistic.

So What do we Mean by 'Leadership' and How is it Different from Management?

This book focuses on leadership reputation and much of the writing in the field of leadership research makes a distinction between leadership and management as different types or forms of exercising authority. Leadership is typically seen as shaping a strategic vision and perspective, focusing on innovation and change, working towards multiple goals and objectives within a longer time frame, examining uncertain complex problems in new ways, managing ambiguous and conflicting events, and being able to attract supporters or followers by virtue of an ability to connect, inspire and galvanise action towards some shared purpose.

Managers, on the other hand, and at the risk of over-simplification, are more typically required to execute agreed methodologies and operating processes in known and predictable environments, implement tried-and-tested solutions to previously experienced problems, manage teams to implement some common purpose, systematically monitor and analyse performance, and address underperformance issues in a timely manner.

Early theories and research suggest that leaders do have special qualities and traits that distinguish them from non-leaders. However, there is still a lack of consensus as to what leadership means and what leadership involves. Leadership is always directly linked to the exercise of power, and some leaders rely on positional power whilst some are defined by what has been achieved by their team and their organisation; and some researchers focus on the process by which leaders get things done through their ability to influence, mobilise and channel the energies of the team.

Leadership Effectiveness as a Relational Process

However, it does seem generally agreed that leadership is a relational process concerning the way in which two or more people are connected and that without followers a person cannot be seen as a leader, no matter how many individual qualities they possess. Leadership is a function that helps people to perform better to increase their output or impact, and all leaders must understand the dynamic relationship between different stakeholders to be successful. However, there are still some highly valued competencies and skills that will enable a leader to optimise their relationships with different groups, and these qualities will be discussed in this book under the section about how reputations are formed.

In this book, I am choosing to refer to leadership in the broadest sense, in that leaders may or may not hold formal positions of authority. There is a leader in every group and when people are deprived of leaders, they tend to look for someone to provide guidance, direction and decision making. The need and opportunity for leadership applies to nearly every group situation in which decisions need to be made. All of us belong to groups of various kinds, from the family to the workplace to sporting clubs, and so maintaining some kind of organisation requires leadership. In all these work and non-work contexts, the assumed leader will make a decision and try to get others to go along with them.

Leadership as a Dynamic Process

When we talk about leadership effectiveness, it is obviously a relative and dynamic concept, and it is assumed that no individuals will fully possess the whole range and spectrum of leadership skills. Leadership competencies are also not a particularly useful guide for understanding leadership reputation as they only indicate gaps between current and desired levels of performance. However, they do not describe what behaviours are necessary to indicate leadership potential and the potential to make the journey to the higher echelons of leadership. There is a very big difference between current leadership competency assessments and genuine high-potential leadership indicators.

There are clearly basic attributes that must be a given for senior roles and there are clearly negative attributes that would eliminate people from contending for senior roles, but the challenge of this book is to identify the relatively few key talent differentiators that ensure that someone will stand out and build a reputation as an outstanding leader.

Leadership effectiveness is also a continuum. Although most people recognise that the requirements for effective leadership change as you move up levels from middle management to senior leadership roles, it is interesting that leadership is often viewed as more or less the same thing at all levels in the organisation. There seems to be little acknowledgement that different levels of leadership exist or that people need to grow, change and make transitions as they progress to different levels.

However, individuals who want to improve their leadership capability often do not know which behaviours or attitudes they need to target, and the process is made more challenging and complicated because the secret of future leadership success may involve giving up behaviours that have enabled them to be successful in the past. The idea of a performance ladder or continuum may help to better understand the notion of a leadership performance continuum, the layers of expectation at different levels of leadership, and what behavioural changes are required to move from a 5/10 to an 8/10 in terms of leadership effectiveness.

The Difference between Reputation and Personal Brand

In this book, there is reference to the concepts of both reputation and personal brand. There is frequent confusion about whether reputation and personal brand are the same thing but, although they are closely linked, they are not synonyms. To put it simply, reputation is past-oriented and retrospective in that it is the sum total of your track record, based on the consequences of your behaviour, whereas a personal brand is a future-oriented statement of what a person can offer an employer or organisation. So while a person's reputation is the accumulation of their actions and behaviours to date, a person builds a personal brand to define their leadership identity and to describe what they stand for as a leader, and what they can offer in any future role. So in this book, in parts 1 and 2, there is an exploration of how reputations are formed, evaluated and damaged, and then in Part 3, there is an exploration of how a personal brand can be developed and promoted with authenticity and integrity.

The challenge for the CV author or the creator of a personal brand profile is to do the analysis of the 'how' – to explain how successes have been achieved – as it is the substance of this analysis that is most valuable when selling oneself to a potential employer or to a senior manager for a more senior role. As so few people are skilled and competent to do this type of analysis, a demonstration of the ability to do this already differentiates this type of person from other candidates as someone with more self-insight and self-awareness about what they can bring to the organisation. Another key step is to understand and embrace the different behavioural requirements for more senior roles, and what behaviours are needed to make the transition from one leadership level to the next.

Who Do I Want to Read this Book?

I have written this book to provide a resource and support for my typical clients, as well as professionals interested in supporting and developing the performance of senior managers and leaders in their organisation. My typical clients have been chief executives, director board members, senior executives, investment bankers or senior partners in professional firms, and my aim is to help them better manage their career and to help them to become even more effective in their current role. The book will hopefully give readers a better understanding of how reputations are formed and the critical importance of reputations in shaping and determining their career trajectory.

My hope is that this book will also have a broad appeal and will be of interest to management consultants, executive coaches, occupational, business and corporate psychologists, HR directors and HR managers; hopefully, some of the issues raised and discussed may help them advise, coach and mentor the leaders and senior executive decision-makers in their organisation. A concept that has particular resonance in the world of sport is the 'aggregation of marginal gains' and hopefully this book will introduce some ideas to help with that journey of achieving marginal gains in building a stronger and more influential personal reputation. The book will also explore the notion of 'marginal losses' and how short-term reputational leakage and longer-term reputation derailment can occur.

The Style of the Book

In terms of my writing style, I have attempted to create an informal read without dumbing down or over-simplification. I have used many sub-headings as I want to signpost the reader to enable them to cover the text quickly and to assist readers with limited time who want to scan the book for certain information.

As a matter of choice, I have also tended to avoid the use of case studies. I have a dislike of books that just fill pages with case studies and examples as I always skip those bits, which are often used as padding, because I want to focus on the central ideas, concepts, insights or arguments being put forward, and examples do not always aid this purpose. Case studies can often lose the essence of the idea by throwing too much verbiage at the reader.

Finally, I hope that I succeed in convincing you that the arguments and discussions in the book are real, in the sense that the book describes what organisations are really like, how people have become successful in the real world and how you can take greater control to make the most of your potential.

The Structure of the Book

The book is divided into three main parts:

Part 1 aims to help the reader to better understand the concept of reputation, how we don't see ourselves as others see us, how our behaviour impacts on our reputation and what drives the perception of colleagues to describe our reputation. This part will also explore the cognitive biases that influence how we are perceived and other psychological factors that shape the way that we view and interpret events and so form conclusions about another person's reputation. Part 1 is thus focused on reviewing some of the theoretical background to understanding how reputations are formed and the principles and concepts that influence the way that we form judgements about people and their reputations.

Part 2 aims to help readers assess and understand their existing reputation, to better understand the types of behaviour which can lead to a successful reputation, and what causes short-term reputational leakage and longer-term reputational damage. The author differentiates between how reputations are formed from an outside-in perspective based on the observable outcomes and impact of one's behaviour, and an inside-out perspective based on intention and personal characteristics. The author proposes the Fundamental Five Outside-in Reputation Winners and the Fundamental Four Inside-out Reputation Winners.

The section also discusses the behaviours that lead to

reputational leakage which is usually short-term and recoverable, and the Fundamental Five Reputation Losers that lead to reputational derailment, which is longer term and may lead to career-threatening consequences. Part 2 also provides many detailed practical tips and suggestions on how to further develop those relatively rare qualities that make a significant difference to the way one's reputation develops.

Part 3 is about turning these insights about reputation into practical help on how to build a personal brand with integrity and authenticity. The personal brand is described as a future-oriented proactive strategy and ideas and suggestions are offered on how to construct a narrative about what a person stands for and what a person can offer an employer or organisation in any future leadership role. Part 3 offers many practical tips, ideas and suggestions in order to help the reader gain specific and personal insights about themselves to develop their own self-understanding and personal career strategy.

How Can This Book be Used?

There are several strategies on how to use the book. The book starts with a theoretical discussion of the psychological principles of how perceptions and judgements on our reputation are formed. However, if you do not want to spend time understanding the underlying theoretical concepts in Part 1, you could look first at Part 2. This part focuses on the key behaviours that will enhance or dilute your reputation and offers practical tips, suggestions and insights which should help you better understand and develop your reputation. Alternatively, you could jump straight to Part 3 for direct advice on how to create an authentic personal brand narrative and how to start to improve your career potential – and then build on this by looking in more depth elsewhere in the book as you choose.

Finally, I also recognise that this is a form of self-help book. Hopefully, it will help to increase the reader's level of self-awareness in forming a better understanding of how their career has developed to date, and help them to gain greater insights into the possibilities for further 'marginal gains'.

PART 1

**REPUTATION –
RHETORIC VERSUS REALITY**

Chapter 1

What is Reputation?

> Reality is what we take to be true.
> What we take to be true is what we believe.
> What we believe is based on perceptions.
> What we perceive depends upon what we look for.
> What we look for depends upon what we think.
> What we think depends upon what we perceive.
> What we perceive determines what we believe.
> What we believe determines what we take to be true.
> What we take to be true is our reality.
>
> Gary Zukav [1]

Chapter 1 Key Points

- What is reputation?
- Strangers to ourselves
- Reputation and self-delusion
- Memory and self-deception
- Reputation and unreliable observations
- Reputation and the false-confidence phenomenon

1.1: What is Reputation?

Reputation can be difficult to describe and difficult to measure and quantify, so when people use the word 'reputation', what exactly do they mean? Reputation is certainly not just rhetoric designed to persuade the opinion of others without substance or meaning. Reputation is real in that it is what other people think of us, so our reputation is based on other people's perceptions and is the result of how we are seen or 'judged' by others based on the consequences of our behaviour.

CHAPTER 1: WHAT IS REPUTATION?

Reputation is really created by two things: what you say and what you do

At its simplest, reputation is really created by two things: what you say and what you do. However, a reputation is a set of perceptions, beliefs and memories that exist in other people's minds, so a single event can be perceived and described in many different ways, and consequently, there can be several different perceptions of a person's reputation. Objective reality can become clouded as different individual perceptions may provide a different insight on what a person is really like. Unfortunately, what you actually do and what other people think of you are not always closely related.

The importance of how we say it and how we do it

Although reputation is created by what we say and do, it is not only what we say that is important but how we say it or how we do it. Furthermore, reputation also reflects a set of memories, behavioural observations, judgements and opinions that sit in the consciousness of many different stakeholders at any point in time. Of course, we all have a reputation. Colleagues already have a view on what is helpful or unhelpful about our behaviour at work. Reputation will also be a function of the extent to which a person meets the expectations of different stakeholders, and the extent to which a person's actions are seen to enhance the objectives and purpose of a particular role. Your reputation will thus be based on other people's beliefs about your value to the organisation, and other people's perception of your credibility as a successful performer in your field.

When some people think about what it takes to build a successful reputation, they quickly focus on measurable tangible results or what are often referred to as 'hard' results. For example, the so-called hard results may include financial revenue or numbers, profits, production figures, sales figures or the successful completion of a functional task or objective; or they may involve customer or client feedback or the achievement of some regulatory changes and so on. However, when people talk about you, whilst they may make reference to these measurable results, they will comment on them in a relatively brief, detached, perfunctory and matter-of-fact manner. They will not speak about these results with any degree of passion, feeling or emotion but these same colleagues will use a certain amount of feeling or emotion when they talk about the kind of person you are, about the kind of values you display, and the way that you treat others or the way that you seem to interact with other members of the team, the decisions you make, and how you contribute to the climate, culture and morale at work.

Different groups use different criteria to evaluate someone's reputation

A person's reputation comprises three basic elements: their actual personal attributes, how these attributes are perceived by others and the value that others place on these attributes. However, different groups use different characteristics or criteria to evaluate someone's reputation. For example, senior managers may place more emphasis on cerebral content, perceived intelligence, interpersonal sophistication, tackling team and individual underperformance, and accelerating the pace for the delivery of agreed plans. Peers or colleagues at a similar level, on the other hand, may place more emphasis on team-working, relationship skills, open-mindedness, adaptability, cooperation, collaboration and helpfulness. Finally, direct reports or junior colleagues may place more emphasis on supportiveness, mentoring, communication, tolerance, encouragement, recognition, compassion and a caring attitude. In addition, language is fluid and ambiguous in that words can mean different things to different people and so all of the above attributes may be interpreted differently by different people. Having a 'caring attitude' will mean different things to different people and 'conscientiousness', for example, has over 20 synonyms in the thesaurus.

CHAPTER 1: WHAT IS REPUTATION?

Career legacy is more about how we did something than what we achieved

The key premise of this book is that our career legacy is more about **how** we did something rather than **what** we did or what we achieved. This is difficult for many to grasp because our employers and bosses condition us to believe that all that matters is **what** we achieved. However, our successful achievements have a limited shelf-life so it is the language used by colleagues to describe **how** we achieved something that is more significant in defining our career legacy. This hidden agenda, of course, is rarely shared with us because our employing organisation wants to minimise unrest and to keep individuals relatively happy, content and motivated in their current role. As a consequence, people get flattered that they are doing a 'good job' when in reality, compared to colleagues or to the level expected if they aspire to a promotion or more senior role, this may be far from the case.

Reputation is based on many different perceptions

Reputation is an intangible asset in that it blends rational and irrational data, as it reflects a set of memories, perceptions and opinions that sit in the minds of many different stakeholders. Everything we do contributes to or detracts from our reputation. However, a reputation is clearly not based on fact but often on fleeting snapshots of our observed style, behaviours, attitudes and values.

Reputation is a combination of the impact of a wide variety of behaviours that people observe either consciously or unconsciously, and if you ask 10 people to describe a person's reputation, you may get 10 different answers depending on the particular aspects of a person's behaviour which are most relevant, and most important in the eyes of the perceiver. Some observers will talk about the person's intellect or their judgement, or their people or relationship skills, their friendliness and interest in others, their sense of humour, their attention to detail and many other negative characteristics that may annoy or irritate. And all the observers will be right in that a person's reputation is whatever others observe it to be.

A single behavioural act can be described in many different ways

Reputation is thus an elusive reality in that a single fact can be perceived and described in as many ways as the number of observers. As a result, more than one reality exists in that there may be an infinite number of perceptions and realities about each person, and in turn, we all may have different reputations with different people. Objective reality can disappear behind these individual perceptions and this awareness is extremely important for those who manage teams or organisations.

Many people believe that they will get promoted because of their year-round performance or because they adopt a model of work that is 'work hard and keep your head down', and they may be confused and perplexed when they are overlooked and managers may tell them that they lack that 'extra something' required to give them an 'edge' to help them stand out from others. Also senior managers are frequently very reluctant to directly share their views on someone's performance. They may often be well-intentioned in seeking to keep the individual motivated and their morale high rather than share the harsh reality of their observed assessments and evaluation.

Reputation may differ in different settings

Some people will have a strong reputation in one setting, but not necessarily in another different setting. Some particular individual who may have developed excellent presentation skills may come across as a charismatic speaker, but they may come across as overly ego-driven and self-referenced when talking to individuals on a one-to-one basis. Some individuals who are described as 'charismatic' may simply display those qualities to people who matter to them, whilst showing a lack of interpersonal interest and concern to those on the periphery of their social or work circle.

CHAPTER 1: WHAT IS REPUTATION?

Reputation may be directly proportional to the extent to which others feel good after each interaction with that person

It is extremely important to understand why individuals have a strong reputation with some people and not with others. Self-interest tends to shape most of what we do and tends to shape the perceptions that we have of other people. Those who have a strong positive reputation with a particular person or group are probably appealing in some way to the expectations and needs of that particular person or group upon whom they have an impact. The extent to which a person is perceived as having a positive reputation with certain people may be directly proportional to the extent to which these people feel good or better after each interaction with that person. This is a key principle and it is important to reflect on whether this critical idea shapes the perception of someone's reputation and the impact they have on others.

A person's reputation may bear only a passing resemblance to what that person has actually done

The way that language is used takes your reputation out of your hands. It makes your reputation not what you do but what other people say about you, usually behind your back. Faced with the power of language to warp reputation, many wise people assess the difference between how the world perceives us and how we truly are. As Abraham Lincoln said "character is like a tree and reputation is like a shadow and the shadow is what we think of it, the tree is the real thing". The real thing unfortunately is often inaccessible and your reputation may bear only a passing resemblance to what you have actually done, because you do not own your reputation or have not developed the skills to access good-quality data on how you are perceived.

1.2: Strangers to Ourselves

Research suggests that we are generally poor at understanding our own reputation because we are generally poor in evaluating our behavioural attributes. Access to our reputation is elusive because accurate self-knowledge of our behavioural attributes is not easily attained. An American journalist, Sidney Harris [2], in the mid-twentieth century proclaimed that: "90% of the world's woe comes from people not knowing themselves, their abilities, their frailties, and even their real virtues. Most of us go almost all the way through life as complete strangers to ourselves". Although an extreme view, this assessment lies closer to the picture portrayed by psychological research. Self-perceptions of competence and character are heavily loaded with bias, misconceptions and illusion, and such self-perceptions often have only a modest relationship with reality.

Immodest and unrealistic views of ourselves

Psychological research (Wilson [3]) suggests that we have immodest and unrealistic views of ourselves when it comes to describing and evaluating our personal behavioural attributes. On average, people think of themselves as anything but average when it comes to describing their personal characteristics. Many surveys have shown that the majority of people tend to believe that they perform better than their contemporaries when it comes to assessing key important and valued personal attributes. Ironically, most people also claim to be better than most other people at producing unbiased and realistic self-assessments. People also tend to think that they are more popular, more talented and more intelligent than the average person, which is usually inaccurate.

In the world of work, it is perhaps possible that people do not really aspire or want to be accurate in their views of themselves in that they might prefer favourable self-promoting self-perceptions, and some people may be willing to deceive themselves by moulding, ignoring or adjusting any feedback about themselves until it conforms to their self-image as a capable, competent and likeable person. In a reputational context, of course, people do not necessarily have all the information to reach accurate conclusions about themselves. Poor performers, for example, are often not aware of how badly they perform because they lack insight into their own incompetence. They may lack awareness to recognise their skill deficiencies and they may lack the knowledge to know 'what good looks like' in a given situation. In many cases, the individual is not wilfully deluding themselves but they are just not in a position to know how far their self-assessment is from reality. In some situations, therefore, some people misjudge their reputation not because of a lack of honesty with themselves but rather because of a lack of the essential cognitive tools to provide correct judgements about themselves. The evidence unfortunately suggests that self-insight into one's reputation is a skill that people believe that they possess to a far greater degree than they actually do.

Limited agreement between our self-assessments and other assessments

Research shows frequent lack of agreement between our self-assessments and those assessments provided by other people. The average correlation between our self-assessments and other people's assessment of specific attributes is as low as about 0.2 (Wilson [3]). Mabe and West [4] reviewed a number of studies and also found a low correlation between self-assessments and assessments by other work colleagues including supervisors and peer appraisals. Thornton [5] concluded that "individuals have a significantly different view of their own job performance than that held by other people". However, it is important to note that a number of researchers have asserted that the general lack of agreement between self-assessments and other people's assessments by different assessors is neither surprising nor problematic in that different assessors may observe different areas of performance, or have different definitions of effective performance, and thus arrive at different conclusions of the same individual performance.

We do not see ourselves as others see us

Nevertheless, the research suggests that we do not see ourselves as others see us. However, the extent of the correlation can depend on the trait and there is more likely to be agreement about personality traits like extroversion and introversion but less agreement on personality traits like social skills, warmth, friendliness, likeability, altruism, collaboration, cooperation, consideration, helpfulness, agreeableness, kindness, generosity, planning, organisation, focus, conscientiousness and so on.

There are a number of reasons why people are poor at predicting their own behaviour, and hence their reputation, including the following four:

Wrong group comparisons

Firstly, many people tend to avoid comparing themselves to high-performing groups, and many individuals seem unaware that they have fallen behind colleagues or that younger and more ambitious fast-trackers have overtaken them. Some people may also falsely compare themselves to the wrong groups and the wrong criteria. We take comfort from what we have achieved but we are less likely to compare ourselves to more senior and successful colleagues, and in general, people are less likely to consider what more could be done by themselves to perform more effectively.

Self-Validation

Secondly, we self-validate. We see what we want to see. We hear what we want to hear. We point the finger rather than taking personal responsibility. We say to ourselves, "I'm busy, therefore I'm effective", "I work 14 hours a day, therefore, I am valuable" or "I've been doing this job for many years so I must be good". However, individuals are often unaware that expectations increase with the number of years that a person has been holding down a job. Furthermore, the more senior a leader is, the less likely it is that colleagues will tell them what is really going on and how he or she is perceived in the organisation. If a senior executive wants to discover the naked truth about themselves, they need to do more than ask questions of colleagues or juniors who report directly to them.

Egocentric bias

Thirdly, there is egocentric bias, and some individuals may be inclined to inflate their self-assessment. For example, it seems that many people believe that they are far more concerned about other people than they really are, in that many people believe that they are more likely than others to perform acts of kindness, that they are more agreeable than others, that they make better judgements about themselves than other people or that they are better at predicting other people's behaviour than other people. And many people do not like to describe themselves as 'average' or 'below average' even though statistically we are more likely to be 'average' on many dimensions when compared to a given population group of similarly qualified colleagues! Another type of egocentric bias is related to attribution theory. According to this theory, individuals tend to attribute good performance to their own effective behaviours and poor performance to external circumstances beyond their control such as bad luck, unhelpful colleagues, lack of support or poor conditions or whatever.

Limited understanding of expectations and success criteria

Fourthly, in leadership, managerial and professional jobs, the criteria for success is more ambiguous. More senior and more able colleagues may have different expectations for a person's performance, and so measure performance differently according to more stringent criteria, and at different levels weight performance dimensions differently. Mid-level or more junior colleagues may be less discriminating in their judgements and have lower expectations.

1.3: Reputation and Self-delusion

> "Our greatest illusion is to believe that we are what we think ourselves to be".
>
> H.F. Amiel [6]

Our positive beliefs about ourselves can help to make us successful but these beliefs can also make it difficult for us to be realistic about our capabilities. Marshall Goldsmith [7] found that many people tend to overrate themselves relative to their peers. When he asked participants on training programmes to rate themselves relative to their peers, 85% ranked themselves in the top 20% and 70% ranked themselves in the top 10% of their peer group. As a corollary to this finding, it has also been found that we tend to accept feedback that is consistent with our view of ourselves, but we tend to deny or reject feedback that is inconsistent with the way we see ourselves.

We are motivated to have a positive view of ourselves

It is interesting that people become so out of touch with themselves and their reputation, making judgements about themselves that tend not to be shared by other people. It appears that people tend to construct theories about their own personalities based around what they would like or prefer to be. In essence, people are motivated to have a positive view of themselves and they avoid looking too closely at flaws in their behaviour or negative aspects of their behaviour. There seems to be a good deal of evidence and psychological research that people see themselves through rose-tinted glasses. We are also more likely to notice the times that we act in accordance with our preferred self-concept – and less likely to notice when we do not act in accordance with it – and we are more likely to dismiss negative evidence as exceptional or isolated incidents rather than as part of a consistent pattern.

However, it might be expected that the vast amount of information that we collect about ourselves should lead to increased confidence in our self-knowledge but it does not apparently lead to greater accuracy in our self-perceptions and self-predictions. It seems that we often have little understanding as to why we have behaved in a particular way and we do not appear to be fully aware of our preferences, often seeming to have difficulty in articulating the reasons for what we have done and why we have done it.

The Dunning–Kruger Effect

David Dunning and Jason Kruger [8] found that low-ability groups tend to overestimate their competence whilst high-ability groups often tend to underestimate their competence. Dunning and Kruger have researched this self-delusion tendency and confirmed that some people have an inflated view of their reputation, clearly suffering from the illusion that they have the skills required to make them a leader when the evidence would suggest otherwise. Dunning and Kruger eponymously referred to this phenomenon as the Dunning–Kruger Effect.

The Dunning–Kruger Effect is a cognitive bias in which low-ability individuals suffer from an illusion about their actual skill level, mistakenly assessing their ability as much higher than it is really. Dunning and Kruger attributed this bias to an inability of those of low ability to recognise their ineptitude, because of a low ability to appreciate what might be possible and what excellence might look like, and so they evaluate their ability accordingly. Their research also suggests that high-ability groups may underestimate their relative competence and may erroneously assume that tasks which are easy for them are also easy for others.

The self-assessment errors of the incompetent stem from an error about the self, whereas the self-assessment errors of the highly competent stem from an error about others

Dunning and Kruger have postulated that the Dunning–Kruger Effect is the result of internal delusion in those of low ability and external misperception in those of high ability. The authors noted that earlier studies suggested that ignorance of standards of performance lies behind a great deal of incorrect self-assessment of competence. This pattern of over-estimating competence was

seen in studies of skills as diverse as reading comprehension, practising medicine, driving a car and playing games such as chess or tennis. Dunning and Kruger proposed that, for a given skill, incompetent people will:
- Fail to recognise their own lack of skill
- Fail to recognise the extent of their inadequacy or lack of skill
- Fail to accurately gauge the excellence or skill in others.

Many people harbour false beliefs about their reputation

David Dunning [9] describes the main discovery from his 20 years of research as being finding out just how unenlightened people are about their competence, and that many people appear to harbour many false beliefs about their competence, character and reputation. If knowing yourself is a task many philosophers have encouraged people to accomplish, it appears that very few of us have taken this advice seriously enough to succeed. However, when it comes to making predictions about other people, people do achieve more accuracy in forecasting how peers or colleagues will behave than in forecasting how they themselves will behave. From Dunning's research, it appears that many people tend to possess useful insight when it comes to understanding other people, but that they fail to apply this wisdom to themselves.

In general, Dunning found that people tend to believe that they are far more likely to engage in socially desirable acts than their peers. Across several studies, Dunning [9] asked people to forecast how they would behave in situations that have an ethical, civic or altruistic dimension, and Dunning asked them to consider the likelihood that their peers would do the same. Consistently, it was found that respondents claimed that they are much more likely to act in a socially desirable way than their peers with regard to donations to charity, cooperating with another person and voting in an upcoming election. However, when we test out whether respondents actually behave in that way, Dunning found that people's peer predictions are more accurate in forecasting someone else's behaviour than predicting their own.

Optimistic self-predictions that are unrealistic and unreliable

It appears from Dunning's research that self-predictions tend to be extremely optimistic but also unrealistic and unreliable. The findings suggest that people exempt themselves from whatever valid psychological understanding they have about their friends and instead tend to think of themselves as special and exceptional. Many people seem to think that the rules that govern other people's psychology fail to apply to them and Dunning has referred to this tendency as "misguided exceptionalism". When people are thinking about themselves, they seem to believe that their intentions and desires will be more accurate in predicting the future than similar intentions and desires will be for other people. In predicting their own exam performance, people emphasise their aspiration level rather than past achievements but they emphasise another person's past achievements more in making predictions about their likely exam success rate rather than their aspirational level.

When forecasting our own behaviour, we should perhaps spend time predicting not what we think we will do but what other people think we are likely to do. The current psychological research suggests that people seem to be more accurate in predicting other people's behaviour than understanding and predicting their own behaviour.

"The fool doth think he is wise, but the wise man knows himself to be a fool"

Although the Dunning–Kruger Effect was formulated in 1999, Dunning and Kruger have noted earlier observations along similar lines by philosophers and scientists, including Confucius ("Real knowledge is to know the extent of one's ignorance"), Bertrand Russell ("One of the painful things about our time is that those who feel certainty are stupid, and those with any imagination and understanding are filled with doubt and indecision" and "The whole problem with the world is that fools and fanatics are always so certain of themselves, and wiser people so full of doubts") and

Charles Darwin ("Ignorance more frequently begets confidence than does knowledge"). It has also been noted that Shakespeare expressed a similar observation in *As You Like It* ("The fool doth think he is wise, but the wise man knows himself to be a fool").

1.4: Memory and Self-deception

It is all too easy to assume that what we remember about ourselves is an accurate reflection of reality. However, memories are not stored as exact replicas of reality but are modified and reconstructed during recall, in that we tend to try to piece together different experiences and make them into a coherent whole picture that makes sense to us, and which often serves a purpose for us. Bartlett [10] describes memory as a reconstructive process that tends to combine different subjective experiences to come up with a new interpretation of events. These narrative fallacies emerge from our attempts to make sense of our world in a way that is compelling and relatively simple. However, because memories are reconstructed, they are susceptible to being manipulated with false information.

When two people produce entirely different memories of the same event, observers usually assume that one of them is lying. But most of us are neither telling the whole truth nor intentionally being deceptive. We are self-justifying rather than lying. All of us, as we tell our stories, tend to omit details and omit inconvenient facts, and we give the story a self-enhancing spin; and if the spin goes over well, the next time we add a slightly more dramatic embellishment and we justify the little 'white lies' because they make the story better and clearer.

Selective memory highlights

Even when we believe that we have a vivid memory of something that happened, and even when we remember the detail and the emotions we experienced, our memory can still be wrong. Even being absolutely and positively sure that our memory is accurate does not mean that it is, as errors in memory support our current feelings and beliefs. At one time, people thought of memory as a

CHAPTER 1: WHAT IS REPUTATION?

library that stores events and facts for later retrieval, and some people think of memory in computer terms in that we assume that just about everything that happens to us is 'saved'. These metaphors of memory are popular and reassuring but they are wrong. Memories are not buried somewhere in the brain and when they are dug up they are not perfectly preserved. We do not remember everything that happens to us and we select highlights.

If we did not forget things, our minds could not work efficiently because they would be cluttered with mental junk. Moreover, recovering a memory is not at all like retrieving a file or re-playing a recording; it is like watching a few unconnected frames of the film and then figuring out what the rest of the scene must be like. When we remember complex information, we shape it to fit into a storyline.

In this way, memory becomes our self-justifying historian: we destroy information we do not want to hear and rewrite history from the standpoint of ourselves. History tends to be written by those who want to look good or who want their story confirmed, so when we write our own histories, we want to justify our actions to make us look and feel good about ourselves, and what we did and what we failed to do. If mistakes were made, memory helps us to remember that they were made by someone else.

When we remember, we incorporate information from many sources

Memory is reconstructive and thus vulnerable to error. The term 'confabulation' refers to the spontaneous production of false memories, which can involve confusing something that happened to someone else with something that happened to you or coming to believe that you remember something that never happened at all. In reconstructing the memory, people draw on many sources. When you remember an event, you may have a direct recollection of the detail but you will also incorporate information that you got later from, for example, a colleague's stories, photographs and videos that you have been shown. You weave all those elements together into one integrated account and it can be difficult to distinguish your actual memory from subsequent information that crept in from somewhere else. This phenomenon is called 'source confusion' to describe how we tend to fuse our memories.

Memories are used to minimise our own responsibility for events

Typically, we tell our stories or memories in the confidence that the listener will not dispute them or ask for contradictory evidence, which means we rarely have an incentive to scrutinise them for accuracy. When we tell a story, we tend to leave ourselves out. "My parents did this and this because of who they were and not because of the kind of kid I was". That is a typical self-justification of memory. This is why, when we learn that a memory is wrong, we feel disoriented – because it makes us rethink our own role in the story. 'Parent blaming' is a popular and convenient form of self-justification because it allows people to live less uncomfortably with their regrets and imperfections. Mistakes tend to be made by other people rather than ourselves. Memory tends to minimise our own responsibility and exaggerates the responsibility of the other person.

Shaping memories to fit our narrative

Memories create our stories but our stories also create memories. Once we have a narrative, we shape our memories to fit it and we spin the stories of our lives. Our memory changes to fit our story. Memories tend to be distorted in a self-enhancing direction in all sorts of ways. For example, research suggests that people remember voting in elections that they did not vote in; they remember giving more to charity than they really did; and they misremember rows, disputes and quarrels to shift blame onto the other party.

If a memory is a central part of your identity, self-serving distortion is even more likely. There is a tendency to rewrite the entire history of any conflict or choice so that a person's memory comes out consistent with how that person wants to see themselves. For some people, their self-concept is based on the belief that they have changed completely and their 'past self' seems like an entirely different person. When people recall actions that are inconsistent with their current view of themselves, they visualise the memory from a third-person perspective as if they were an impartial observer. But when they remember actions that are consistent with their current identity, they tell a first-person story as if they were looking at their former selves through their own eyes.

Getting what you want by revising what you had

Conway and Ross [11] described this self-serving memory distortion as "getting what you want by revising what you had". We have a tendency to misremember our history as being worse than it was, thus distorting our perception of how much we have improved to make us feel better about ourselves now. All of us grow and mature but generally not as much as we think we have. This bias in memory explains why each of us feels that we have changed profoundly but our friends, enemies and loved ones are the same, and generally do not notice such significant change.

1.5: Reputation and Unreliable Observations

It has been shown that people often cannot tell the difference between something they were told or something that actually happened to them. If people overhear others exchanging rumours about some person, many will later come to believe that they actually experienced the event themselves. Of course, it is uncomfortable to realise that some of our colleagues are presenting unfounded ideas about someone's reputation. However, if there is evidence that they were wrong in their beliefs, it is difficult to admit to mistakes because they would have had to realise that they may have caused harm and personal damage to a person's career. It is usually much easier to preserve their beliefs by rejecting the evidence as being irrelevant. As soon as a person begins to justify their beliefs, it becomes difficult to go back without enormous psychological discomfort.

We choose to defend our judgement even when confronted with conflicting evidence

Scepticism teaches us to be cautious about taking what people tell us or what we see at face value. However, if a person is presented with evidence that they made an error of judgement or expressed a false opinion about a person's reputation, their first impulse will be to deny their mistake for the obvious reason of protecting their own reputation as someone who typically makes sound judgments. If they want to think of themselves as an honourable, competent person who makes sound judgements about people, then they need to convince themselves that the 'new evidence' is poor or patchy, as the alternative conclusion (that they have made a wrong assessment) may be very unpalatable to their view of their competence. As a consequence, they may go through mental 'hoops' to convince themselves that they could not possibly have made such an error of judgement in the first place.

We fit the evidence to support our conclusion

When we try to interpret the reason behind our own or someone else's behaviour, we often instinctively decide we know what happened and then fit the evidence to support our conclusion, ignoring or discounting evidence that contradicts it. Social psychologists have studied this phenomenon extensively by putting people in the role of jurors and seeing what factors influence their decisions. Most people immediately construct a story about what has happened and then, as evidence is presented, accept only the evidence that supports their conclusion or version of what happened, which is referred to as 'confirmation bias'. Those who jumped to a conclusion early were also the most confident in their decision.

1.6: Reputation and the False-Confidence Phenomenon

A core principle of scientific thinking is the importance of examining the ruling out of other possible explanations for a person's behaviour before deciding which one is the most likely.

CHAPTER 1: WHAT IS REPUTATION?

In making judgements about people's reputations, experience in making judgements about people does not necessarily increase accuracy. However, it does increase people's confidence in their accuracy of observation and interpretation, and this is something that has been called the 'false-confidence phenomenon'. Once we have placed our bets on someone's reputation, we don't want to entertain any information that casts doubt on that judgement.

Overconfidence is the enemy of making good reputational judgements

Doubt is not the enemy of making good judgements about someone's reputation but overconfidence can be the enemy of making good judgements about someone's reputation. Currently the professional training of most leaders includes almost no information about their own cognitive biases, how to correct for them, and how to manage the conflict and discomfort they will feel when their beliefs meet disconfirming evidence. Many leaders will make comments like "I saw it with my own eyes, therefore I am right"; "I know that I am right because I have been doing this for years"; and "I know what is right when I see it".

Chapter 1 Key Summary Points

- Reputation is elusive as many different observers can perceive and describe facts and behaviours in many different ways.
- Reputation is really created by two things: what you say and what you do. However, a reputation is a set of perceptions, beliefs and memories that exist in other people's minds, so a single event can be perceived and described in many different ways and, consequently, there can be several different perceptions of a person's reputation.
- An understanding of our own reputation is also generally poor as psychological research suggests that we have immodest and unrealistic views of ourselves; and so we need help to achieve greater insight about our own reputation.

- A person's reputation comprises three basic elements: their actual personal attributes, how these attributes are perceived by others and the value which others place on these attributes.
- The extent to which a person is perceived as having a positive reputation with certain people may be directly proportional to the extent to which these people feel good or better after each interaction with that person.
- Many individuals hold mistaken views about themselves based on self-delusion, unrealistic optimism and overly optimistic views of themselves.
- We do not see ourselves as other see us because we make wrong group comparisons, we are prone to self-validation, egocentric bias, and poor understanding of changing expectations and success criteria.
- Our memories are reconstructed and are susceptible to being distorted with false information about our own reputation.
- It has been shown that many people often cannot tell the difference between something they were told or something that actually happened to them, which can make reputational judgements unreliable.
- Most people are more accurate in predicting other people's behaviour than their own. In predicting their own performance, people emphasise their aspiration level rather than past achievements but they emphasise another person's past achievements rather than their aspirational level.
- Overconfidence about the accuracy of one's ability to observe and interpret behaviour can be the enemy of making good judgements about someone's reputation.

Chapter 2

The Importance of Reputation

> "Reputation, reputation, reputation! Oh! I have lost my reputation. I have lost the immortal part of myself, and what remains is bestial. My reputation, Iago, my reputation!"
>
> Shakespeare, *Othello, the Moor of Venice*, Act II, Scene III, 242–4

Chapter 2 Key Points

- The importance of reputation
- How our behaviour impacts our reputation
- How our reputation is assessed and evaluated
- The career paradox: how the rules of the game change

2.1: The Importance of Reputation

Reputation is our biggest asset. No-one ever questions the importance of reputation. In fact, people tend to care more about their reputation than about reality, and Tetlock [1] found that we care more about what other people think about us than we do about what may have actually happened or how we may have actually behaved. In other words, we care more about looking good than about truly being good! We cut ethical corners quite often when we think that we can get away with it, then use our retrospective reasoning to manage our reputations and justify ourselves to others. In some ways, our moral reasoning about our reputation resembles a politician searching for votes rather than a scientist searching for the truth.

Most leaders recognise that their reputation is critical to their success and thus has a central role in building a successful career. At its simplest level, it is what others think of us. At a more complex level, it impacts on our credibility in everything we do, everything we say, and how people react to us at a personal and professional level. While reputation may be difficult to describe and difficult to quantify, many of us will instinctively and intuitively have a sense of those colleagues who have 'good' reputations and those colleagues who have 'less good' reputations.

If an individual is perceived as having a 'good reputation' this implies that he or she has raised the confidence levels of their colleagues that the 'appropriate' behaviours, attitudes and strategies are being employed in their role which will, in time, produce 'good' results. However, many people think that their reputational value lies entirely with their functional and technical competence and their ability to do their job. Some colleagues advise that we should not care what people think as long as we are able to 'deliver'. However, you may know of some colleagues who have enormous talent but who never achieve the success their level of work deserves because they have not learned how to leverage their assets to represent themselves in the best and most authentic way.

Reputation makes the difference between success and failure

The world of business has seen some tough times in the last few years, and in these challenging times many people's reputations have ebbed and flowed. Reputation matters because it can make the difference between the success or failure of a person's career, as a person's position in an organisation is created by what others say and think. However, many senior managers, directors and chief executives have now realised that even their best-intentioned efforts and successes at work are not enough to secure a solid reputation. The reality is that being skilled and

CHAPTER 2: THE IMPORTANCE OF REPUTATION

knowledgeable in one's chosen profession is insufficient and passively hoping that the world will notice you is not a good career strategy. It is also not a good career strategy to be an attention seeker but it is important and emotionally mature to learn how to manage other people's perceptions and expectations.

Everyone, of course, has a reputation with potentially both positive and negative consequences. We judge people in organisations the same way that we judge people in our personal lives. We listen to what they say, how they say it, the language they use, how they behave and act, and from these perceptions we might use half a dozen adjectives to describe the person. This essentially forms their reputation.

As an illustration of the importance of reputation, at a funeral or wedding, we try to capture those aspects of a person's character or personality that reflect their reputation and the behaviours that make their reputation different from those of most other people. We try to capture the essence of a person's life. The signature characteristics and qualities that tell us the deeper story are rarely included in a CV, but at a funeral or wedding, we try to capture those aspects of a person's character or personality that reflect their reputation.

Reputations evolve in an uncontrolled way

Individuals are unaware of the way their reputations evolve. For example, a client, 'Joe'*, was technically and intellectually smart, but he was disorganised, would miss meetings and needed to be chased to complete work. Over time, to his horror, he gained the reputation of being 'unprofessional' as he did not deliver what had been agreed and disrespected the time of his colleagues. Another client, 'Dan', was a great 'ideas person' who was always morphing from one idea to the next, but he developed a reputation of being 'not to be trusted' because his position was always changing. Another client, 'Steve', was a poor listener and developed a reputation for having 'poor judgement' because he

---

* All client names have been changed.

did not access enough information from other people to factor into his decision making. Steve became marginalised from the team because he was 'unrewarding' to communicate with, due to his lack of listening ability. Finally, we have all met the 'good news messenger' who is over-positive and who always glosses the message. Another client, 'Larry', tarnished his reputation because he was perceived as consistently presenting 'good news' and so offering an 'unbalanced judgement'. So Larry, who was extremely well-intentioned with a very positive attitude, became known as someone who could not be trusted to 'tell it as it is' and his judgements had to be taken with a 'pinch of salt'. His colleagues learned to 'discount' what they heard from Larry. Of course, all these examples illustrate how reputations can be career threatening because they attack an individual's 'political capital' in terms of their credibility, gravitas, influence and value within the organisation.

Our reputation precedes us

A reputation is very powerful and is critical to our success because our reputation precedes us. Reputation is clearly important because in order to be the go-to person for what you do, you must create, build and sustain the best possible name for yourself. A good reputation will open doors, help to build relationships, encourage discussion and engagement, help to foster support, enable us to receive the benefit of the doubt, encourage trust and enable a quicker recovery when things do not go to plan.

2.2: How our Behaviour Impacts our Reputation

At work, our reputation is formed by the language people use when they talk about us. As a consequence, any individual who aspires to drive and shape their career needs regular access to good-quality data based on how they are perceived. There are four ways in which the 'how' can enable us to stand out:
- How do you say it? Do you use appropriate language? Do you articulate your position well? Do you speak with conviction? Do you convey energy and passion? Do you

demonstrate the values in which you believe? Do you demonstrate sufficient balance in your language to suggest that you will listen to an alternative view and perspective? Do you regularly ask questions to find out what and how others think about an issue?
- How do you behave? Do you come across as confident and respectful of others? Do you appear to be genuine in that your behaviour reflects your words? Do you appear humble and self-deflecting? Do you ask questions and do you ask multiple questions to convey more sincerity and interest to uncover what really matters?
- How do you react? Do you respond well to other people's different views? Do you show the courtesy and respect that other people expect? Are you included in discussions because you are valued and show respect for others' views? Are you sufficiently humble to change your views and listen attentively to the views of others? Are you capable of changing your mind? Do you have the generosity of spirit to applaud and congratulate someone for their success?
- How do you make people feel? Do you question other people about their feelings? Do you share your own feelings to establish a meaningful engagement? Do you make others feel valued? Do you show interest in others and do you create a 'feel good' factor in others? Do other people feel that you are reliable and trustworthy and that you want to help them? Do you make others feel that you are interested in their well-being? To what extent do people often or usually feel better after spending some time with you?

Of course, we know from research that many people will inflate their self-assessment of their ability to behave well with other people but we know that most people do not successfully create a 'feel good factor' in others. Many people at work are qualified to execute the 'what' but very few will stand out if judged by the 'how'. However, the relationships that will last the longest and those colleagues who are most trusted and admired will be based on the 'how' rather than the 'what'. The simple fact is that those individuals with strong relationships will be tolerated and given time when there are problems, errors or events do not go to plan, but those colleagues with weak relationships will find that even the simplest mistake or problem will not be tolerated.

2.3: How our Reputation is Assessed and Evaluated

'Reputation capital' is a short-hand term that refers to the amalgamation of many non-tangible variables which reflect an individual's value, worth and influence in an organisation. Many people think that their reputational value lies entirely with their ability to do their job, and many people think that measurable 'hard' results are the only thing that matters in determining their career success, pay or promotions.

People often refer to 'hard results' and they often seem to imply that 'soft skills' are of less value and importance. Nothing, of course, could be further from the truth. Obviously, hard results are critical factors in achieving success and it would be naive to think otherwise, but these hard results can only be achieved by an individual leader if he has a strong reputation. For example, based on the leader's reputation, colleagues will either trust their decisions or not. Colleagues will either believe in what they say or not. Colleagues will either believe whether they have the team's interests at heart or not. Colleagues will choose to follow and 'go the extra mile' or not.

Therefore, strong leaders know how to make the connection between reputation and results, and they also know that it is reputation which will endure because the results will become history in a few months. When people talk about the results we achieved, it tends to be rather brief and matter-of-fact because people talk about these results without any particular feeling or emotion. However, when we talk about a person's behaviour, the conversation is more animated because people are more interested in talking about the person's reputation, how they treat people, how they behave, whether they are respected and whether their values stand out compared to those of their colleagues.

CHAPTER 2: THE IMPORTANCE OF REPUTATION

Reputation is only built on achieving results if results can be linked directly to personal behaviours

This book is intended to help the reader discover their personal value by becoming familiar with variables that impact on their reputation. Although the bottom-line ability to do the job well is always essential, critical and non-negotiable, it is not a differentiating factor if many others can do a similar job. In the longer term, reputation is built on achieving results if results can be linked directly to personal behaviours, and in the shorter term, reputation and an individual's organisational worth is a function of how a person's behaviour is described by colleagues.

2.4: The Career Paradox: How the Rules of the Game Change

The career paradox is that people get promoted to a senior role because of their ability to deliver and execute tasks in a given functional area, but then the rules of the game are changed in that different behaviours are expected at senior executive levels. Unfortunately, no-one typically tells the person involved that the rules have changed. Also typically, no-one gives the person involved any honest feedback on their performance or how to play with these changed rules. The person may have been an 8/10 or 9/10 in terms of their functional ability to deliver specific technical tasks in a given area, but all of a sudden they are asked to do a leadership role in which their 'relationship-management' expertise may be only 3/10 or 4/10. Many of these new managers or leaders have never had any authentic feedback around their ability to influence, lead, motivate or galvanise teams, and more critically they have a very slim grasp of the differences between managing and leading.

Hired for what you know and fired for who you are!

An individual's career starts by learning a skill, training for a career in a specialist area and developing an expertise and proficiency in a particular role. Then as a result of their technical expertise and experience, they may be put in charge of the team and may then get appointed as a supervisor, then a manager of people and then a leader of the function, organisation or business. However, there is a significant difference between the evolved relationship-based leadership qualities required for superior performance as a senior executive and the functional requirements at lower levels. Leadership is something that is learned over a period of time and, in general, only about 20% involves technical or functional knowledge and experience. The other 80% of leadership is about demonstrating the right kind of relationship skills and leadership behaviours.

Many managers are promoted to senior positions because they are doing an excellent job but they are often ill-equipped to lead a team because they have not developed the leadership, interpersonal and relationship skills required to engage with other parts of the organisation. In senior roles, there is also a requirement for leaders to inspire, motivate, coach and upgrade the talent of their team. Leaders learn that leadership is more about getting the right people into the right positions, establishing the right collaborative relationships, communicating effectively across functions and working through others. This requires a significant change in how they organise their day-to-day working life. Essentially, leaders are trying to multiply their abilities by managing through others, and by so doing, they will be able to make time to broaden their sphere of impact and influence.

Chapter 2 Key Summary Points

- Reputation impacts on our lives in a fundamental and highly important way that affects our personal and career legacy.
- As an illustration of the importance of reputation, at a funeral or wedding, we try to capture those aspects of a person's character or personality that reflect their reputation and which make them different from most other people.

CHAPTER 2: THE IMPORTANCE OF REPUTATION

- Reputation matters because it can make a difference between success and failure in terms of a person's career and their position in an organisation.
- Reputations evolve in a way of which the individual concerned is unaware based on how they say things, how they behave, how they react and how they make people feel.
- Reputation is a legacy based more on how we behave than on what we achieve. Reputation is only built on achieving results if results can be linked directly to specific personal behaviours.
- The career paradox is that people get promoted to senior roles based on their ability to deliver and execute tasks in a given functional or technical area, but then the rules of the game change, in that their performance is now assessed on their leadership, interpersonal and relationship skills rather than technical or functional competence.

Chapter 3

Reputation, Bias and Prejudice

"O wad some power the giftie gie us
To see ourselves as other see us!
It would frae mony a blunder free us
An' foolish notion"

Robert Burns [1]

Chapter 3 Key Points

- How reputations are shaped by our personal bias
- Reputations and potential sources of error
- Reputation and memory distortions
- Cognitive dissonance as a perceptual filter
- Attribution errors in describing reputations
- Personal construct theory and how reputations are shaped
- Misunderstandings
- Judgement errors that distort reputation
- Ten common cognitive biases that impact on reputation
- Eight subliminal perceptual effects that impact on reputation

3.1: Reputation and Personal Bias

Our reputation is based on other people's perceptions and is thus a combination of the impact of a wide variety of behaviours that people observe either consciously or unconsciously. If you ask six different people to describe a particular individual's reputation, you may get six different answers depending on the factors, attributes or constructs that are most important for each particular observer. Depending on the observer's level of discernment and psychological-mindedness, level of seniority or relationship with the other person, they may choose to emphasise intellect, judgement, friendliness, interpersonal skills, collaboration, compassion, kindness, sincerity, perceptiveness and so on. Moreover, they may all be right, in that reputation is whatever others observe it to be.

Our accounts of what happens in our lives cannot be understood as 'factual' in any straightforward sense as we all look at things in an idiosyncratic and selective fashion. Understanding how people cognitively construct their world is fundamental to our understanding of how another person's reputation is formed. We all process information differently and we all have cognitive biases that help us to filter information, and these filters are used to take shortcuts to form a view about someone else's reputation.

Reputation is a blend of the rational and the irrational

Reputation is a blend of rationality and irrationality, and the irrational feelings or biases of colleagues can influence their perspective as much as their rational conclusions. Unconscious prejudice does tend to complicate the way in which reputations are perceived. We seem to find it difficult to retain a huge number of facts about a person so our decision making is influenced by our emotions and relatively trivial details. We are influenced by our initial impressions and by the most recent, eye-catching and memorable information we have observed or been informed of about the person. We then tend to seek out information that confirms rather than challenges our assumptions as we tend to look for evidence to support our view as opposed to rationally weighing up the evidence on both sides.

We also tend to seek out the company of people who agree with us and we look to justify our conclusions based on hindsight bias in order to minimise any conflicting evidence. So regardless of the personal or career consequences of the formulation of our opinion about someone else's reputation, we tend to hold steadfastly to the views that we have originally formed.

Our reputation may vary from situation to situation

Our reputation is a consequence of the combination of how we behave, the actions we take, the words we use, our body language and many other things, and all of these factors contribute to a greater or lesser degree to our perceived reputation. Therefore, our reputation is based on our perceived behaviours and actions in many different situations. However, some people will have a strong reputation in one setting but not in another different setting. In essence, everything we do contributes to or detracts from our reputation and some individuals may be selective in how they display certain qualities to people who matter to them. For example, there are some individuals who choose to be friendly, charming and amenable to colleagues who they respect and value, but choose not to demonstrate these behaviours to other colleagues who do not hold their interest and attention.

We all tend to be hard-wired to make assessments and judgements about other people. It is very hard to meet someone without forming a view or opinion about them – in fact, those who are not able to form an opinion are probably less emotionally intelligent or less emotionally aware. Although we might like to think that we make judgements based on sound hard observable data, we tend to make our judgements based on more subjective feelings about a particular person.

3.2: Reputations and Potential Sources of Error

This chapter explores how our perceptions can be distorted, and how we might observe and interpret other people's behaviour in a way that does not necessarily reflect the reality of the reputation they deserve. The process by which reputations are formed is a direct consequence of the perceptual filters used by observers of our behaviour and these filters are subject to many potential sources of error, bias, unconscious subliminal effects, unsound reasoning and logical fallacies. We all have perceptual filters at play and we all have expectations of others. The truth is that our perceptions are often inaccurate, but particularly if we feel

CHAPTER 3: REPUTATION, BIAS AND PREJUDICE

emotionally engaged or emotionally affected by another person or by a specific situation.

Of course there is no such thing as objective truth or reality. There is only 'our' version of reality, which is essentially our perception. We all have an in-built psychological tendency to interpret behaviour, particularly in uncertainty, through the lens of our predetermined labels. It may be assumed that if someone uses a label to describe someone else's behaviour then there is some sort of common understanding of what the term means, but this is not the case as the same label can mean many different things to different people. In essence, giving someone a label is an illusion not an explanation, in that a label does not allow us to look more carefully at the detail and context of the specific actions being observed and so there is no opportunity to check out the validity of the reputation description.

We make sense of observed behaviours in a very individualistic way

We make sense of observed behaviours in a very individualistic way. Information is absorbed and filtered according to specific mental mechanisms that assign meaning. Our emotional reactions to events are a product of our interpretations of these events. However, different individuals bring different sets of criteria to their interpretation of events in terms of their biases, experiences and preferences in the way that they process observational data and information. As a consequence, similar information about an individual will be interpreted in different ways and different conclusions about their reputation will be formed.

Reputation and blindspots

Our perception of a person's reputation can also be influenced by our blindspots. We all have blindspots in our view of ourselves but we often delude ourselves into thinking that we do not have any. Even the most rational people have blindspots but people develop defensive structures over time that make them blind to their dysfunctional behaviours.

We have self-serving habits that allow us to justify our own perceptions and beliefs as being accurate, realistic and unbiased. Social psychologists, Ross and Ward [2] call this phenomenon "naive realism". It is the tendency to believe that we perceive objects and events clearly "as they really are". We assume that other reasonable people see things the same way that we do. If they disagree with us, then they are obviously not seeing things clearly. Naive realism creates a logical paradox because it presupposes two things: people who are open-minded and fair ought to agree with my reasonable opinion of someone else; and secondly, any opinion that I hold must be reasonable because if it wasn't, I wouldn't hold that opinion.

Therefore, we tend to delude ourselves into thinking that if we could only get the other person to sit down and listen to us, we could tell them how things really are and then they would agree with us. And if they don't agree with us, it must be because they are biased. Even when each party recognises that the other party perceives the issues differently, there is a tendency for each party to think that the other side is biased while they themselves are objective, and that their own perceptions of reality should provide the basis of an agreement.

Ross and his colleagues found that we believe our own judgements are less biased and more independent than those of others because we rely on introspection to tell us what we are thinking and feeling, but we have no way of knowing what others are really thinking and feeling. We tend to take our own involvement and thinking on an issue as a source of accuracy but we regard such personal feelings on the part of others, who hold different views, as a source of bias.

George Orwell said that we are all capable of believing things that we know to be untrue, but then, when we have finally been proved wrong, we twist the facts so as to show that we were right!

CHAPTER 3: REPUTATION, BIAS AND PREJUDICE

How we process information to make sense of other people's behaviour

Social psychologists have developed models of the way in which people process information about their social world and they have tried to explain how we build stereotypes of other groups, judge other personalities, make causal attributions based on other people's actions and interpret other people's behaviour. However, it is also true that we are not typically aware of the processes that we use to form these judgements and opinions about other people, and there seems to be a great deal of unconscious processing and perceptual filtering.

It is well known that first impressions are very powerful in shaping the reputations that we form about other people but what we do not know is how much of the other person's behaviour is being interpreted by us using perceptual processes and filters of which we are not aware. One of the most important judgements that we make on a daily basis is our interpretation of the motives, intentions and personality of other people, and in practical terms, it is usually to our advantage to make these judgements quickly.

If reputation is based on other people's perceptions, then we need to strengthen our understanding of how reputations are formed by exploring how perceptions are formed and what perceptual filters are in play. There are a number of different perceptual patterns, cognitive perceptual biases and perceptual illusions that shape the way we think. As a consequence, reputations are not always fair or objective and the following sections offer some explanation of why this is the case. The different perceptual filters discussed below are:
- Memory distortions
- Cognitive dissonance
- Attribution errors
- Personal constructs
- Misunderstandings
- Unconscious biases
- Subliminal conditioning effects.

3.3: Reputation and Memory Distortion

We construct entire reputational narratives about other people on the basis of memories that may often be wrong. It can be frustrating when things happen that we do not remember but it is more concerning when we remember things that never happened, and the consequences can be profound for ourselves and the reputations we form about other people.

Loftus [3], a leading scientist in the field of memory, refers to "imagination inflation" because the more that you imagine that a particular person is likely to behave in a particular way, the more likely you are to inflate it into an actual memory. Specific details may then be added to make the memory more real. The more people tell someone how an event might have happened, the more real it starts to feel to them. Once people have retrieved their memories, they discuss with other people who may share similar views and who are able to confirm their explanation or description of someone's behaviour or reputation. They may also firmly reject any inconsistent evidence or any other way of understanding why someone may have behaved in a particular way.

It is important to appreciate the possible distortions of our memory caused by 'imagination inflation'. If we appreciate that even deeply felt memories can be wrong, it might encourage people to hold their memories more lightly and to drop the certainty that their memories are always accurate. We must be careful which memories we select and use as a base for justifying the reputations that we hold about other people.

Changing one's mind about a memory can be difficult

Even in situations in which the reputation we have formed about someone is based on memories that are proved false, it is always an easier choice to justify the memory because to change one's mind can be difficult and, at times, it is easier to retain the original perception about a particular person's reputation. It is very difficult when the truth gets in the way of a good, interesting story! And it is not easy to change one's perception because it means taking a fresh, critical look at the memory of the other person that we have promoted rather than re-evaluating and letting go of the memory.

Where there is smoke, it does not necessarily mean there is fire!

There is a common view that if you are utterly convinced that your memories are true then they are true – but research suggests that this is not the case. We tend to attribute blame or negative descriptions about people because of the cliché "where there's smoke, there's fire" but we should know better. None of us like learning that we are wrong, that our memories are distorted or that we made an embarrassing mistake. If you hold a set of beliefs about a person's reputation that guides your behaviour and you learn that some of the beliefs are mistaken, you must either admit you were wrong and change your perception or reject the new evidence. If the mistakes are too threatening to your view of your competence and perceptual judgement, and if you have not taken a public stand defending them, then you will probably change your perception and be grateful to have a more accurate one. However, if some of those mistaken beliefs have made someone's problems worse or created damage for an individual's career or if you have stated your view of a person publicly, then you will have a serious conflict to resolve.

3.4: Cognitive Dissonance and the Failure to Process Information Logically

Festinger's [4] cognitive dissonance theory proposed that we all have an inner drive to maintain consistency in the attitudes and beliefs we hold, and that we also have a drive to avoid disharmony (or dissonance). Festinger argued that it would be troubling and uncomfortable if two friends, say Joe and Tom, were very close and fond of each other but had polarised opposite feelings of like and dislike about a third person, Ben. In this case, the tension can only be eased by Joe either liking Tom less or liking Ben more. In terms of reputation, the cognitive dissonance theory suggests that we try to form consistent patterns of thought about a person, but these thoughts can work in both a positive and negative direction.

Cognitive dissonance theory suggests that we do not process information logically. For example, if new information is consistent with our beliefs about a person, we think it is well-founded and useful but if the new information is inconsistent with our beliefs about a person, then we may consider it biased, foolish or mistaken. So powerful is the need for idea alignment that when people are forced to look at conflicting evidence, they will find a way to criticise, distort or dismiss the conflicting evidence so that they can maintain or even strengthen their existing belief. The more information that emerges to question our perspective, the more creatively we search for new justifications, and the more entrenched we may become in our original view or our perception of someone else's reputation.

Evidence is revised to fit our assumptions

In many cases, evidence is even revised to fit our assumptions, a process of which we are usually unaware, as we reframe or interpret situations to suit our purpose and back-up the decisions and judgements we have previously made. In 2003, after it had become clear that there were no weapons of mass destruction in Iraq, Americans who supported the war and President Bush's reason for launching it were thrown into a state of cognitive dissonance or internal conflict. For Democrats, who had thought that there were no weapons of mass destruction, the resolution was relatively easy in that the Republicans were wrong or the President had lied or that they had been too eager to listen to faulty intelligence information. For Republicans, however, the cognitive dissonance or conflict was sharper and some resolved it by refusing to accept the conflicting evidence, in that they believed that weapons had been found, destroyed or had previously existed; or alternatively, they may have believed that the decision was right, given the intelligence that was provided for the President.

It certainly seems the case that once minds are made up, it is hard to change them. Indeed, neuroscientists have recently

CHAPTER 3: REPUTATION, BIAS AND PREJUDICE

shown that these biases in our thinking are built into the very way the brain processes information. For example, in a study of people who were being monitored by MRI scanners (magnetic resonance imaging), the research showed that the reasoning areas of the brain virtually shut down when participants were confronted with dissonant or conflicting information, and the emotion circuits of the brain lit up when consonance or compatibility between ideas or actions was restored.

People like to think that they make choices based on good rational reasons

Indeed, even raising information that goes against your point of view can make you all the more convinced you are right. The more costly a decision, in terms of time, money, effort or inconvenience, the greater the dissonance may be and the greater the need to reduce the dissonance by overemphasising the good things about the choice made. So, when you are about to make an expensive purchase, move house to a new area, buy a car or a computer or decide whether to undergo plastic surgery, do not ask someone who has just done it for their advice because that person will be highly motivated to convince you that it is the right thing to do.

People want to believe that, as smart and rational individuals, they know why they made the choices they did, so they are not always happy when you tell them the actual reason for their actions. Even when the reasons for their choices are explained to people, there is a tendency for individuals to say that they understand the theory but it doesn't apply in their case: they are different and made a decision for their own reasons. However, when senior managers are wrong in their judgement of someone else's reputation, their professional identity is threatened and so cognitive dissonance theory would predict that a successful senior manager is less likely to admit mistakes in their judgement about someone's reputation if it will damage their own professional reputation.

3.5: Attribution Errors in Describing Reputations

Attribution theory is concerned with explaining how we describe and explain other people's behaviour. Heider [5] introduced attribution theory, which assumes that people try informally to analyse in a common-sense way why people do what they do, then attribute one or more causes to that behaviour so that it makes sense to themselves. Quite simply, however, people perceive their own behaviours very differently from how others perceive their behaviours.

According to attribution theory, there is a fundamental attribution error that is frequently observed when people try to explain and attribute a cause to someone's behaviour. The fundamental attribution error is as follows. When we succeed, we tend to attribute our success to our personality characteristics, abilities, attitudes or motivations; when we fail, we tend to attribute our failure to other external factors beyond our control such as poor conditions, the quality of the competition, bad luck (or the good luck of others), the unhelpful weather and other factors that dilute our performance. On the other hand, there is a tendency for most people to attribute exactly the opposite causes to the success and failures of others. For example, if our opponent wins a contest, we are often inclined to explain it as a consequence of external circumstances like their good luck, the conditions or weather being favourable, or the existence of other external factors in their favour; whereas if our opponent loses or performs poorly, we are more inclined to believe that they lack talent or competence, or that they were simply just not good enough on the day. It seems that nearly every person has been, at some time, prone to making this kind of fundamental attribution error although we are rarely aware of how we have deluded ourselves into seeking this type of causal explanation.

Attribute substitution error

Another form of attribution error, the attribute substitution error, occurs when an individual has to make a judgement that is very complex and they attempt to replace the complex problem with a more simple variation. The individual replaces a complex question with a simple question, rather than engaging with the complexity of the actual question. Therefore, when someone tries to answer a difficult question, they may actually answer a related but different question without realising that a substitution has taken place. In the majority of cases, individuals may be unaware of their own biases and unaware that they have simplified the problem in order to make it more accessible to themselves. The attribute substitution error can clearly lead to erroneous judgements about someone's reputation when the observer fails to engage with the complexity of a particular situation and prefers to simplify their decision-making process about someone's behaviour.

At a broader level, the attribute substitution phenomenon is one major reason why a referendum question about serious complex issues does not work. In the case of the referendum about whether the UK should stay within the European Union, some people simplified the question by making it a decision with regard to immigration or emigration, some focused on unnecessary bureaucracy, others prioritised economics, security or the NHS, limited resources or value-led questions about tariff-free trade, unrestricted movement, being a member of a political union or a defensive alliance. It appears that politicians have learned very little from psychological research about the decision-making errors that stem from attribute substitution, and the inevitable process of replacing complex questions with simple questions.

3.6: Personal Construct Theory of Reputation

In 1955, George Kelly [6] presented personal construct theory as an alternative explanation to help us understand how we make sense of other people's behaviour. Kelly chose the word 'construct' to refer to the adjectives that we choose to use to describe other people and to differentiate it from the word 'concept' – the crucial difference being that 'construct' is a label that has a specific opposite whereas a concept does not. Kelly argued that 'good' only has meaning when related to 'bad' and 'beautiful' only has meaning when related to 'ugly', and he believed that all constructs that we use about people are bipolar. The constructs that we use are based on our values, priorities, personal preferences and life experiences, and each person's system of constructs is unique based on their preferred ways to look at and interpret the people in their world.

Kelly introduced the idea that we all develop personal constructs or labels or preferred adjectives as "mental representations" to make sense of the way we interpret events, people and situations. Kelly thought that we experience the world through the lens of our constructs, but that we may all use different constructs to interpret our own personal world as we see it. Some of us will look for and place more importance on constructs like intelligence, humour, sociability, likeability, kindness, attractiveness and so on, and our preferred labels will be a consequence of which attribute has a higher value or importance for us. We will then repeatedly test these constructs based on what we see and observe: if we find evidence to support these constructs, we strengthen our beliefs about a particular person; whereas if we find evidence which does not support these constructs, we are more likely to change our perception about that person.

We tend to choose constructs according to the criteria we believe to be relevant for a particular situation or person, according to our expectations as to how someone should behave and act in a particular situation. We might also use the construct at the time that we observe the behaviour or we may reflect back on the situation to use a construct to interpret a person's behaviour in a different way. For example, if a colleague consistently needs to be chased and followed up to supply information, we could describe them as 'lazy', 'disrespectful', having 'poor attention to detail', 'inconsiderate', 'deceptive', having 'low emotional intelligence', not being a 'team player' or 'unprofessional'. Most probably, we will choose the description that best fits our view of what is most important in a given situation. Kelly believes that we all have a fundamental need to predict how

CHAPTER 3: REPUTATION, BIAS AND PREJUDICE

people will behave and so we use a system of constructs that we have found to be useful in predicting behaviour and in helping us to build a picture of a person's reputation.

3.7: Misunderstandings

Misunderstandings may occur when we listen to someone and believe that we understand their message, when actually we are quite wrong. This situation can easily lead to wrong reputations being formed as a result of a mistaken understanding of a particular narrative. The situation will often be compounded by the fact that the person with whom we are communicating believes that he or she has been understood when in fact he or she has not. A misunderstanding can be defined as a situation in which at least two people have subjective and opposite interpretations, yet both think that they see the same thing and agree. People eventually act on their respective misunderstandings and discover that the basis for their behaviour was incorrect, then they apologise and say that they thought that you meant that you were in agreement with their feelings and opinions and that we had a common understanding.

We hear what we want to hear

However, the major point of a misunderstanding is that we hear what we want to hear and tend not to explore further or check our understanding of what the other person means. This is a major source of problems between individuals and it is due primarily to the following four attitudes:
1. We believe in our own assumptions and forget that we should question our assumptions periodically.
2. We fall into the 'attribution trap' by which we explain things according to our own mental programming although different people use the same words with different meanings.
3. We take shortcuts when communicating with other people and, at times, we don't even listen to the completion of the other person's message, but cut them

off by saying that we understand in order to speed up the process of getting to the point and moving forward.
4. In interpreting some behaviour, we assume that there is a rationale behind every act and that all behaviour has an explanation, and as observers, we tend to look for meaning in irrational events. The level of success in doing this may depend on an individual's level of emotional intelligence.

We should all be aware that the assumption that we understand each other when actually we do not can have damaging consequences, possibly leading to distorted views about a person that may impact on their reputation.

3.8: Judgement Errors that Distort Reputations

In the early 1970s, Daniel Kahneman and Amos Tversky [7] demonstrated three types of errors that people make when reaching judgements. In their research, they identified three types of judgement error, which they described as 'availability', 'representativeness' and 'anchoring'. Availability is the ease with which a particular idea or thought about a person or situation can be brought to mind or the speed at which an idea or adjective is associated with a person. Representativeness is when people use categories or stereotypes and make a judgement based on perceived likeness with a particular stereotype or category in order to find causal relationships between people because they may appear to resemble one another. The anchoring effect is the subconscious phenomenon of having expectations about someone else's behaviour due to our existing knowledge of, or previous perceptions and conclusions about, them.

In the busy information-overloaded world in which many operate, we need to be able to filter information quickly about other people to get what is really relevant and important at the time. We have many decisions to make each day and it is not surprising that we have developed a quicker and easier way to get through this constant stream of decisions. However, this habitual automatic way of making decisions based on availability, representativeness and anchoring means that we may be disproportionately influenced by our past experience, assumptions, judgements and preconceived ideas about people, which can get us stuck in a cycle of applying the same old historical perceptions about a person's reputation.

3.9: Ten Common Cognitive Biases

Our perceptions differ greatly on so many things and just because we see something a particular way does not make it true or accurate. We can be so insistent sometimes that our way of seeing something is more right than someone else's way of seeing something. Many people convince themselves that they are 'telling the truth' but this doesn't mean they have been doing so. Many truths are preserved and felt differently, perspectives harden into fixed narratives, and the stories people tell about other people's reputation are often warped and distorted by private agendas.

Most of us believe that we are unbiased and objective

One way of better understanding how we form a view about someone's reputation is to consider the ways in which our perceptions may be inaccurate or biased. Most of us, of course, believe that we are unbiased, good at appraising people and coming to some sensible judgement about a person's reputation that is fair and rational. But in practice, most of us come up short.

The following section looks in more detail at 10 common cognitive biases which may potentially distort our views about a person's reputation.

Halo Effect Bias: A person's reputation can be positively or negatively skewed as research suggests that we have tendency to maintain a consistent view of other people by liking or disliking everything about the person. We may have either a very positive or negative perception about another person in terms of some particular attribute, and then as a consequence, we believe that the other person is positively endowed or negatively deficient on a whole range of other unrelated attributes.

Leniency Bias: A person's reputation can be positively inflated if we have a tendency to be very generous, tolerant and accommodating in our assessments of other people, and consequently there is a lack of discrimination, colour and accuracy in our assessment of their reputation.

Availability Bias: A person's reputation can be positively or negatively influenced when our assessment is overly influenced by the most recent events or memories. This is a mental shortcut. The recent event may have been a successful project or an unsuccessful task or just a recent pleasant or unpleasant experience, and can disproportionately influence our perception of the other individual.

Affinity Bias: A person's reputation can be enhanced because we are more likely to think well of people who appear to have a similar personality to ours and who appear to share similar interests. When our perception of the other person correlates highly with the extent to which they are seen as similar to us, this similarity is allowed to overly influence our perception of their performance and reputation.

First Impression Bias: A person's reputation can be positively or negatively influenced when we tend to overly focus on the first impression an individual has made; draw conclusions about the person based on relatively insubstantial situation-specific issues, which carry inappropriate or disproportionate weight; and our perception of their reputation tends to remain unchanged over a long period of time.

Confirmation Bias: When we have an idea in our mind about another person, we tend to look for evidence that supports that idea and tend not to pay attention to evidence that does not support or contradicts the idea. Therefore, a person's reputation can be positively or negatively influenced when we seek to focus on information about a person that confirms our beliefs, perceptions and preconceptions, and also tend to ignore or filter out facts and opinions that do not support our beliefs.

Stereotype Bias: We all have a tendency to classify people into categories or stereotypes as this is a convenient and easy way to understand and make sense of people. Moreover, it helps us predict the way we think that people will behave. However, we may tend to classify or categorise people incorrectly and we often tend to ignore information if it contradicts our perception and the stereotype we have formed.

Self-Perception Bias: Our view of ourselves can also affect our perception of other people. If you consider yourself a caring person then there may be a tendency to avoid offering unflattering descriptions of another person as you would not like to appear uncaring in the reputational description you provide.

Hindsight Bias: A person's reputation can be influenced when we describe a person's reputation based on the outcome of events and we then retrospectively try to create a coherent picture of the other person to explain the successful or unsuccessful outcomes. This is also known as 'being wise after the event'.

Memory Reconstruction Bias: When we have gaps in our memory, we have a tendency to reconstruct our memories into a credible and consistent narrative. Therefore, our memory of how someone behaved is rarely as accurate as we might think, and so we might complete the picture and fill in the gaps to form a reputation about another person that is not a representation of what actually happened.

3.10: Subliminal Impact on Reputation – Eight Subliminal Conditioning Effects

Subliminal impact on our perception of someone's reputation may occur when we are not aware of how our thinking may be primed or conditioned by prior or associated events. In effect, our thinking is conditioned in a way that predisposes us to think in a particular way about people. Eight subliminal effects are described below.

Eight Subliminal Conditioning Effects

Priming Effect: A person's reputation can be positively or negatively influenced by the 'priming effect', which occurs when other people tell us what they think about the person, positive or negative, or selectively share examples of their behaviour that may then influence our view of the person's reputation.

Framing Effect: A person's reputation can be influenced by the different ways in which information is 'framed' or presented by someone describing how that individual might be expected to behave. The same information presented in different ways to us will evoke different emotional reactions from us and so influence our perception of someone's reputation.

Anchoring Effect: The 'anchoring effect' refers to the benchmark or informal norms we use when we are seeking to make sense of information given to us. A person's reputation can be influenced by the choice of anchor or benchmark. Our first impression is often the 'anchor' or 'base' upon which subsequent perceptions are established. If our first experience of a particular person was negative then that experience will influence and colour

CHAPTER 3: REPUTATION, BIAS AND PREJUDICE

subsequent interactions. Also, if we have certain expectations of a person at a particular level of seniority, our 'anchor' or reference group will be more demanding and challenging, and consequently, we may be more demanding of the standards expected.

Selective Attention Effect: A person's reputation can also be influenced if we spend little time thinking about them, then choose to focus on a small but not necessarily representative sample of their behaviour and mislead ourselves by not thinking through all the available evidence as a consequence of a lack of time.

Competition Neglect Effect: A person's reputation may be influenced when we do not make meaningful comparisons with how someone at the person's level might be expected to behave. As a consequence, we may choose to overestimate or underestimate a person as a result of using an inappropriate comparison group.

Impulsive Thinking Effect: We may over-react impulsively and emotionally or jump to a conclusion without waiting for sufficient information before reaching a conclusion. Our opinion of a person may often be based on feelings and impressions rather than evidence that backs up our position.

Polarisation Effect: A person's reputation can be distorted if we have a tendency for black-and-white binary thinking and if we have limited tolerance for shades of grey. If we think in black-and-white terms, we can become very judgemental and polarised in our thinking because we may only consider the extreme options and may fail to consider alternative interpretations of what happened.

Catastrophising Effect: A person's reputation can be negatively exaggerated if we have a tendency to think catastrophically. If we perceive some behaviour as wrong, we may have a tendency to exaggerate the consequences and then get things completely out of perspective. This can lead to extreme negative feelings about a person's reputation.

3.11: Distorted Perceptions and the Impact on Reputational Value

So what do we make of all these different ways in which our perceptions are influenced? Can any weight or value be placed on a person's reputation when our perceptions differ greatly on so many things? Just because we see a person behaving in a particular way and form a reputational judgement about that person, this does not mean that our way of seeing the person is any more accurate than the view of another person unless we have a process in place to form these judgements.

Intuitive thinking and rational thinking

The Nobel Prize-winning author Daniel Kahneman [8] offered another view of how human intuition works. The basic idea presented by Kahneman is that we have two basic modes of thinking. He referred to the first mode of thinking as 'System 1': this is our intuitive thinking processes, which are fast, impulsive, automatic and emotional, and usually reflect our cognitive biases that result in impressions, feelings and inclinations. Kahneman's second mode of thinking, 'System 2', is our rational thinking processes and this mode of thinking is usually slow, evidence-based, reflective, deliberate and systematic, and it is usually the outcome of a considered evaluation that results in logical conclusions. Therefore, the more we can use System 2 processes before we pronounce a judgement on someone's reputation, the more accurate will be our description of a person's reputation.

CHAPTER 3: REPUTATION, BIAS AND PREJUDICE

Reality is a fluid concept

Reality, therefore, is a very fluid concept. Our version of what is real is only our perception of it. Therefore, at one level, it does appear that the accuracy of a person's reputation is unique to the perception of one individual. However, at another level, if several people sample similar types of behaviour and form similar conclusions then we would assume that there is a higher degree of probability that the reputation does reflect the character of the person.

Although it is only our perception, we do have a choice about how we perceive things and we have a choice about how we respond and react to the behaviours we observe. As we try to make sense of the world around us, we use our beliefs to make assumptions about a person's probable future behaviours. However, once established, our beliefs are usually accepted by us as facts and rarely challenged, and so a person's reputation can persist for a very long time. We also create an emotional attachment to our 'map of reality' and this process tends to take place at a subconscious level. However, our map is not reality as it is only our version of what is real and so, from time to time, our map needs to be updated.

Chapter 3 Key Summary Points

- Our reputation is based on the perceptions of others and this may give rise to our having different reputations with different people. Our reputation may vary from situation to situation and from group to group.
- Reputation is a blend of rationality and irrationality, and our irrational feelings, prejudices and biases can influence our perception as much as our rational conclusions. We make sense of observed behaviours in a very individualistic way.
- Different individuals use a different set of criteria to interpret behaviour based on their version of reality, which reflects their perceptions, biases, experiences and preferences. Similar information about an individual will

- be interpreted in different ways by different people and different conclusions will be formed about their reputation.
- The process by which reputations are formed is a direct consequence of the perceptual filters used by others and these filters are subject to sources of error, bias, unconscious subliminal effects, unsound reasoning and logical fallacies.
- Our perception of someone's reputation can be distorted by our fallible memories. We construct entire reputational narratives about other people on the basis of memories that may often be wrong.
- Cognitive dissonance theory proposes that we try to form consistent patterns of thoughts about an individual and may reject conflicting evidence in order to maintain a consistent pattern of ideas about that person, and this can work in both a positive and negative direction for a person's reputation.
- According to attribution theory, we look for causes to explain other people's behaviour. The fundamental attribution error is that we are more likely to attribute personal characteristics to explain our own successes and attribute external causes beyond our control to explain our failures. Conversely, when we seek to explain other people's behaviour, we attribute external factors to explain their successes and personal characteristics to explain their failures. As a consequence, this error may lead to misleading interpretations of someone's reputation.
- According to personal construct theory, we all have preferred constructs or labels that we use to describe people based on our values and life experiences. We place more emphasis on certain constructs or descriptors so as to reflect the attributes which are more highly valued by us.
- Misunderstandings about a person's reputation may occur because we hear what we want to hear. We assume that

CHAPTER 3: REPUTATION, BIAS AND PREJUDICE

we understand what the other person is saying or doing when we may not understand, which may lead to our having a distorted view about someone's reputation unless we look for evidence to check our assumptions.
- Judgements about other people's reputation are often inaccurate because of perceptual errors and cognitive biases, and ten cognitive bias examples are introduced such as halo effect bias, leniency bias, recency bias, affinity bias, first impression bias, confirmation bias, stereotype bias, self-perception bias, hindsight bias and memory reconstruction bias.
- Subliminal conditioning impacts on the way we perceive others and eight subliminal conditioning effects are described such as the priming effect, framing effect, anchoring effect, selective attention effect, competition neglect effect, impulsive thinking effect, polarisation effect and catastrophising effect.
- The accuracy of a person's reputation is unique to the perception of one individual but if several people sample similar types of behaviour and form similar conclusions, we can assume that there is a higher degree of probability that the reputation does reflect the character of the person.

PART 2

HOW REPUTATIONS ARE WON AND LOST

Chapter 4

Reputation Perceived from Outside-in and Inside-out

"A leader is like a shepherd. He stays behind the flock, letting the most nimble go out ahead, whereupon the others follow, not realising that all along they are being directed from behind… You put others in front, especially when celebrating victory and when nice things occur. You take the front line when there is danger. Then people will appreciate your leadership".

Nelson Mandela

Chapter 4 Key Points

- Reputations formed will differ depending on whether a person is viewed from an outside-in perspective (the impact of their behaviour) or an inside-out perspective (the intention behind their behaviour)
- The unwritten rules of leadership effectiveness
- The secret language
- The leadership capability continuum
- High Potential Reputation Outside-in Model
    - Culture creating capability
    - Strategic thinking capability
    - Delivering excellence capability
    - Team leadership capability
    - Organisational influence capability

CHAPTER 4: REPUTATION PERCEIVED FROM OUTSIDE-IN AND INSIDE-OUT

4.1: Outside-in and Inside-out Perspectives

Reputation is a consequence of what a person does: however, some behaviours may only be known to the person themselves whilst other behaviours have more observable consequences and are known to others. We tend to judge ourselves by our intentions as we tend to assume that our behaviours reflect our good intent, but we tend to judge others by the impact of their behaviours rather than their intentions.

It is self-evident that many of our behaviours and intentions are not immediately obvious to others, but over time, they may become a key element of our reputation. On the other hand, it would be difficult to establish a reputation if others were not able to see the impact and outcomes as a consequence of our behaviour.

Therefore, there are two ways to look at a person's reputation: from the outside-in perspective, which is outcome-focused or results-focused and refers to the impact or evidence-based consequences of our behaviour that can be perceived by colleagues; and the inside-out perspective, which is focused on behavioural intentions, refers to our motivations and how we aspire to behave, and which may often be only known to ourselves.

Colleagues perceive the outside-in perspective, but if they get to know a person well they may also have a glimpse of their intentions and motivations and have an inside-out perspective. Therefore, a comprehensive understanding of reputation needs to both include an appreciation of the outside-in perspective and the inside-out perspective if we are to form a complete picture of how reputations are formed.

The people with the best reputations, of course, will make an impact both from an inside-out perspective and from an outside-in perspective. Individuals with a strong reputation are mindful of how they need to behave to achieve good results and good outcomes, but they are also aware that they need to demonstrate observable, objective and tangible success in certain areas.

Key talent differentiators

This book is focused on identifying which leadership attributes are most noteworthy and most significant in enabling someone to have a stand-out reputation. So what are the key differentiators from an outside-in or an inside-out perspective that cause some people to stand out in relation to their peers? What types of impact or types of behaviour need to be evidenced to make someone stand out as a future leader or a potential leader?

Some people believe that there is an agreed set of essential and required leadership behaviours and abilities, but of course in reality, no such clarity of agreement exists. In addition, the overuse of certain terms leads to tired and over-used 'motherhood statements' that no longer have much meaning, and so the language used to describe desirable leadership behaviours can often appear very dated and lacking colour and differentiation.

In addition, the higher a person rises in an organisation, the more demanding we tend to be about the impact and behaviours that we expect to see. Some outcomes and behaviours are essential but nevertheless not noteworthy because we expect them as a minimum standard for individuals in senior positions. Other variables are 'knockout factors' that will definitely rule out potential candidates from senior positions and destroy a person's career. The most pressing need in a discussion about reputation is to identify those factors that are most significant and powerful in differentiating between the best, most outstanding leaders and the only moderately good or average leaders.

The unwritten rules

In most organisations, promotions are governed by unwritten rules that reflect the intuitive, often poorly expressed feelings of senior executives regarding an individual's ability to progress. Decisions about who gets promotions can often seem mysterious and arbitrary. Individuals with strong performance reviews and a strong track record often get passed over and, in most companies, performance feedback is often vague and confusing because no-one wants to demotivate or to demoralise senior managers.

However, the key focus of this book is to identify the key attributes that will shape the development of a positive leadership reputation. I want to focus on the select number of 'leadership talent differentiators' that enable a small number of talented people to stand out from the vast majority of would-be leaders with regard to their reputation.

The rules of the game change

There is a familiar adage popularised by Marshall Goldsmith, that 'what got you here, won't get you there' and Goldsmith used the phrase as the title of a book. The paradox is that you get promoted on the basis of specific outcomes, functional skills and attributes, and then these attributes may cease to be as important because the new leadership role values 'relationship skills' more than 'doing skills' or just tangible outcomes and results.

Many new leaders do not even know that the rules of the game change as individuals progress to more senior levels of leadership; once they realise, they are often highly uncomfortable in letting go of 'what got them there' and at the same time become resentful of the organisation, making comments like "they never told me this".

The days of muscle, machismo and masochism are giving way to the need for cerebral and emotional elasticity

At senior levels, it is no longer sufficient to 'know your stuff' and to be seen as a good functional and technically competent manager. Just because someone is performing well in their current job does not indicate that they will be successful in a more senior leadership role. At increasing levels of seniority, there is a different, more critical and more demanding layer of expectations, and typically these expectations are implicit, and not transparently expressed.

Each senior executive will have a different set of beliefs about the type of person who should be promoted to join them. Some talented individuals may emerge at the top because of outstanding results, excellent functional knowledge, good analytical skills, hard work and long hours. Unfortunately, they may struggle in other areas relating to people, politics, persuasion, perception, personal efficiency and positioning. The days of muscle, machismo and masochism are giving way to the need for cerebral and emotional elasticity.

Learning to give up behaviours that got you there in the first place

It is clear that technical and functional proficiency can be very important at junior and mid-management level, but there is a point in a career at which functional expertise and knowledge become less important as the individual gains promotions. At a certain level of seniority, it can even prove to be a liability if the manager ends up micro-managing and becoming a bottleneck by telling people how to do things rather than focusing on what needs to be achieved. The leader's role is to energise other people, empower and help them to perform but not to do their job for them.

Successful leaders appreciate that they are no longer the producer, instead having to multiply their influence and impact by learning how to grow and develop others, and learning how to work through others rather than focusing on how they can produce themselves. As a consequence, they must learn to give up behaviours that may have resulted in them being successful in the past but which are no longer appropriate.

The leadership capability continuum

The task of identifying the core theme of effective leadership competencies is further complicated by the fact that every person performs to a greater or lesser level on each competency. Each leadership competency is a relative concept, and there is a continuum or performance scale that needs to be climbed.

Identifying star performers is subtle and complex. The required qualities are typically not well understood and many senior executives cannot see what makes the difference between a 5/10 and a 7/10 performance when it comes to evaluating their own behavioural skills or attitudes. Few senior executives would rate themselves a 5/10 but statistically most of them are! And if they knew that they were rated a 5/10 by senior managers, what would they do about it?

Leadership competencies do not predict high potential

The understanding of leadership competencies is not the answer to understanding how leadership reputations are formed or how high potential leaders are identified. The problem is that the skills needed to be effective in the present are not the same as the skills needed to be effective in the future.

Individuals who are very successful in their current role may have a narrow functional focus and lack the broad-ranging skills and behaviours required for more senior roles. Leadership competencies typically describe an end state – what leaders will look like when they are successful in their current role – but they do not describe future high-potential indicators. The leadership competencies only tend to indicate the gaps between current and desired levels of performance. Therefore, we need to establish a methodology or a framework in an attempt to develop a better understanding of how reputations are formed and can be enhanced. An essential part of the 'high potential reputation model' is a realisation that:

1: There are some leadership attributes that are necessary or desirable but not sufficient in themselves;
2: There are some other leadership attributes that can block or derail progress; and
3: There are some key talent differentiators that strongly predict future outstanding leadership effectiveness and career progression, and these factors are described in the High Potential Reputation Outside-in Model and the High Potential Reputation Inside-out Model presented in the following pages.

Minimum requirements

For the purposes of analysing what makes a good leadership reputation, we are taking it as a given that successful leaders need a number of core skills. However, these are basic skills that are not in scarce supply and do not differentiate between the average and most successful outstanding leaders.

The minimum requirements tend to refer to those attributes that are basically essential if a person is to be seen as a serious contender for a leadership role. It is clear that someone who is to be considered for leadership positions must have a strong functional and technical competence, and a good track record of achieving well in previous roles. When asked to define the ideal leader with a high reputation, many would emphasise such traits as vision, intelligence, decision-making, relationship-building, organising and executing, adapting, stamina, energy, enthusiasm, resilience and integrity. All these skills may be necessary but they are not sufficient qualities for a leader to be outstanding.

Knockout factors

In addition to these minimum requirements to become a potential leadership candidate, there are a number of other characteristics that would eliminate a person from any list of potential leadership contenders. These 'knockout factors' would include very poor or limited interpersonal skills that rub people up the wrong way, and they may refer to an abrasiveness, insensitivity or bullying personality. If someone is seen to act predominantly out of self-interest or to lack integrity, there is limited possibility that they would be able to attract the followership necessary for individuals to succeed in a leadership role.

4.2: The Fundamental Five Outside-in Reputation Winners

There are some key talent differentiators that will strongly predict future outstanding leadership effectiveness and career progression, and in the author's view, distinguish outstanding performers from those who are merely average or adequate. The author is proposing a High Potential Reputation Outside-in Model and a High Potential Reputation Inside-out Model. The High Potential Reputation Outside-in Model looks for evidence that successful high-potential leaders are able to demonstrate their ability via observable outcomes as reflected by the impact of their behaviours. The Inside-out Model looks for evidence in their intentions, the way they think and approach their job.

The Outside-in Model is based on the premise that successful leaders will only succeed in enhancing their reputation if they demonstrate practical, observable achievements in the following five areas:

- **Culture Building:** The ability to create an environment in which people can give of their best.
- **Strategic Thinking:** The ability to set vision, direction and initiate change.
- **Delivering Excellence:** The ability to execute given tasks and maintain excellent operational standards.
- **Team Leadership**: The ability to deliver high performance through others.
- **Organisational Influence**: The ability to influence others at all levels and across all functions for optimum impact.

Outside-in Reputation Winner 1: Culture Building

Successful leaders create an environment and an atmosphere in which people have the opportunity to give of their best. All top leaders tend to make us feel very special and valued. They manage to make us feel noticed and we are pleased when we are singled out for attention. The outstanding leader must also be a defender of standards, a moral compass, a spiritual leader in the way that they shape the culture of the team, influence the thinking, attitudes and values of the team, and the leaders must be a driving force to get things done quickly, to get people to challenge themselves and constantly reflect on how they can improve to do things better.

Outside-in Reputation Winner 2: Strategic Thinking

Successful leaders are forward thinkers who have a clear sense of the organisation's mission and who provide shape, direction and purpose as to what the organisation wants to achieve. Top leaders must be able to innovate and set direction in the pursuit of some long-term strategy and goal. The primary role of a strategy is to focus on the few things that matter most for the achievement of competitive advantage. All top leaders need to be able to think strategically about how their organisation can compete in the market place and develop an edge over their competitors. Successful leaders are forward thinking, lateral thinking and intellectually curious, but 'strategic thinking' may also refer to the ability to innovate and change so that internal processes and systems are also optimally efficient. This strategic focus must also include the ability to communicate a shared vision of the direction in which the organisation needs to travel in order to galvanise colleagues and staff, and help others understand the team or organisation's overall direction. Finally, the successful leader needs the perspective and ability to balance the tension between the challenge of daily tasks and operations and the strategic delivery of actions that may impact on the long-term success of the organisation.

Outside-in Reputation Winner 3: Delivering Excellence

Successful leaders must be able to deliver the organisation's agenda and achieve objectives by careful use of tactics, astute judgement and decision-making. Delivery and planning efficiently are about doing things right and producing success through careful forecasts, planning, monitoring, measurement and analysis. All top leaders must have the ability to execute operational plans and monitor and analyse performance. The top leader needs to be personally efficient and develop appropriate skills to organise and manage their time to choose between competing priorities, and not get sucked into too low a level of detail so that they cannot see the bigger picture or continue to steer and monitor the organisation. This skill clearly involves a high level of judgement and decision making, good personal organisation, great time management and being consistent and reliable in following through on promises and agreed plans. It requires the ability to accept responsibility and accountability, and to be sufficiently motivated and able to use systems to monitor and track progress. Very importantly, it also means having the ability to analyse how progress has been successful or unsuccessful so that appropriate remedial action can be taken.

Outside-in Reputation Winner 4: Team Leadership

Successful leaders must have a clear sense of what is involved in compiling a high-performing team and must have the capability to select, inspire, motivate and coach individuals to achieve high performance levels. They must be able to engage with teams and make individuals want to follow them and be led by them. All top team leaders need to have the psychological insight and behavioural analytical skills to select and identify talent, set direction, coach to challenge, raise and develop performance, motivate and tackle underperformance in a controlled and timely manner. It requires the ability to stretch, challenge and energise as well as the ability to demonstrate care and compassion for the team, and perhaps a hard-headedness and toughness to remove underperformers.

Outside-in Reputation Winner 5: Organisational Influence

Successful leaders must have the ability to make an impact and influence across functional boundaries and at different levels by recognising the need to adapt and tailor their influencing and communication style to different groups. They must also have the ability to influence across vertical, horizontal, stakeholder, demographic and geographic boundaries. The best leaders have multi-faceted and adaptable influencing styles tailored for the needs of specific people, specific situations and specific messages. They also need to demonstrate political savvy in networking wisely to gather information, ideas, insights and contacts to develop a broad perspective to strengthen their judgement and develop an understanding of who needs to be influenced in order to get things done. They need to be prepared to communicate regularly to manage expectations and understand how to present information in clear unambiguous language that is succinct, relevant, memorable and tailored to the needs of different audience groups.

4.3: The Fundamental Four Inside-out Reputation Winners

The Inside-out Model is based on the premise that successful leaders will build an outstanding reputation if they are seen to possess and demonstrate well-developed attributes and personal characteristics in the following four areas:

- **Self-awareness:** The ability to be realistic in self-assessing their strengths and weaknesses, and to be driven by the need to self-improve and search for marginal gains.
- **Likeability:** The ability to connect with a wide range of people at different levels and in different roles in such a way that colleagues are inspired and motivated to work with and for them.
- **Wise judgment:** The ability to reflect and think broadly and deeply about problems with an open, curious mind and broad perspective to enable high-quality decisions and judgements.
- **Perceptiveness:** The ability to be insightful and intuitive, and interested to explore how and why other people behave, think and feel in the way they do to enable a more insightful approach to influencing others and attracting followership.

Inside-out Reputation Winner 1: Self-Awareness

Successful leaders will constantly assess their performance and look for ways to improve. An essential requirement for all high-potential leaders is to be self-aware with the ability to recognise their strengths and personal development areas. They need to demonstrate a curiosity to explore different ways for self-improvement, and the curiosity to search for 'marginal gains' as a leader as opposed to focusing only on trying to improve the organisation's functioning.

Inside-out Reputation Winner 2: Likeability

Successful leaders need to be likeable, in that individuals need to enjoy working with them if they are going to offer support and follow them. Leaders need to be able to connect and collaborate with colleagues who may have different styles, different personalities and different backgrounds. The likeable leader needs to be considerate, encouraging, and compassionate as well as challenging in a constructive way.

Inside-out Reputation Winner 3: Wise Judgement

Successful leaders need to have well-developed critical-thinking skills that lead to wise judgements. This is more than being intellectually smart as wise judgement requires an open-mindedness, curiosity and broad perspective to consider a range of different hard and soft variables. It requires the ability to think widely and deeply about different options, and the ability to recognise and control personal biases in their thinking. It involves asking questions about specific assumptions and the consequences of specific actions, thinking beyond the boundaries to make unexpected connections in order to improve or reframe a particular solution or outcome. Many intellectually bright, clever people are good linear thinkers in situations that require the application of knowledge to find a finite solution or in which there is a binary 'black or white' answer to a problem. However, that is being smart rather than wise: wisdom requires the ability to suspend judgement, think 'divergently' and analyse in breadth and depth about the pluses and minuses of various options and possibilities before converging on a proposal, plan of action or a sound considered judgement.

Inside-out Reputation Winner 4: Perceptiveness

Successful leaders need to be psychologically minded and perceptive about others, which means being insightful and intuitive about other people. This requires the curiosity to explore how and why people behave, think and feel in the way they do rather than in just what they do. A perceptive person is a good judge of how people feel and what they think about things, and they are very good at noticing things about people which other people may miss.

Chapter 4 Key Summary Points

- Reputations will differ depending on whether you view a person from an outside-in perspective, which is outcome or result focused, or an inside-out perspective, which is behaviour, intention or value focused.
- In most organisations there is a secret language that refers to the key attributes and characteristics which differentiate high performers but which do not typically appear in formal performance review documentation.
- Leadership competencies are relative concepts, but the leadership capability continuum is not well understood by most senior executives.
- The High Potential Reputation Outside-in Model includes the Fundamental Five Reputation Outside-in Winners that drive and shape a person's leadership reputation:
  - Culture-building
  - Strategic thinking
  - Delivering excellence
  - Team leadership
  - Organisational influence.
- The High Potential Reputation Inside-out Model includes the Fundamental Four Inside-out Reputation Winners that drive and shape a person's leadership reputation:
  - Self-awareness
  - Likeability
  - Wise judgment
  - Perceptiveness.

Chapter 5

The Fundamental Five Outside-in Reputation Winners

> "If we were all judged according to the consequences
> Of all our words and deeds, beyond the intention
> And beyond our limited understanding
> Of ourselves and others, we should all be condemned".
>
> T.S. Eliot, *The Cocktail Party* [1]

Chapter 5 Key Points

- How to develop a reputation for culture building
- How to develop a reputation for strategic thinking
- How to develop a reputation for delivery and execution
- How to develop a reputation for team leadership
- How to develop a reputation for organisational influence

The following chapter looks in more detail at the Fundamental Five Outside-in Reputation Winners that will help to win an outstanding reputation, and describes how to build a strong reputation in each of the fundamental five areas. For each of the Fundamental Five Outside-in Reputation Winners, we look at the following two questions:
- Why are these behaviours important for winning a strong reputation?
- How can these behaviours be developed to improve a reputation?

5.1: How to Win a Reputation for Building Strong Cultures

Why is building a strong positive culture important for developing a reputation?

The capability to build a strong positive culture is important in developing a reputation because culture impacts on everyone's ability to perform at their best. Organisational culture gets talked about a lot by people discussing successful organisations, and senior leaders are highly influential in shaping the culture in which people work. Every leader has a significant role to play in creating, nurturing and maintaining the organisational culture. In many ways, the leader or boss is the face of the culture and the biggest contributing factor to it, and so each leader needs to consider what they can do to have a positive impact on changing or maintaining a culture that enables others to give of their best.

To put it simply, culture is about what it is like to work where you are and how things are done in the organisation; we all impact on the organisation culture with everything that we do and how we behave. The type of culture an organisation develops is considered an important factor in improving job satisfaction, retention, trust levels, productivity levels and much more. However, a culture is not static: an organisational culture is always fluid and always adjusting.

Spiritual leaders

Successful leaders need to be seen as 'spiritual' leaders in the sense in that they are the champions and defenders of desirable values. They should be able to demonstrate consistent standards and values by having a clear philosophy about how people should behave with one another, how business should be conducted, what behaviours are desirable and appropriate, and what behaviours are undesirable, inappropriate and unacceptable. This usually involves a recognition of the importance of showing humility, demonstrating integrity and being aware that the leader needs to be seen as a role model to set the standards for the culture and the organisation. People need to see leaders as competent to do the job but they also need to believe that leaders will do what they say they will, and that they have the best interests of the team and organisation as their priority, as opposed to acting out of self-interest. Good leaders need to be focused on building a positive optimistic culture. It is expected that they will treat colleagues and direct reports with respect and integrity.

If high-potential individuals perceive their values as being incongruent with the values of the organisation, high-potential individuals will seek to work in other organisations. Conversely, those individuals who have values congruent with the organisation will be more likely and more motivated to stay with the organisation. Corporate values should influence selection procedures and decisions, and a good leader should ensure that their values are transparent to all levels within the organisation.

Successful leaders must be prepared to champion the key values of the business, which involves being an exemplar and role model for the type of culture the organisation wishes to espouse and a defender of the standards that the organisation wishes to promote. Good leaders win trust and respect because they 'walk the talk', they are role models and they are exemplars for maintaining standards and creating a positive work environment.

Values guide our work behaviour

Values are those things that are important to us. Values influence our choice of behaviour, how we choose to relate to others and the way we choose to act towards other people. Whereas skill and competence are no guarantees of success, values reflect a set of assumptions about how a leader will behave. Values are important because they set the agenda for how we see things and our values control how we evaluate and react to events around us.

Although values are important, we also need to know about how a leader prioritises their values and what weight they place on their values. For example, if I say that honesty is important to me, you might expect that I will always tell the truth. However, in fact, knowing that honesty is important to me will give you little idea as to whether I will always tell you the truth, unless you know the priority I place on honesty relative to my other values. If I place a higher value on being liked than on honesty, then I may not give you honest feedback, if I fear that doing so would create tension in our relationship or alienate you in some way.

How can the capability to build a strong positive culture be developed to improve a reputation?

The capability to build a strong positive culture can be developed to improve a reputation by focusing on the following four strategies and behaviours:
1. Leadership philosophy
2. Team code of conduct
3. Career development
4. Employee surveys.

1. Leadership philosophy

When we refer to cultural values, we are referring to the leadership philosophy that a leader wishes to develop and promote. Basically, it refers to the leader's philosophy or beliefs about how they should lead an organisation, how they should manage people, how they expect people to behave with each other, how they expect leaders to behave with their direct reports, how they expect to manage upwards to their senior managers, and how people are expected to behave to get things done in the organisation. A leader should also feel confident about articulating their leadership philosophy as an explanation or justification of why they are choosing to behave in the way that they do, and why it is important, for example, that they do not attend every meeting or spend their time 'in the trenches' or ensure that they are not managing at too low a level of detail.

It is important, therefore, for a leader to communicate a leadership philosophy to build a desired culture in the following ways. Firstly, it is important for the leader to communicate a clear vision of the culture they want to develop, and so the leader should write this down and talk about it. Secondly, the leader needs to make sure that their behaviour matches the culture they want to reinforce. They must therefore be a role model. Thirdly, the leader must communicate clear expectations. The leader thus needs to let others know what behaviours they are looking for, how they can demonstrate evidence of displaying these behaviours, and agree as to how to hold people accountable for their ability and motivation to develop these behaviours. Fourthly, the leader needs to ensure that their decisions will be consistent in the impact on the culture they are trying to create, and seek feedback from others. Finally, every leader makes an important decision when they bring people into their team or organisation. It is important that the leader considers the culture when they hire, assessing whether the person will fit and whether they will contribute naturally to the culture the leader is trying to nurture.

A senior leader would benefit from writing down their values and sharing these with their teams to increase the visibility of the type of culture that they would like to develop. It is clearly a very personal challenge to own and articulate a personal philosophy based on sincerely held values but the following are examples of some typical values:

- Integrity: As demonstrated by honest, truthful relationships, putting the interest of the team and organisation above self-interest, keeping promises and being trustworthy.
- Respect: As demonstrated by treating others with dignity, empathy and compassion.
- Interest and concern for others: As demonstrated by a preparedness to ask questions about personal interests, feelings and reactions so that you get to know the person and show care and concern for their well-being.
- Generosity of spirit: As demonstrated by the preparedness to give others the benefit of the doubt, to be generous in recognising good work, giving credit where it is due, and to be generous in public praise and recognition of what others have achieved.

- Authenticity: As demonstrated by transparency in actions and the types of behaviours that one chooses to exhibit. It is important to reflect on whether or not you are comfortable with who you are and the decisions you have made about yourself. There is thus no place for pretence or trying to make up a story about oneself that is not genuine.
- Courage: As demonstrated by standing up for one's beliefs, taking a stand in the face of adversity, being prepared to act for the common good, and to confront and stand up to senior managers or colleagues when necessary.
- Humility: As demonstrated by a self-awareness of one's limitations and how others will produce a superior performance in certain areas; being open to the feedback and the perspectives of others.
- Balanced judgement: As demonstrated by the willingness to seek out and embrace different views and perspectives, and the avoidance of polarised, black-and-white judgements and convictions not based on reason and logic.
- Curiosity: As demonstrated by the preparedness to question what 'good' looks like and to share best practices with others. Curiosity is the desire to learn more about something and is the catalyst for innovation and strategic change.
- Going the extra mile: As demonstrated by the preparedness to offer help and support to colleagues both within and outside your team and functional area in situations where the job does not require you to offer this type of support to others.

As an action step, try to make a list of eight key values that you believe reflect your leadership philosophy to create a positive work culture. Then write down how those values can potentially be demonstrated by certain behaviours and how you demonstrate those values in your day-to-day behaviour. Then write down those day-to-day behaviours that do not support your espoused values and how you feel when you fail to demonstrate a particular value. Finally, using this information, write down one or two sentences to describe the philosophy that encapsulates and prioritises what is important to you as a leader.

2. Team code of conduct

In order to create the framework to enable a team culture to evolve, a leader could draw up written guidelines or a 'team code of conduct' on what standards of behaviour are expected and how people should behave towards their colleagues, their direct reports and their senior managers. These guidelines may also contain behavioural suggestions on how to resolve team disagreements. There should be an agreed process, which is put down in writing, on how to manage conflicts, how to manage a failure by colleagues to live up to the agreed expectations, or how to hold the team leader accountable for meeting their leadership expectations and commitments.

3. Career development

In order to create a culture that will enable others to give of their best, it is important for the leader to invest time in the individual personal and career development of their team members. This means making time to be accessible, to motivate, and to make time for career planning and individual personal development discussions. This individual strategy will typically involve organising regular quarterly meetings with individual staff to discuss their personal and career development plans. These types of discussion show that the leader cares and will breed loyalty in team members. Every team member should have clarity about their career path and transparency on what they need to demonstrate to get to the next level.

As a starting point, the leader needs to communicate how individual performance will be measured in terms of task achievements and behavioural evidence. Ideally, each individual should have clarity in writing as to what behaviours they need to develop in order to continue to grow and optimise their contribution to the organisation. The leader needs to be transparent about whether opportunities exist for individuals to move to new assignments and roles as part of their career development. Finally, it goes without saying that the leader needs to ensure that fair compensation is linked to performance.

4. Employee surveys

Another good idea for the leader is to plan how to create a culture that enables individuals to give of their best by organising an employee/team survey every 6 or 12 months to take the temperature of the team's attitudes about various aspects of the work environment relating to how work is managed, management style, stress-inducing pressures, communications and what people would like to know.

Culture building key summary points

- Culture is about what it is like to work where you are and how things are done in the organisation; we all impact on the organisation culture with everything that we do and how we behave.
- A leader should be able to articulate their leadership philosophy and write down and share their values in relation to how he or she plans to demonstrate how they are promoting integrity, respect, interest and concern for others, generosity of spirit, authenticity, courage, humility, balanced judgement, curiosity and going the extra mile.
- A team code of conduct should be drafted with written guidelines on what standards of behaviour are expected, desirable and unacceptable, and how conflicts should be managed.
- In order to create a culture that will enable others to give of their best, it is important for the leader to invest time in the individual personal and career development of their team members.
- Employee surveys should be regularly conducted to allow feedback and contributions on a range of organisational,

management and leadership issues that impact on the organisation's culture.

5.2: How to Win a Reputation for Strategic Thinking

Why is strategic thinking important in developing a reputation?

Strategic thinking is a core competence for leaders and aspiring leaders because they need to understand the context in which the organisation operates, identify goals and explore options on how to move forward, close gaps and achieve these goals. Good strategic thinkers will be well informed about marketplace events and trends, and will continuously look for ways of reacting to changes in the marketplace or actions taken by competitors, and plan and respond accordingly. However, strategic thinking does require the ability to think conceptually and think about abstract problems, possibilities and opportunities, so there will be a wide variation in different people's ability to engage in these types of strategic thinking skills.

One golden rule of leadership is to be clear about strategy, objectives and direction, and never lose sight of the big picture and the common purpose. Strategic thinkers will also take a long-term view of their organisation and think about threats as well as opportunities for the organisation. Finally, good strategic leaders must be able to communicate a plan, a vision and a story in a compelling way that will inspire and motivate their colleagues to act, and ensure that their colleagues understand the overall direction of the organisation.

Making time to think ahead

Time needs to be set aside for strategic thinking and planning, during which leaders can avoid getting sucked into reacting to the needs of today. Leaders need to try to create the impression that they are in control of steering the organisation, anticipating future events, avoiding problems and not missing significant opportunities that could beneficially impact on the business. Therefore, leaders can send the wrong messages if they are seen to be too hands-on in 'rowing the boat'. They should be seen to have their 'head up' so that they can steer, anticipate and shape where the organisation is going. Followers need direction and guidance and they need to be encouraged to be enthusiastic about the future direction and how things can be better in the future. As a consequence, leaders need to be forward looking and to broaden their perspective to know and understand the aims of other functions and departments within the organisation. They need to be aware of external influences and external game-changers, and 'needle-moving' developments that may affect their organisation.

How can strategic thinking capability be developed to improve a reputation?

Strategic thinking skills can be developed to improve a reputation by focusing on the following five strategies and behaviours:
1. Thinking holistically
2. SWOT analysis
3. Facilitating innovative ideas
4. Strategic discussions
5. Create a compelling narrative.

1. Thinking holistically

Thinking holistically requires leaders to scan backwards, forwards and sideways in order to understand current patterns, future possibilities and possible connections. It is important that leaders make time to understand history and context, and to find out what is going on in the world. The best leaders understand geographical, demographic, industrial sector, function and organisational history. Leaders need to be well informed about their sector, their competitors and current challenges, being curious about what is happening in their function and industry, and knowing what questions to ask.

Leaders can learn to think holistically by reading extensively

CHAPTER 5: THE FUNDAMENTAL FIVE OUTSIDE-IN REPUTATION WINNERS

and by networking to build connections with competitors and influential opinion shapers. Leaders need to look beyond their organisation to understand how other organisations perform and operate, and remain open and flexible to explore how to learn new approaches.

Making time to think

Leaders need to make time to think and plan by scheduling thinking time in their calendar like any other activity. Thinking time is productive time. Thinking about future possibilities requires the ability to be reflective, to be well informed, to be able to spot patterns and make connections that may lead to a new, eclectic way of doing things. However, this is a major challenge as many leaders will complain that they are not able to make time for such activities. Therefore, leaders need to learn to delegate effectively and reduce their direct involvement in day-to-day management activities by developing improved delegation techniques, which includes asking direct reports to provide specific progress information at certain intervals to allow for monitoring of progress and provide confidence that the operational agenda is on track.

2. SWOT analysis

It is important that leaders undertake a regular analysis of the business by using a simple SWOT analysis of strengths, weaknesses, opportunities and threats as a means of generating new ideas.

3. Facilitating innovative ideas

Leaders do not have to be the source of strategic ideas. It is important to use other team members who may excel in this area but leaders can broaden their perspective by networking internally and externally with clients and customers so that they can develop a broad perspective about the business or organisation. However, to make strategic networking most effective, it is advisable to predetermine a list of questions on which the leader would like to hear different perspectives. It is also a great plan to write down what people say about specific topics and issues so that the leader can aggregate and analyse their responses, and compile a database on what colleagues or clients think about different issues. In such a way, the leader can initiate discussions with other senior colleagues based on the findings, and so be seen as an 'idea leader' or 'thought generator'. In order to optimise the leader's contribution as an idea generator or thought leader, it is important to network in a systematic, purposeful way. If the leader collects quality views from six-to-ten colleagues around two or three specific areas, they will gather 'good quality data' to offer judgements with gravitas and credibility, but they can also use the data to generate further discussion. They will then be able to say, for example, that on the basis of the group consulted, we know that 80% think x!

Thought leaders are usually good facilitators who have accumulated a breadth of opinion and then use this information to stimulate improved discussions and proposals. In this simple way, a person can become associated with ideas and be seen as a strategic thinker. In essence, the leader has become a facilitator who may not have new or original ideas themselves, but by bringing together the ideas of other people, they may be able to identify connections and links and introduce themes, trends and patterns that may not previously have been apparent.

4. Strategic discussions

If a leader is to develop a reputation as a strategic thinker, they need to be heard to be talking about strategic issues on a regular basis. This will be highly significant in shaping perceptions about their strategic skills. If they are seen and heard to be talking about competitors, or new products or different client feedback, and future possibilities and options shared from networking meetings with senior managers and leaders, then they will reinforce their image and reputation as a strategic thinker.

Developing and maintaining a reading list of current journals and managerial journals will also ensure that the leader is up to speed with any recent developments in their field. It is also advisable that aspiring leaders make some notes on their reading around strategic issues as potential topics for discussion with senior leaders.

5. Create a compelling narrative

A key element of strategic thinking is to be able to communicate a strategic vision in a compelling way. The first step is to simplify a potentially complex series of plans, and an excellent skill is to be able to draft single-page notes, flowcharts or mind maps so that complex ideas or proposals can be simplified and easily understood, possibly with the aid of diagrams. Not everyone is able to deliver a message or a plan in a way that will inspire but it is important not to kill a presentation about a strategic plan or vision with too much data and detail.

The challenge in communicating a strategic vision is to tell a story or provide anecdotes that might resonate with an audience. If the leader is not comfortable presenting to large groups then they need to find a smaller forum in which they can talk about a strategy but it is important that the leader conveys their personal commitment and try to appeal to the emotions of their audience. It can also be a useful tactic to invite different direct reports to introduce different parts of a strategic plan. This will help with the buy-in to the plan as long as they are seen to own what is being communicated.

Strategic thinking key summary points

- Outstanding leaders need to be clear about strategy, objectives, direction and the common purpose, and they must be able to communicate the plan or vision in a compelling way.
- Leaders also need to demonstrate that they are in control of the organisation, that they are steering it and forward-thinking about how things can be better in the future.

- Strategic thinking can be developed by making time to think holistically, for forward-thinking, undertaking a SWOT analysis, facilitating innovative networking discussions, engaging in discussions about strategic issues, learning how to plot future direction with the aids of flowcharts, one-pagers, or mind-maps, and learning how to create a compelling narrative to communicate the vision.

5.3: How to Win a Reputation for Delivery and Execution

Why is delivery and execution capability important for developing a reputation?

The capability to deliver and execute well is important because most successful leaders initially gain their reputation as doers who are able to deliver results; this is what gets them noticed and promoted to more senior roles. The ability to deliver, execute and get results involves the leader in working through others, improving their delegation skills; improving their time-management skills; learning to monitor, measure and analyse processes and procedures to ensure they are working efficiently for the team to implement on time; and to undertake tasks to a good level of quality that will attract repeat business and enhance the team and leader's reputation.

Avoid spending time on low-value activities

Most leaders spend too much time on low value, unproductive tasks at a level below their pay grade that may only create small incremental value to their organisation. With micro-managers, time is frittered away on too many meetings, on minimally important processes and too many 'status quo thinking' discussions, with the boss needing to make the final decision on most major issues to such an extent that the micro-managing boss may become a decision-making bottleneck.

Successful leaders are expected to be able to understand what is involved in the implementation and delivery process. However, as a leader gets to more senior levels, their job is not personally to manage the tasks but to learn to delegate effectively, and create an infrastructure with processes and procedures to ensure that tasks will be implemented, measured and monitored without drawing the leader into the detail of the tasks. As a leader's responsibilities increase, the leader needs to think through where they want to focus their time and energy, and they must be able to learn how to make other direct reports and colleagues accountable. If they are unable to empower others then they may become a bottleneck and an obstacle to delivering and executing the organisation's tasks and plans.

How can a capability to deliver and execute well be developed to improve a reputation?

The skills to deliver and execute well can be developed to improve a reputation by focusing on the following seven strategies and behaviours:

1. Delegation strategies
2. Using templates for delegated meetings
3. Analysis and evaluation
4. Creating roadmaps to track progress
5. Diary management
6. Learning to say 'no'
7. Personal development roadmap.

1. Delegation Strategies

Delegation skills can be greatly improved by rehearsing tasks with an individual direct report in the form of using carefully structured questions to rehearse how a task is to be completed by a specific person or team. Typical questions might include:
- What do you understand by the task?
- What do you see as the main issues and problems associated with the task?

- What support do you need from me or other parts of the organisation?
- How confident are you that you can complete the task?
- How confident are you that you can meet the deadline?
- If you are to miss the deadline, what is likely to be responsible and what can you do to minimise these disruptions or delays?
- What kind of issues do you feel appropriate to elevate to senior managers?
- How frequently should we follow up, measure and review progress?
- How do you assess the capability of your team to carry out the task, what are your major concerns and how will you seek to prepare the team to cope with the challenge?
- What metrics should we use to assess how well the task is progressing, and how will we measure how well the task has been undertaken and whether the task process has been successful?
- What criteria will you use when I ask you after the task completion to write an evaluation note on what could be done differently or better next time?

2. Using templates for delegated meetings

If the leader has to delegate and ask a direct report to attend a meeting on their behalf, a useful idea is to prepare a template of five or six issues on which you would like the delegated person to exercise their judgement, report back and analyse the contributions of different parties at the meeting. These issues may relate to less factual matters, perhaps to the dynamics of the meeting, the level of agreement in the meeting, the apparent alliances that were formed, the level of disagreement at the meeting, the amount of time different individuals spoke, the key influencers, the disengaged persons, the prioritisation of specific issues and so on. It may also include questions for your direct report to exercise their judgement on the atmosphere or temperature of the meeting, the level of consensus, the confidence that people will act on whatever agreement was reached and so on.

3. Analysis and evaluation

In the context of delivery and execution, a weakness of many operational managers is to focus on recording and reporting information without any in-depth analysis or evaluation of the information or data on which they are reporting. A common practice is to use a traffic-light system to provide progress reports. However, a major problem is that this tempts direct reports to get into the habit of reporting and recording, and not investing enough time in analysis, evaluation and interpretation of the facts, data and performance to date.

The key step-up strategy is to ask direct reports to analyse, evaluate and interpret information, and ask them to form a judgement on the significance of their analysis. There are two key questions the leader, line manager or team leader should be asking their direct reports. The first question is concurrently orientated in looking for an assessment of the current status of the task or project. The second question is future-orientated in looking for an assessment of their confidence that future targets will be achieved. For example:

- In your best judgement, taking everything into account that you know about the task, team and competing priorities, how satisfied are you, in percentage terms, with the current status or progress on this specific task?
- In your best judgement, taking everything into account that you know about the task, team and competing priorities, how confident are you, in percentage terms, that you will complete the task by the agreed date?

In the first instance, of course, it is not appropriate for a direct report to tell you that they are 100% satisfied with progress or 100% confident about the future. This would be a clear red warning light prompting you to probe further and deeper, being indicative of an assessment that is too simplistic.

Action plans should be recorded in writing. It is important to break down tasks or strategic plans into a series of action steps so that milestones are agreed, providing opportunities to monitor progress. Follow-up reports should always be in writing so that there is a trail to revisit if a task is not completed on the lines the direct report predicted or forecasted. The follow-up processes can involve monthly reports, roadmaps or dashboards.

4. Creating roadmaps to track progress

A 'roadmap' is a device for enabling a person to keep a line of sight on all their key priorities. It is usually drafted as a single-page document that is like a radar screen in that the roadmap highlights the six-to-eight key issues on which you or your team are focussing. It may contain headings like Key Focus/Priorities, Key Challenges/Difficulties and Success Measures. The idea is to focus attention on the key enablers and challenges to help the individual to step back and consider their goals for the next six or 12 months and focus on the prioritised tasks to achieve these goals. An example of a roadmap is reproduced below.

	Issue 1	Issue 2	Issue 3	Issue 4	Issue 5
Key Priorities					
Key Challenges					
Success Measures					

5. Diary management

It may be a valuable exercise for a leader to maintain a daily or weekly diary to track how they use their time and rigorously analyse which meetings they need to attend, which pieces of work they need to delegate and which strategic issues they should be prioritising.

It is also valuable for a leader to be able to schedule a one-hour personal time slot in their calendar on a consistent and regular basis. This gives them quality time to think about some of the bigger issues, to prepare for important meetings and to ensure that they are timely in their responsiveness and delivery to meet deadlines, as well as the needs and expectations of colleagues.

It is also important for a leader to review the extent of external

CHAPTER 5: THE FUNDAMENTAL FIVE OUTSIDE-IN REPUTATION WINNERS

networking activities carefully to ensure that time is well spent and to review whether colleagues could be attending some of these external events so that they can gain appropriate experience.

6. Learning to say 'no'

Leaders need to learn how to say 'no' in a polite, constructive and helpful way whilst using language that indicates that they do not want to let down the other person or produce work of inferior quality but have to prioritise other tasks that have been given higher priority. It is important that leaders are seen to be managing and shaping events as far as possible rather than getting into a reactive mindset where they are just responding to the pressures of the moment without stepping back to consider longer-term goals and priorities.

It is important to remember that leaders do not convey a good impression if they are constantly running around like headless chickens and are seen as being overly reactive to day-to-day tasks: colleagues will feel that they are not in control. It is more impressive and more expected from a senior manager to appear to have the time to be seen to be 'steering the ship' and in control of their functional area of responsibility, coaching their direct reports and available to allocate time selectively for the most pressing needs of the organisation or business.

Managing email traffic

It is important that leaders learn to be very responsive to emails as a matter of courtesy and respect to colleagues as well as a matter of judgement in managing colleagues' expectations. The purpose of responding to emails is to demonstrate that the leader can be trusted, that they are reliable and that they are considerate of their colleagues' time and agenda. If time is short, a simple technique is to learn to use 'holding emails' to thank a colleague for their email and let them know when they might expect a fuller response. Unfortunately, the more common practice is not to respond promptly, which can cause a huge amount of frustration and reputational damage.

7. Personal development roadmap

As a time-management tip, the one-page roadmap described above can also be used as a personal development tracking and monitoring device. This type of personal development roadmap aims to take a broader 'bigger picture' view of the leader's personal development goals by mapping out what they hope to achieve in the next 6 or 12 months. The personal development roadmap can be used to facilitate regular discussion with your boss by creating a 'clear line of sight' on how you are using your time. It also provides an opportunity for your boss to input into your thinking, and gives your boss confidence that you are addressing the key issues.

Delivery and execution key summary points

- It is important for leaders to avoid spending time on low-value activities.
- It is crucial to learn to delegate but not abdicate by using delegation rehearsal techniques.
- Delivery and execution excellence can be developed by learning to work through others, learning to monitor, measure and analyse the different processes, adopting efficient delegation strategies, and using templates for direct reports to record and analyse meeting outcomes in the leader's absence.
- It is important that leaders focus on analysis, interpretation and evaluation of results rather than just reporting and recording.
- The idea of a roadmap is introduced in order to track progress on different priorities, specific challenges and difficulties that may impede progress and potential success measures to evaluate progress.
- Time management tips and strategies are presented on learning to say 'no', being responsive to emails, and adapting a personal development roadmap to facilitate regular discussion with the leader's boss, and create a vehicle for their input and provide confidence that they are addressing the key issues.

5.4: How to Win a Reputation for Outstanding Team Leadership

Why is team leadership important in developing a reputation?

Team leadership is important in developing a strong reputation because successful leaders do not act by themselves but surround themselves with a trusted, capable team of people who support the leader and who are able to deliver and execute agreed plans. Leaders, who aspire to win a good reputation, demonstrate their ability to lead a team, create the optimum environment for individuals to give of their best and know how to develop talent and manage underperformers.

The key ability is to be able to create a culture in which everyone can give of their best, motivate different individuals in different ways, inspire team members by appropriate use of language and by setting appropriate goals, objectives and purpose. There is also a sense of creating optimism and hope by increasing awareness of what is important, and what behaviours and actions will be most highly valued. A good leader must have the behavioural insight to recruit and select talent, and identify team members who have the behavioural profile potentially to be successful in roles to enable the leader to achieve their objectives. Finally, good leaders also focus on the individual behavioural development and career development of their direct reports, and they are quick to tackle underperformance issues. Good leaders achieve a balance between support, care and compassion, and the right level of challenge and stretch.

How can team leadership be developed to improve a reputation?

Team leadership skills and a team leadership reputation can be developed to improve a reputation by focusing on the following nine strategies and tactics:
1. Setting direction

2. Team communication
3. Team empowerment
4. Team recruitment and selection
5. Managing team performance
6. Team motivation
7. Team coaching
8. Team leader consistency
9. Team visibility.

1. Setting direction

It is important that the leader sets the direction for their team with an outline of purpose, objectives, tactics and key priorities. As part of this process, it is essential to establish and communicate appropriate team success factors and metrics by which the team's performance can be assessed, evaluated and judged.

2. Team communication

It is also important to be transparent and predictable about how and when communication will take place in terms of frequency, and how written and oral communication should be used. A publicly shared communication plan will go a long way to build morale, credibility and trustworthiness.

3. Team empowerment

The devolution of power and the empowerment of the team are essential if the leader is going to have the time to evolve into a more senior leadership role. Therefore, it is essential for the leader to delegate systematically and hold others accountable for their actions, and as part of this process, the leader can send a positive signal by taking their name off the distribution list on selected issues in order to give others full authority and to ensure that team members accept accountability for the achievement of agreed goals and tasks.

4. Team recruitment and selection

In order to ensure that the leader has the optimum level of talent within their team, a key starting point for any team leader is to undertake a behavioural assessment of their direct reports so that the leader has a clear analysis of the team's strengths and less-well-developed attributes. The first real challenge is for the leader to select or recruit team members who have the capacity to carry out the team's expectations. This skill is a huge talent differentiator because the skill to identify the desirable behaviours is in short supply. The first task is to identify the criteria that differentiate the outstanding from the average or poor performers and create a table similar to the following:

Selection Analysis Table

	Below Average Match	Average Match	Good Match	Very Good Match
Experience			√	
Technical Skills			√	
Drive, Planning and Organisation		√		
Strategic Vision	√			
Team Leadership		√		
Influence and Impact	√			
Team Fit			√	
Culture Fit		√		

In building team strength, some leaders typically consider a team's mix as consisting of A, B and C team players. This strategy was made popular by Jack Welch in his days as CEO at General Electric. Welch argued that a team needs a blend of star A performers, who are going to move on to more senior roles, B performers, who are more consistent and steady but will probably have narrower specific functional skills to contribute to the team, and C performers, who are probably underperforming and will need to be moved on or out of the organisation to roles that might better fit their skills.

Therefore, in summary, the team leader's task in building a successful team is to identify the skills and behaviours required for the team to be successful; to select a team or new recruits by assessing individuals against a desired behaviour and skill profile; and then to plan how to develop and close gaps in their performance, and agree and commit to the behavioural change objectives by preparing a written note outlining the areas in which the individual needs to demonstrate more growth.

5. Managing team performance

A leader's ability to address underperformance issues is a very important attribute. The leader needs to be sufficiently tough minded to remove weaker or disruptive team members in order to allow the team to perform to their optimum level. In an ideal scenario, the individual direct report should be encouraged with questions to identify the gaps in their performance for themselves. The resulting conversation needs to be recorded in writing and the individual team member tasked with providing evidence in writing on a regular basis as to how they have demonstrated progress in agreed development areas.

Such an approach requires the individual to adopt an analytical approach and to focus on not just what they have done but also on what they have learned and how they and the organisation have benefited. The insight and ability to describe what a person has learned is the key point that will give others confidence that any progress or change will be long-lasting.

Taking responsibility to demonstrate progress

Making team members responsible to provide evidence on changes in their performance is an essential leadership performance-management attribute. The leader might suggest that a person uses the following types of evidence:
- 'Compare and contrast' with how the person was operating or behaving six months previously

- Reference to any insights about a new skill, attitude or way of behaving which has been learned
- Make reference to any particular technique or behavioural strategy which has been learned
- Demonstrate an understanding of different priorities and different types of activities on which the person plans to focus
- Demonstrate an awareness of how the person is perceived by others and how it may be changing with examples.

It is important for the leader to invest in individuals by managing their performance and giving them signposts on how to develop their career and optimise their earning potential. Ideally, the leader should try to ensure that each individual has clear signposts not only on what they are expected to deliver now in terms of success factors but on what they need to achieve to develop their career in the longer term.

At the subsequent individual performance review meetings, it is also a good idea for the leader to prepare a template of the questions they want their direct report to ask themselves so that they come prepared to 'sell' what they have achieved to the leader. This forces the direct report to anticipate and prepare for the kind of questions that they need to ask of themselves. The questioning process will also train the direct reports to be more thoughtful and considered in their approach.

6. Team motivation

The leader needs to understand what motivates individual members of their team. A direct and transparent way of uncovering and identifying the motivational triggers for each person is to ask the following questions:
- What three things have I done that you have found motivating in the last 12 months?
- What three things have I done that you found demotivating in the last 12 months?

The leader can then use the findings to shape how they manage and motivate each individual.

7. Team coaching

The purpose of coaching is to help team members play at the top of their game and to maximise their effectiveness by a process of 'marginal gains' in different areas. The essence of coaching is to help individuals to learn about themselves, see themselves as others see them and search for marginal gain opportunities in all aspects of their role and contribution at work.

The best leaders are always excellent individual coaches of their direct reports because they recognise the importance of building a strong team whose members can increasingly step up to take on more responsibilities and run parts of the organisation – which should enable the leader to focus on other priorities. For example, if the leader's team are able to function well, the leader can invest more time on the strategic forward-looking issues of the day, the external-facing communications and relationship building necessary for any leader, as well as to enable the leader to selectively invest time in the parts of the business or organisation that may have problems to be resolved or which will benefit from the leader's experience and intellectual insights.

8. Team leader consistency

The leader needs to try to be consistent in responding to emails. They should try to be punctual for meetings to respect others' time and try to avoid fluctuating moods and emotions. Leaders need to make sure that they do not over-commit or over-promise. It is important to remember that clarity, consistency and reliability in sticking to deadlines will be essential if they are to build respectful, trusting working relationships with their team. It may also be very relevant for consistency to share responsibility with the team, as long as the leader has clear systems for tracking progress and holding people accountable for their actions and outputs.

9. Team visibility

The leader also needs to make the team visible outside of its immediate functional area and help its members to influence cross-functionally so as to facilitate relationships across the organisation. This should ensure that others know what the team is about and what it is seeking to do. It is important that the leader ensures that there are multiple points of contact in the team who are trusted and respected by colleagues in other departments and functions. If all contacts outside the function are channelled to the leader then the leader will very quickly become a bottleneck, and the efficiency and speed of processing and completing tasks will be compromised.

Team leadership key summary points

- Successful leaders surround themselves with a capable, talented team of people who support the leader and deliver on agreed plans.
- Team leadership skills can be developed by setting team direction in relation to purpose, tactics and priorities; communicating clearly and transparently; and empowering the team by means of systematic delegation and accountability processes.
- Team recruitment and selection is essential to build team strength and to have the insight to identify the critical success criteria, and the knowledge and awareness to use the appropriate behaviour-assessment methodologies to identify the degree of fit for any individual to a new team role.
- Team performance needs to be managed by making team members accountable for demonstrating evidence of key behaviours and demonstrating evidence of progress.
- Tips and strategies are introduced for team motivation, team coaching and the need for team leadership consistency.

- Finally, it is important that the team leader ensures that the team is visible to the rest of the organisation and that the team has the opportunity to build cross-functional connections independently of the team leader.

5.5: How to Win a Reputation for Outstanding Organisational Influence

Why are organisational influencing skills important in developing a reputation?

Organisational influencing skills are important in developing a reputation because the ability to influence, to be streetwise and politically savvy, and to be able to align disparate groups to aim for a common purpose is essential for all successful leaders. Very successful senior leaders do not just focus on the task in hand but look for opportunities to influence cross-functionally, and think about how they can add value to the welfare and success of the whole organisation. However, influencing skills are one of the most difficult skills to develop well as there is constant pressure and expectation from a range of different stakeholders. The key challenge is to get buy-in from others on the direction of the organisation, persuading different groups to align to a common purpose, and guiding people towards a course of action or accepting new ideas or changes of direction. Leaders who aspire to have influence must be able to make genuine connections with other people as a precursor to being able to influence.

How can organisational influence be developed to improve a reputation?

Organisational influencing skills can be developed to improve a reputation by focusing on the following nine strategies and behaviours:
1. Executive presence
2. Self-confidence
3. Political savviness

4. Incremental progression.
5. Influencing groups
6. Building connections
7. Communication sharpness
8. Enquiry and advocacy
9. Mastering presentation skills.

1. Executive presence

Executive presence is important in any senior role if you want to have influence in order to give others confidence that you are worth listening to, and that you understand what is expected in the organisation. The awareness to know how to dress and how to act, and which work-related topics to discuss with senior managers and at what level of detail, is very important to convey credibility. Good influencers must know how to communicate their passion to succeed and have the ability to assert themselves in an appropriate authentic way that is consistent with their personal style.

An influential leader must be able to put their ego to one side, wholeheartedly engage with the other person or persons in the moment, and be able to share their own passions in a very compelling way. However, the ability to connect with the person or persons that you are trying to influence is often associated with gravitas. Gravitas is about commanding a high level of attention and attracting followership from others. Gravitas is often personality related, in that people with high levels of confidence and independent thinking often stand out from the crowd, but the ability to influence does not come in one type of personality. We have become accustomed to the classic extrovert being synonymous with strong influencing skills but it is also the case that a thoughtful introvert can have equal impact through the use of powerful questions as opposed to powerful personal statements.

2. Self-Confidence

High-potential leaders have the self-confidence to believe that they are valuable in terms of what they can potentially contribute to the thinking of colleagues in unstructured discussions, even though different parties may play different roles at different levels in the organisation. Therefore, high-potential leaders need to be able to have the self-confidence to talk as equals with their senior managers in the hope that they create the impression that they are on an equal footing in terms of the value of their ideas and their value-added contribution.

3. Political savviness

Political savviness is both a mindset and a skill set. Savvy leaders view politics as a necessary part of organisational life, in that all organisations have an informal structure that more often than not represents how things really get done. Political savviness in action involves targeted networking to build alliances and partnerships with like-minded colleagues who may be able to help with the execution of a course of action. Politically savvy leaders will listen well, ask good questions and be reflective, analysing how things are being done and how things might be changed.

Being described as 'political' is often seen as an unattractive quality, associated with negative concepts like being opportunistic or manipulative, but it is also possible to redefine political as meaning influential or emotionally mature or, charmingly and more prosaically, as having 'savviness'. Savviness is being seen as streetwise and knowing how the system, culture or organisation works, and how things can best get done or be achieved as quickly as possible. In all organisations, the savvy political activists and pragmatists are successful influencers. It is common sense for people to use their judgement to appraise the dynamics of their organisation, and assess those who may have more ability and who are respected opinion shapers. Idealists and political avoiders, who believe you should get ahead only by doing the job, following the rules and working harder, tend to have lower impact and influence.

CHAPTER 5: THE FUNDAMENTAL FIVE OUTSIDE-IN REPUTATION WINNERS

Politically savvy leaders tend to exhibit the following three successful factors:
- Knowing who's who
- Being attentive and insightful
- Building large networks.

(i) Knowing who's who

Firstly, political savvy leaders know who's who. They can work out the real structure within the organisation and who truly holds power and influence. Savvy politicians will map the organisation so that they will know that X can be influenced by Y. They know what the real agendas are and they can see through the smokescreen of organisational flannel. They will network effectively and they will know and understand key relationship connections and how to accelerate the process of getting things done. People can build their influence by building constituencies of supporters because they know who is connected to whom, why and how.

(ii) Being attentive and insightful

Secondly, politically savvy leaders are perceptive, charming, socially astute and good at assessing and understanding the motivations of others and what makes them tick. They are attentive and insightful, have a learned ability to pick up on non-verbal cues and are often known for their charm. The leader will use the opinions of others and show that he understands and values people. A good influencer reaches out to people and has the ability to connect with others by using questions to better understand their concerns, priorities and difficulties. As a consequence, a successful leader will always be accessible.

(iii) Building large networks

Thirdly, politically savvy leaders build large networks and will strive to develop strong bonds of trust with useful colleagues. The savvy leaders will find important issues to progress and share agendas with like-minded colleagues, thus raising their visibility because of an association with organisation-wide projects that have cross-functional relevance. The politically savvy individuals tend to be well liked and will usually have an impact beyond their immediate functional area.

4. Incremental progression

Good influencers have a sound appreciation of the length of time often involved in the influencing process and the need for incremental gradual progression. When progress stalls in the influencing process, it is important to use probing questions to uncover blocks and reservations.
- What would be your reservations for taking the next step?
- What would be the benefits and upsides of buying into this proposition?
- What are your concerns and what are the downsides of buying into this proposition?

Pull rather than push

It is important that leaders have the ability to make a compelling case for a particular proposal or point of view since they will need to be able to attract and win over others – which may include team members, board members, customers or clients. However, it is even more important for the leader to place themselves in the other person's shoes. The leader can then try to 'pull' the other party towards the influencer's position with astute questions rather than 'push' the influencer's views and opinions on the other party without necessarily knowing the other person's starting position.

Many leaders, in their attempt to influence, focus on content at the expense of strategy, structure and tactics. Planning, therefore, is essential and the best influencers will work out and calculate a gradual progression campaign of influence over several meetings, possibly over an extended period. If the other party to be persuaded has a 2/10 strength of feeling about a position or action and you want to get him or her up to 9/10, this change will not come about as a result of one meeting: the other party needs to save face and not convey that their original opposition was not

CHAPTER 5: THE FUNDAMENTAL FIVE OUTSIDE-IN REPUTATION WINNERS

well thought through. In reality, several meetings may be required in order to move the other party by small increments. Every time a block appears, it is important that the influencing party makes a point of uncovering reservations so that the influencer has the opportunity to address these reservations and remove any concerns. It may often then be necessary to call a halt to the meeting, and revisit at a later date, in order to take the next steps.

5. Influencing groups

There is a major difference between the techniques used for one-to-one influencing discussions and those for influencing a group. To be successful in influencing at group meetings, leaders need to control meetings they call by having a clear agenda and clear action points. The meeting preparation should involve an analysis of the pluses and minuses of each point to be proposed and the various options available, what milestones to monitor progress may be relevant and how success can be measured.

It is very important prior to important meetings to analyse the needs of the audience and how the leader's communication style should change or be tailored for different groups. Therefore, it is good practice to write down the purpose of the meeting and what it is hoped to be achieved, and the three-to-six key takeaways that you wish to leave with your audience. It is important to think through the three-to-six key points that you wish to communicate or discuss, and how they can be most easily remembered in the form of a story, metaphor, number of points to remember or mnemonic.

It is important to make use of headings, sub-headings and numbered points to focus the mind of the listener in all forms of communication. If the meeting involves the presentation of data, it may be important to explore how you make numbers meaningful in terms of 'best-case scenarios' and 'worst-case scenarios'. Most statistics are relative although many are presented as absolute concepts!

Influencing informal groups

In informal communication situations, it is important that the influencer learns to make extensive use of the language of questions in order to facilitate between different groups, and learns to use questions to manage conflicts and differences of opinion, and uncover reservations and different perspectives. "How did you arrive at that conclusion?" is more constructive than "I don't agree with you."

It may be important that you learn some prefacing phrases or concluding phrases that might include questions to invite people to add or contribute to your thinking. For example, you might encourage others to comment by saying "I am not fully committed to this point so I would welcome any additional thoughts." "I am not necessarily confident or clear about the range of options available so I would welcome ideas to broaden my perspective."

Active listening

A successful influencer in all group meetings needs to be able to listen well, to attend to the other person and use questions to uncover both the thoughts and feelings of the other party about an issue. Good listening involves summarising, so that the influencer can demonstrate that they have understood the other person's point of view, and may also involve helping the other person with suggestions for a particular plan of action to make progress.

6. Building connections

It is always a good idea to build an engagement strategy with senior stakeholders. The aim is to better understand the priorities and expectations of senior stakeholders but if there is some agreement about frequency and purpose of meetings, then the periodic engagement can more easily be achieved. Another key reason for meeting consistently with senior stakeholders is to exchange ideas, information and insights to broaden a person's bandwidth and perspective, in turn strengthening the breadth of their judgement and credibility.

CHAPTER 5: THE FUNDAMENTAL FIVE OUTSIDE-IN REPUTATION WINNERS

In terms of building connections and expanding influencing reach, good leaders must be able to persuade people to work with them and support them, which means that they need to treat others with respect. An individual's talents will go further if combined with good manners and generosity of spirit. At the end of the day, it is all about these relationship skills because if a colleague cannot contemplate sitting through a senior manager meeting or engaging in difficult conversations or discussions with their leaders then they will not buy-in to a leader's vision.

It is important to remember when relating upwards to senior managers that the more junior manager should aim to treat their senior with respect but not deference, and that the more junior manager should aim to aspire to an adult–adult relationship. By so doing, the more junior manager will win respect as a valued business partner as opposed to a deferential relationship that will only reinforce the impression that the more junior manager is subordinate and of lower value.

The content of the discussions with senior stakeholders is vitally important to create the right impression. The discussion and dialogue should focus on strategic or 'big picture' issues or analysis of operational events, or some learning and insight that will help to shape future strategy rather than just focusing on transactional detail and delivery.

Finally, try to be a part of the story or to contribute to the story. More than anything, the role of the leader is to sell the idea and the vision of the organisation's strategic goals and objectives. The strategy is the story and the strategy can help to increase the confidence of the team and provide a sense of direction. The subtext is that the strategy is under the leader's control. Every successful leader has a good story that speaks to the type of person they are, the values that they hold and the challenges they have overcome rather than referencing any specific operational policy details. However, the 'story of the future' is also not necessarily true or accurate, in that the leader is making a best-guess estimate about how things might unfold.

7. Communication sharpness

A leader with strong influencing skills usually has a particular way of speaking and communicating. They have an ability to be sharp, concise and succinct, to assimilate a lot of information and extract the key salient points, and are skilled at providing summaries of diverse discussions. The leader with excellent communication skills is able to deliver information in headlines and then backfill with detail if necessary. Clarity will often mean being able to deliver the key point of the message in around 10–20 words. Having influence means not delivering a dissertation or 'brain dumping' on your audience to show off how much you know. Rather, you should communicate key points in bundles of, say, three-point groupings so the information is easily digestible and intelligible. A long-winded, pedantic, verbose person has no chance of having strong influence. It is also important to avoid speech mannerisms by repetitively using terms such as 'like' or 'you know' or 'do you know what I mean' or 'if you understand what I mean'. Filler language like 'um' and 'so' should be avoided and language like 'sort of' or 'this may not be a good idea but' does not convey authority or presence.

A person with strong influencing skills also usually exudes personal ease in that they know what matters and they are comfortable in their own skin. They are usually not acting out of self-interest nor trying to prove anything. They appear curious, gracious and challenging but with respect – and without appearing to have a strong personal ego. The confident communicator defends the points that matter but they do not seek praise, nor do they mind criticism or pushback from others.

Communication style has a great deal to do with demonstrating that the leader has the judgement to understand what different styles are required in different communication situations and with different audiences. The most impressive skill for a leader is the ability to develop the barrister-like data-reduction technique. This means being able to assimilate a lot of information and distil an argument to three-to-five key points with possibly the pluses and minuses of each point if relevant. It is important to develop a concise communication style in both written and spoken forms. Good leaders are aware of the need to signpost and headline what they are going to say, and learn how to summarise with key headings.

It is obviously important that email content is sharp and clear. However, emotionally intelligent leaders also use emails to build relationships, so it is important always to invest the time and effort in topping and tailing emails with a more personal connecting link or comment that will make the recipient feel good and feel valued.

8. Enquiry and advocacy

One of the failings of many communications and meetings is that people just focus on talking at each other, expressing their opinions and not benefiting from what other people know by facilitating between different perspectives or building bridges between different points of view.

Advocacy is about making statements, saying what you think and giving your point of view, and enquiry is about asking questions in order to understand the other person's point of view. High advocacy and low enquiry is one-way communication and although it can be useful for giving information, it doesn't lead to exploring different points of view or agreeing to a common action. On the other hand, high enquiry and low advocacy is a different form of communication, in that the speaker does not state his or her views. However, whilst it is useful as a way of finding out information, it can create difficulty if the speaker has a hidden agenda or if he or she is using questions to get the other person to discover what the speaker already thinks is right. A better strategy is to strive for high advocacy and high enquiry that fosters two-way communication and learning, and encourages both parties to state their views and enquire into the other person's points of view. A good guideline is to seek to understand before trying to be understood.

9. Mastering presentation skills

The ability to speak clearly and concisely to a large group of colleagues, clients or customers is an important and rare quality. Anyone who possesses this skill to a high degree will certainly have a strong advantage over their peers. However, there are a number of techniques and verbal tactics that can make a person's presentation more effective and more influential. These verbal tactics might include the following:

- **Metaphors, similes and analogies:** Metaphors can be very effective in a professional context but it does require a creative and innovative mind to think about the right kind of metaphors that will work in particular communication situations. On the other hand, it is easy to overcomplicate a message through the use of metaphor.
- **Stories and anecdotes:** Even people who aren't born raconteurs can employ this tactic in a compelling way as stories can help to make the message more engaging.
- **Contrasts:** Contrasts are one of the easiest tactics to learn and use. Leaders with presence might talk about saving goals and scoring goals, being defensive or being offensive. John F. Kennedy dramatically used the phrase "ask not what your country can do for you – ask what you can do for your country".
- **Rhetorical questions:** Rhetorical questions can be used to encourage engagement. For example, if a colleague is feeling demotivated, a manager might motivate by saying "So where do you want to go from here? Do you want to prove them wrong? Do you want to demonstrate that you possess the skills that they may feel are lacking? Or do you want to go home and give up and feel that you are a failure?"
- **Three-part lists**: This is a well-used verbal tactic as people can easily remember three things. You could also say that there are three things that I want you to take away from this presentation and under each of the three headings you might describe another three sub-headings. For example, a common three-part list for developing a

business strategy might include: What have we done to get to where we are? Where do we want to go? How do we get there?
- **Moral conviction**: Expressions of moral conviction work very effectively if they manage to reflect the sentiments of the majority of the group. A leader will increase their influence if they can establish their credibility by revealing the quality of their character by making others identify and align themselves with their statements.
- **Passion:** Passion can effectively be conveyed by setting high aspirational goals and conveying confidence that these high goals can be achieved. The leader can convey passion by taking the opportunity to convince their team members that they have the intelligence, the experience, the technical knowhow, the ability and the necessary attributes – and that all they need now is the will and ambition to succeed.

Organisational influence key summary points

- The ability to influence cross-functionally and at different levels, and to align disparate groups to work together for a common purpose, is an essential leadership skill.
- A leader with a strong influencing capability will have good executive presence, self-confidence and a good image in order to get attention; they will act the part, convey gravitas and appear to be politically savvy and streetwise.
- Developing political skills is extremely important by knowing who's who to get things done, being attentive and insightful in the way that relationships are managed, and knowing how to build large networks of constructive relationships.
- It is important to develop a variety of influencing techniques. The key skill in influencing successfully is to cultivate the ability to sell ideas where the strategy is the story and the story narrative is about a more successful, more rewarding and more profitable future.

- Influencing skills can be developed by the way formal communication meetings are conducted, by improving facilitation skills at informal communication meetings, time management of meetings and developing more obvious active listening skills.
- Developing stakeholder relations is an important element of being a good influencer and tips are offered on developing an appropriate engagement model, the importance of showing respect but not deference, and engaging in big picture, analytical discussions.
- Communication style and presence are important in terms of acting the part. Use enquiry rather than advocacy as a communication style.
- Some suggestions are also provided on how to sharpen and develop one's presentation skills.

Chapter 5 Key Summary Points

- This chapter focuses on how strong reputations can be won and offers practical tips and suggestions on how to develop a winning reputation in the following Fundamental Five Outside-in Reputation Winning areas:
  - Culture building
  - Strategic thinking
  - Delivering excellence
  - Team leadership
  - Organisational influence.

Chapter 6

The Fundamental Four Inside-out Reputation Winners

"We know what we are, but know not what we may be."

William Shakespeare

Chapter 6 Key Summary Points

- The Fundamental Four Inside-out Reputation Winners are described and ideas are presented on how to build a strong reputation in each of the following areas:
  - Self-awareness
  - Likeability
  - Wise Judgment
  - Perceptiveness.

The purpose of this chapter is to explore those qualities and attributes that distinguish outstanding performers from those who are merely average or adequate from an inside-out perspective. As with the outside-in perspective, we implicitly assume that other baseline or minimum competency requirements exist. So the key differentiating inside-out attributes for outstanding leadership are as follows:

- **Self-Awareness:** The ability to be realistic in self-assessing strengths and weaknesses, and be driven by the need to self-improve and search for marginal gains.

- **Likeability:** The ability to connect with a wide range of people at different levels and in different roles in such a way that colleagues 'feel good' by the nature of the work interaction and the work relationship.
- **Wise judgment:** The ability to reflect and think broadly and deeply about problems with an open, curious mind and broad perspective.
- **Perceptiveness:** The ability to be interested, insightful and intuitive in wanting to explore how and why other people behave, think and feel in the way they do.

For each of the Fundamental Four Inside-out Reputation Winners, we look at the following two key questions:
- Why are these behaviours important in developing a strong reputation?
- How can these behaviours be developed to improve a reputation?

6.1: How to Win a Reputation for Self-awareness

Why is self-awareness important for developing a reputation?

Self-awareness is probably one of the least-discussed leadership competencies but possibly one of the most valuable and rare leadership attributes. Self-awareness is having the ability to understand one's strengths and weaknesses relative to others at a particular level and the ability to understand what differentiates one person from another at senior levels in particular. This is a highly valued skill and experience suggests that accurate insight of this nature is rare. A key driver for high-performing leaders is the desire to constantly improve their performance. As the philosopher Aristotle postulated, a "Man who competes against his fellow man is noble but true nobility is man who competes against his previous self".

Most people overestimate their capacity to know themselves and make accurate assessments of their colleagues. Peter Drucker, the acclaimed management writer and leadership thinker, espoused that "Most people think they know what they're good

CHAPTER 6: THE FUNDAMENTAL FOUR INSIDE-OUT REPUTATION WINNERS

at. They are usually wrong".

Self-awareness is the outstanding attribute of all great leaders. Moreover, knowing what good or great looks like and having the self-awareness to identify the gaps between oneself and other top leaders allows the individual leader to take responsibility to drive their own development. Their self-awareness also allows them to use other team resources to complement any gaps in their skill profile. If people do not have this self-awareness then it may be assumed that they lack the capacity to drive their own development and that they may lack any stretch capability to raise their game when required.

Only 5% of respondents said their managers were self-aware and empathic

A survey by management consultancy Orion Partners in 2012 found that 24% of employees thought that their bosses had a bad style of leadership that damaged the productivity of the organisation. Just 5% of respondents said that their managers were self-aware and possessed empathy, and led in a way that would create workplaces in which employees felt rewarded, valued and recognised. A survey by Forbes found that, on average, 40% of employees do not respect the manager to whom they report.

This research is consistent with other research findings that suggest that many leaders have limited psychological depth, in that they are as unaware of their strengths as they are of their weaknesses. They do not know how their actions are perceived or how their reputation has developed. However, the more seriously leaders take their personal growth, the more seriously colleagues will take them. The challenge for leaders is to question themselves about what they could be doing differently, seeking feedback, resisting the temptation to explain and defend, and enjoying seeking new solutions outside of their historical comfort zone. Self-aware leaders are prepared to ask for honest feedback and they are open to the process of listening and hearing feedback rather than being defensive in blaming others or looking for external causes when things do not go to plan.

Drive for self-improvement

A drive for self-improvement is essential for success at all levels in organisations, and this attitude has become a very important predictor of success as a leader. In fact, you cannot be a good leader without wanting to improve your own performance and without constantly looking for marginal gains. If any person wants to improve their leadership skills, a basic first principle is to understand what great leaders do and do not do. If someone is going to improve as a leader, they have to believe that they can do what they do better. People who think leadership or competence is an innate talent tend not to fulfil their potential because they do not work on their performance and they are more focused on preserving whatever status they currently have. This leads to defensiveness and a lack of openness to feedback from others.

Appetite to grow and learn

Self-awareness can be developed but first we need to become more aware of what an outstanding performance looks like and how our performance matches these expectations. We need to see the gaps between our actual profile and the ideal profile, and understand how these gaps can be closed. The best leaders are able to use self-reflection to increase self-awareness but research tells us that people perceive their own behaviours very differently from the way that others perceive them. We have a tendency to see our own challenges or errors as situationally based rather than caused by our possible lack of ability, competence or underperformance in a particular area.

How can self-awareness be developed to improve a reputation?

Self-awareness can be developed to improve a reputation by focussing on the following seven strategies and behaviours:
1. Learning agility
2. Leadership narrative
3. Self-assessment

4. Honest feedback
5. Maintaining a journal
6. Compare and contrast
7. Psychometric assessment.

1. Learning agility

The most important quality in a leadership role is to have the ability to learn. In particular, leaders need to learn what type of behaviour, attitude, characteristics and values they need to develop if they are to be an outstanding successful leader. Leaders who have self-awareness and a self-improvement or a self-development drive are essentially curious and open minded, and they have an appetite to learn and grow, to develop new skills and a desire to respond in innovative ways to new and unforeseen circumstances. Leaders with self-awareness do not assume that the skills that got them to their current level will still be the relevant skills that will take them to the next level. Leaders with self-awareness are also self-driven, in that good performance review evaluations are less relevant than their self-motivated desire to improve their performance.

There may not be any one best leadership style but what matters is that the more a person learns, the better they get. Malcolm Gladwell [1] in his book *Outliers* and Matthew Syed [2] in his book *Bounce* both suggest that it takes about 10,000 hours of practice to get really good at something. Both these authors refer to developing skills in tennis, music and other areas, but becoming a great leader is no different.

Carol Dweck [3] researched individual mindsets, which are the beliefs individuals hold about how they think about their intelligence, their talents and their personality, and whether these qualities are simply fixed traits carved in stone or whether they can be cultivated throughout their life. Dweck found from her extensive research that people with a "fixed mindset" believe that their attributes are fixed and relatively immune to change, and so they try to preserve the status quo and the current perception of their capabilities. However, people with a "growth mindset" recognise that they continue to learn and grow throughout their life, and they understand that no-one has accomplished great things without years of focused practice and learning.

Leaders and managers will often complain that they do not have sufficient time to focus on self-development, self-improvement or new learning activities. However, many observers believe that it is self-evident that for leaders to focus on their on-going development has to be a non-negotiable if they want to stay ahead and on top of their game. It is also true that if a leader acknowledges areas of their behaviour that they need to develop, colleagues will give them credit and assume that any weaknesses that are probably apparent to others will be improved as a consequence of their focus to improve them.

If people do not have this self-awareness and self-improvement drive, it may be assumed that they lack the capacity to drive their own self-development and may lack any stretch capability to raise their game when required. However, the more seriously leaders take their self-improvement and personal growth, the more seriously colleagues will take them. The process is to challenge oneself about what one could be doing differently.

2. Leadership narrative

A second strategy to improve self-awareness is to draft a 'leadership narrative' to describe your career journey and career progress. This requires a good deal of calm reflection and should focus on your education, career and individual development from a leadership perspective. One of the essential expectations of outstanding leaders is that they possess an ability to define and explain who they are, what they stand for, how they would differentiate themselves from other successful colleagues and what they need to do to get better – and they need to be able to do this in a way that is genuine, credible and authentic.

In the narrative, you should be able to describe behavioural differences between yourself and others at your level. If a potential leader is unable to do this well, they do not really have

leadership potential. The narrative may cover the following areas:
- Did you have any formal or informal leadership roles at school or further education or did you see yourself as a social group leader amongst your peers?
- If involved in any leadership roles, describe how you got involved in those roles, what motivated you and what you learned from the experience.
- Was there any influential person or informal mentor who shaped your thinking and influenced your career direction?
- Describe the pattern of your career development, your satisfaction with your rate of career progress, and the responsibilities and leadership roles you have experienced.
- Whether you actually have a leadership role or not, describe what being a 'good leader' means to you.
- Describe your key signature strengths and your self-perceived shortcomings as a leader or potential leader, and describe what you need to continue to work on and to develop.
- Describe how you think you differ from friends from a similar background or colleagues who function at a similar level. What makes you different?
- Describe how you plan for your future career to develop, which skills and behaviours you already have to make this happen, and what existing and new skills and behaviours you still need to develop.

3. Self-Assessment

Another strategy to build self-awareness requires you to step into the role of observer of yourself and describe what has happened to you from an evidence-based perspective. The observer's mind enables us to notice more about how we make decisions, how we interact with others, how different situations make us feel, what energises us and what depletes us. The following list of questions may be used as a starting point to develop greater self-awareness as well as a more in-depth understanding of your current level of self-awareness.

Childhood experience:

- What were the most significant influences in your early life? What individuals were influential in shaping the person you have become?
- What were the three most positive events in your childhood and why were they significant for you?
- What were the three most negative events in your childhood and why were they significant for you?
- In what ways has your childhood experience contributed or hindered the development of self-awareness?

Educational experience:

- How well did you perform at school academically? Did you have any sporting successes or did you hold any leadership positions at school?
- If you continued to further education, what led you to choose a particular degree or college course?
- Why did you choose your college/university?
- What did you like and dislike about university/college?
- Did you have any non-academic positions, successes or interests at university/college?
- In what ways has your educational experience contributed to or hindered the development of self-awareness?

Career experience:

- What career plans did you have on leaving college/university and were there specific career expectations for you?
- Why did you choose your first job and what factors have shaped your career?
- How many different types of job have you undertaken? Which of those jobs did you like the best? Which of those jobs did you like the least?

- What have been the key highlights and disappointments of your career to date?
- What are three of your greatest strengths?
- What are three of your greatest weaknesses or shortcomings? Which of those three have caused problems for you or for others?
- To what extent have you been active in planning your career as opposed to reacting to career opportunities?
- What is your definition of career success? How successful would you rate your career on a 0–10 scale? Have you met, surpassed or under-delivered on your parents' expectations and your own expectations?
- How satisfied are you with your career and rate of progress on a 0–10 scale?
- In what ways have your career experiences contributed to or hindered the development of self-awareness?

Life experience:

- What period of your life have you liked the most and what was it about that time that you enjoyed so much?
- What period of your life have you liked the least and what was it about that time that you disliked so much?
- Who are three people you most admire? And what characteristics do they possess that you admire?
- What three personal accomplishments fill you with the greatest sense of pride?
- What is the one specific situation in which you felt the most upset or frustrated?
- In what ways have your life experiences contributed to or hindered the development of self-awareness?

Social experience:

- What types of people do you enjoy spending time with?
- Do you seek out people who are similar to or different from you and why is that?

- How many close friends do you want to have? Why that number?
- Where have you met most of the friends you currently have? What can you learn about yourself by looking at where you met those friends?
- What topics do you most enjoy discussing with your friends? What is it you enjoy about those topics?
- How do you handle disagreements with others?
- In what situations and with whom do you feel the most free to be totally yourself?
- What qualities do you dislike in others? Which of those qualities do you yourself have?
- What qualities do you admire in others? Why do you want to have those qualities?
- What kind of impression do you try to make on others? What specific things do you say or do to make this impression?
- Whose approval have you sought the most? Why that person?
- What is the single biggest change you would like to make when you interact with others? What specific thing could you do to make that change?
- In what ways have your social experiences contributed to or hindered the development of self-awareness?

4. Seek honest feedback

A fourth strategy for helping to increase our self-awareness is to seek honest feedback from friends or colleagues. We all have traits that others see but we are unable to see in ourselves and we refer to these as our 'blindspots'. Nobody is fully aware of how we come across to others, so we have to rely on feedback from friends and trusted colleagues who are prepared to be truthful in their assessment. The recipient of the feedback, however, needs to be able to ask the right questions and make the friend or colleague 'feel safe' in giving direct feedback. For example, it is easier to give feedback if you ask a colleague "Which two or three characteristics could I change, develop or modify to become even more competitive or successful at my level?" The next stage is to accept the feedback without comment, defensiveness or self-justification. You do not need to agree with the feedback but, in the next few weeks, it would be a very powerful strategy to compile some written evidence to demonstrate either why the feedback may not be deserved or how you have addressed the feedback issues, and then share this with the person who provided the feedback.

5. Maintain a journal

A fifth strategy to help to increase self-awareness is to maintain a journal and write down specific tasks or roles undertaken over a two-week period. Write down the feelings you experienced with the task or role, what went well and what went less well, and possibly rate your feelings and your perceived success on a five- or ten-point scale. Over time, you will see patterns emerge that will give some indicators about your relative strengths, weaknesses, areas of job satisfaction and dissatisfaction, and identify opportunities for further self-improvement and self-development.

6. Compare and contrast

A sixth strategy that may provide some further insights with regard to increasing self-awareness is to focus on comparing and contrasting yourself with different people at your level or at a more senior level.

Step 1: Write down every person whom you admire and respect. It can be anyone – celebrity, politician, author, scientist, musician, philosopher, family member, friend, teacher, etc. They do not even have to be real. You can list fictional characters.

Step 2: Next to each name, write the characteristics, abilities or qualities you like about that person.

Step 3: After you have written your list for each person, go through the list of qualities and compile them into a single list.

Step 4: Then answer the following questions:
- How would you rate yourself on these qualities on a 0–10 scale?
- Which qualities would you like to develop to a greater degree?
- What is one small action step you could take to develop that quality more in yourself?

7. Psychometric assessment

The seventh self-awareness improvement strategy is to undertake a personality-type assessment. There are many questionnaires available on the market but the Myers–Briggs Type Indicator (MBTI) is one of the most frequently used psychometric instruments. The MBTI is an introspective self-report questionnaire with the purpose of indicating differing psychological preferences in how people perceive the world around them and make decisions. The MBTI was constructed by Katharine Cook Briggs and her daughter Isabel Briggs Myers. It is based on the conceptual theory proposed by Carl Jung [4], who had speculated that there are four principal psychological functions by which humans experience the world – sensation, intuition, feeling and thinking – and that one of these four functions is dominant for a person most of the time. The underlying assumption of the MBTI is that we all have specific preferences in the way we construe our experiences and these preferences underlie our interests, needs, values and motivation. The four principal psychological functions, as described by Jung, that we use to experience our world are as follows:

CHAPTER 6: THE FUNDAMENTAL FOUR INSIDE-OUT REPUTATION WINNERS

Extraversion and Introversion – The first pair of styles is concerned with the direction of your energy. If you prefer to direct your energy to deal with people, external situations or the 'outer world', then your preference is for Extraversion. If you prefer to direct your energy to deal with ideas, information, explanations or beliefs, or the 'inner world', then your preference is for Introversion.

Sensing and Intuition – The second pair concerns the type of information that you process. If you prefer to deal with facts, what you know, to have clarity, or to describe what you see then your preference is for Sensing. If you prefer to deal with ideas, look into the unknown, to generate new possibilities or to anticipate what isn't obvious then your preference is for Intuition. The letter 'N' is used for intuition because 'I' has already been allocated to Introversion.

Thinking and Feeling – The third pair reflects your style of decision making. If you prefer to decide on the basis of objective logic and reflection, using an analytic and detached approach, then your preference is for Thinking. If you prefer to decide using values and emotions – i.e. on the basis of what or who you believe is important – then your preference is for Feeling.

Judgement and Perception – The final pair describes the type of lifestyle you adopt. If you prefer your life to be planned, organised and well-structured then your preference is for Judging. This is not to be confused with being judgemental, which is quite different. If you prefer to go with the flow, to be spontaneous, to maintain flexibility and respond to things as they arise then your preference is for Perception.

All possible permutations of preferences in the four dichotomies above yield 16 different combinations, thus defining 16 different personality types. The MBTI is a development tool that can be used to identify strengths and blindspots, so they can help individuals further leverage their strengths and compensate for their blindspots. The MBTI tool can provide an opportunity to acknowledge that we all have personality diversity and gives us a common language to talk about how we might differ from our colleagues.

However, this does not mean that someone who tends towards introversion cannot necessarily perform a more extroverted role. What it does do is help them understand that, if they are to be successful, they need to invest more of their energy into a role with which they may not be naturally comfortable. The MBTI does not, of course, define everything that there is to know about a person and there are many other psychometric tools that serve different purposes. These self-report instruments provide a large sample of data on the way a person thinks about themselves and these tools can be used to prompt some exploratory thinking about how you behave at work. You can then explore the positive attributes demonstrated by different personalities and you can take a view on which behaviours, skills or aspects of your performance may benefit from further development.

Self-awareness key summary points

- Self-awareness is a rare skill. Few senior executives are seen as having accurate self-insight and most are seen as lacking psychological depth.
- Successful leaders who have a high level of self-awareness have a desire to constantly improve and a curiosity and capacity to continually learn.
- The following seven self-awareness improvement strategies are discussed:
  1. Learning agility
  2. Leadership narrative
  3. Self-assessment
  4. Seek honest feedback
  5. Maintain a journal
  6. Compare and contrast
  7. Psychometric assessment.

CHAPTER 6: THE FUNDAMENTAL FOUR INSIDE-OUT REPUTATION WINNERS

6.2: How to Win a Reputation for Likeability

Why is likeability important for developing a strong reputation?

Likeability is important for developing a reputation because all the evidence suggests that being likeable will help to make you successful. Likeability matters in all walks of life and it is very important to be seen as likeable in a working role. Likeability matters because likeable people are more likely to be hired, to be promoted, to get others to help them, to be successful in influencing others and to get others to offer them useful information. Likeable people are less likely to be fired and their errors and mistakes will be more easily tolerated, forgiven or ignored. Furthermore, if two equally impressive people are under consideration for selection or promotion, it will be the most likeable one who is chosen.

Most people probably hope that they would score highly on a 'likeability spectrum' as most people try to be pleasant in their interactions with others. It is reasonable to assume that most people try to make a reasonably good impression on others. The key question here is how likeable does one need to be in order to be successful in a senior leadership role and to build a reputation as someone who is likeable?

Some will say that being likeable isn't required to be a successful leader and that it is more important to be respected than liked. However, there is clearly a link between how well a person is liked and how successful they are. However, this is not a definitive linear correlation – plenty of successful people are not well liked – but it makes sense that if you have the necessary talent and you are also likeable, success in any particular role will be achieved more easily. If a person is regarded as likeable, this will inevitably raise their self-esteem and self-confidence. Moreover it will make networking easier, which in turn creates opportunities to optimise a person's range of influence and for a person to receive more information. This will in turn strengthen their judgement.

More likely to persuade

Likeable people are more likely to persuade others because they are likeable rather than because of the strength of their argument itself. So many decades of research have found that the choices and decisions that are made about individuals in their career are often influenced by the likeability of the person involved. Likeability pulls people towards you, enabling you to attract followers and supporters who will go the extra mile because they want to befriend and help you. Remember that there is a likeability spectrum. It is a long continuum and only a few people are near the top, so likeability matters because it separates the likeable person from others and in essence it gives them a career advantage. It is also the case that the Halo Effect is applied to likeable people in that likeable people are rated as above average across a whole range of diverse attributes far removed from their interpersonal charms.

There are many talented managers with similar levels of skill, talent, knowledge and expertise but the most successful leaders build up a broad and deep reservoir of goodwill at all levels in the organisation that largely reflects the extent to which they are seen as likeable by colleagues. There are many effective, powerful but unlikeable leaders who tend to treat those they see as the 'little people' with indifference at best and contempt at worst. In contrast, the way that good likeable leaders treat these 'little people', or the secretaries, cleaners, receptionists, janitors and catering staff, becomes part of the DNA of the organisation.

President Bill Clinton was remarkably skilled in the way that he built and developed relationships. Many people who have met him have commented on his interpersonal charm and likeability. Clinton reflects on this skill in the following way: "I've come to believe that the most important thing is to see people. The person who opens the door for you, the person who pours you coffee. See them. Acknowledge them. Show them respect. The traditional greeting of the Zulu people is 'sawubona'. It means, 'I see you'. I try and do that".

CHAPTER 6: THE FUNDAMENTAL FOUR INSIDE-OUT REPUTATION WINNERS

How can likeability be developed to improve a reputation?

Likeability can be developed to improve a reputation by focusing on the following eight strategies and behaviours:
1. **Reaching out and engaging** by showing interest and curiosity, and using multiple cognitive and non-cognitive questions
2. **Giving behaviours** like active listening, compliments, smiling, lightness of demeanour, humour, kindness, polite manners, generosity of spirit, compassion
3. **Creating warm positive connections** like handshaking, eye contact, name contact, remembering personal information, sharing personal information
4. **Conversational connections** like using matching language, regulating conversational ratios, mastering 'small talk'
5. **Respectful attitudes** like displaying humility, punctuality and respect
6. **Positive approach** like displaying optimism, open-mindedness, focusing on balance and accuracy
7. **Genuineness** like authenticity, sincerity, avoiding chameleon-like tendencies, avoiding insincerity and pretentiousness
8. **Acting the part** like demonstrating appropriate dress and appearance.

1. Reaching out and engaging

Reaching out questions

It is often said that people will forget what you said but remember how you made them feel. The basic essence of the likeability factor is making engagements with other people less about you and more about them, and making them feel good about an interaction with you. Self-centred people are usually not likeable so when you are involved in a conversation, it is important that you focus more on the other person than yourself. The easiest way to charm someone else is to ask more questions and do less talking about yourself. The secret of asking good questions is to ask open questions with different layers and that start with how or why or when or 'tell me about'. Learn to use multiple funnelling questions that build on earlier questions. As Dale Carnegie said: "To be interesting, be interested".

Asking one question may come across as polite and formal so multiple questions are necessary to come across as genuinely interested and engaged. If you use the right kind of questions to engage with the other person, listening to them closely and backing this up with another more engaging question, then it will be relatively easy to appear likeable and charming to a number of people with little effort.

Curiosity

In order to appear likeable, it is important to show curiosity about other people and what they do, what they think, what pleases and displeases them, and how they feel about things. Most people like to talk about themselves, so it is easy to engage with someone by asking them about what they have been doing and what they plan to do. Interpersonal curiosity is a desire to uncover new information about someone's life experiences and their thoughts and feelings about a range of different events or activities. Curiosity about someone's feelings is a guaranteed likeability gain rather than asking factual questions about their experiences. The biggest compliment you can pay anyone is showing an interest in what they think and their views and opinions. How many times do you ask someone what they think about something? Another fruitful avenue is to try to establish some interest in people and their non-work lives. What books have they read lately? Are they following any TV programmes just now? What new skill would they like to learn if they had the time? What talent do they wish they had developed and why?

Asking 'feeling' questions

Many conversations at work are focused on what might be described as cognitive fact-based interactions and what people think about particular issues from a factual perspective. However, when the question-asker is able to move from a cognitive question to an emotional feeling-type question, by asking the other person how they feel about a particular issue rather than what they think about it, they will probably make a far greater positive impact on the other person. This is a major transfer of focus in any conversation and will usually open up and elicit a whole range of different words, feelings and opinions as well as move the conversation from a possibly polite superficial discussion to something that is more meaningful, personal and intimate.

2. Giving behaviours

Active listening

If a person takes the time to listen to other people, they will paradoxically have more influence over the other person. However, listening well and intently is not easy and we have to put a lot of effort into it so that we understand the other person's world. Being a good listener does require the listener to talk less than the other person and be an attentive presence, maintain eye contact, lean towards the listener and provide occasional positive verbal reinforcements. It is also good practice to clarify and interpret what a person is saying by occasionally summarising or restating what is being said or asking for clarification if there is something you do not fully understand. It can also be impactful to paraphrase to reflect the essence of what was said and to move beyond what was actually articulated to the perceived implication behind the meaning, beliefs, values, assumptions or goals behind the words.

Compliments

Most people respond well to compliments. Compliments can be made about a range of things – a person's appearance, their shoes, the words they use, their thoughts, their interests and so on. However, the most powerful form of compliment is based on a specific accomplishment or achievement rather than a general comment. It is, of course, important to be sincere and authentic and not to compliment people if it is not a genuinely held feeling. It can be extremely attractive and likeable to go out of your way to personally acknowledge and compliment someone for some particular successes. Everyone likes to hear that their efforts are being recognised.

Generosity of spirit

Perhaps the most powerful form of generosity of spirit for a leader is to cultivate magnanimity. This means giving credit where it is due, ensuring that credit for success is spread as widely as possible and taking personal responsibility for failures. Spread the fame and take the blame. Generosity of spirit is an extremely important leadership quality and a real differentiator between likeable and unlikeable leaders.

Compassion

Another key differentiating attribute in regard to building likeability is the capacity to show that you care for individuals and that you treat them with individual compassion rather than as one of a group, one of a team or a statistic. When you show that you care, you make people feel respected and valued. Compassion and caring is an important framework for your likeability.

Smiling

A smile can be very contagious and welcoming, and makes a person appear very accessible. It is easy to do but if we calculate how many times we smile during a day, the answer might surprise us by being a lot less than we expect. When we smile, we suddenly appear more approachable, warm and friendly, and so people that smile often are more likely to appear more likeable.

Lightness of demeanour

This refers to the importance of not taking ourselves too seriously, being prepared to laugh at or make fun of ourselves in a gentle way. Lightness usually involves an ability to react with humour or self-denigration if errors are made. It may also involve an attitude of mind that looks on the bright side and that refuses to catastrophise unsuccessful events. Self-deprecation is another form of lightness and involves making our achievements or our abilities seem less important. However, false modesty can be irritating so self-deprecation requires a gentle skill to soften a perception about oneself by referring to good luck, being in the right place or pointing out that application has its rewards and so on. Teasing good-naturedly will reduce barriers as long as the teasing does not attack a person's identity or tease about something that is not changeable. Humour and laughter are also highly infectious although it can be very difficult to be quick-witted. Moreover, it can be risky until you 'get' the other person and know what represents appropriate humour. It also goes without saying that humour needs to be context specific as, if used inappropriately, it can cause others to feel that you are not taking the discussion topics sufficiently seriously or you may be seen as lacking maturity of judgement.

Kindness

We often lose sight of the simple things that make us likeable, which are often the things that make us human. For example, people notice small acts of kindness, like giving helpful advice or a helping hand not required by the nature of the helper's job role. Conveying kindness, of course, is about giving to others and that includes being caring, and supportive. If you show kindness by sparing time for others, going out of your way to help others or sending an email of congratulation or condolence when appropriate then you are more likely to be seen as likeable by others.

Polite manners

The likeable person is more likely to be polite in their manners, to say 'please' and 'thank you', and to express appreciation with sincerity. This is an art that might involve using a personal touch like writing hand-written notes to show appreciation. It is also the case that showing appreciation should include careful avoidance of well-worn platitudes: an effort should be made to find a different and personal way of expressing thanks. It is also self-evident that expressions of appreciation should be timely and prompt in response to an act that requires thanks.

3. Connecting strategies

Eye contact

It is clearly important to be able to hold direct eye contact with others; indeed, this can be one of the most compelling forms of communication. However, the key is to be able to make eye contact without staring, so it is important to know when to look away so that you do not appear intimidating or threatening. When executed in an appropriate way, eye contact can lead to a very close form of interaction that in turn will lead to likeability. The appropriate amount of eye contact is about 60%. Too much can make you appear threatening and intimidating; too little can make you appear disinterested, shy, bored or as if you are not listening.

Handshaking

A firm handshake can lead to a very positive first impression, whereas a weak or limp handshake will very clearly lead to a negative first impression. The opportunity to shake hands is an opportunity for tactile communication. A handshake can also be used effectively to congratulate someone on a particular success. Some people appear to feel a little self-conscious about giving and receiving handshakes but not mastering the ability to feel comfortable with handshakes may well detract from their potential to be likeable.

CHAPTER 6: THE FUNDAMENTAL FOUR INSIDE-OUT REPUTATION WINNERS

Name contact

Most people enjoy it when others use their name in conversation. Likeable people tend to be very successful in remembering names and using them in both oral and written communication. President Clinton had a reputation for making a point of remembering the names of relatively low-level officials and was well remembered and liked because of his effort to recognise individuals and remember their names. Many people will rather glibly say that they have a terrible memory for names but may thus immediately make themselves less likeable because they do not seem prepared to invest the time or effort to ensure that they develop a system for remembering names. It is easy to keep notes on your smartphone to help you remember names of colleagues or clients and it is easy to refresh your memory before the next meeting.

Remembering personal information

When we meet someone again after a time interval and the other person remembers the previous conversation, perhaps remembering a family name or a business or social holiday or a trip planned, then we feel valued, special and recognised and we like the other person more for showing such interest. It is an extremely likeable characteristic if someone can recall and retain these conversations but it is also relatively easy to give oneself some help by writing notes on a smartphone against the contact's name. Then prior to the next meeting, it can be easy to quickly remind oneself of the previous conversation or any family or social detail that may be relevant. Most people will be amazed at the positive impact it has on the other person.

Sharing personal information

Sharing personal information helps people to get to know you and this is part of the process of becoming likeable. Some people feel that they have to be guarded about their personal life at work, but in most cases, people will enjoy getting to know you better and finding out about the 'real you'. They thus have more opportunities to find common ground, which is often the basis of likeability. If the leader restricts themselves to showing an occupational persona, they will never be liked in the same way as there will be a cognitive, fact-based relationship centred on job requirements without an emotional relationship based on a feeling of wanting to help the leader to be successful.

4. Conversational connection strategies

Matching language

In order to be likeable, it is important to use language that other people understand. This means avoiding jargon or complex language that may be difficult for others to understand. Mirroring the other person is a common technique that involves using similar language to a certain extent, so that if we use similar phrasing, a similar level of vocabulary, a similar amount of time speaking, then it will contribute to the likeability factor.

Conversational ratios

Conversation is like a tennis match in which one person speaks for a short time then, ideally, hits the ball over the net to give the other person an opportunity to speak. It is rarely appropriate to speak for more than two or three minutes at a time before the other person switches off and loses interest but you can check the level of interest by the amount of eye contact they display or the amount of reinforcing comments that they provide. It may be possible to tell an anecdote or a story that lasts for a longer period of time but most anecdote or story tellers overestimate the other person's interest in their story. There are people who think that they can entertain their social group by telling stories or talking for a long time or telling jokes but most of the audience will usually lose interest. It is a constant source of surprise that many people do not achieve a balance in one-to-one verbal conversations, speaking excessively because they want to fill the silence rather than using questions to give their attention to the other person and allowing the other person to fill the silence. Anyone who speaks for more than a couple of minutes is at risk of being seen as boring and less likeable and so they may lose the interest of the other person. So it is important to keep checking back to determine whether the other person is keen for you to continue.

Small talk

To be likeable, it is important to be able to conduct small talk. It can be difficult at times trying to find common ground with people you do not know but the strategy must always involve asking questions and asking questions – preferably that are not tired, ritualistic and well-worn. Try to avoid using "How are you?" questions that are often ritualistic and devoid of meaning. As an alternative to asking fact-led questions, you could try asking feeling-led questions. For example, there is a difference between asking someone "What is your job?" and "How do you feel about your job?" It may be helpful to think of the move from cognitive to emotional questions as crossing a bridge from the polite semi-formal superficial conversation to a more meaningful intimate personal conversation. In small-talk conversations, there is also a need to give information to allow the other person to build and participate in the conversation so that there is a constant flow between two people. However, the biggest failing in small talk is to talk too much and ask too few questions of the other person.

5. Respectful attitude

Humility

One of the greatest attributes in appearing likeable is to demonstrate humility for one's successes and achievements. Humility is expressed by appearing self-effacing and also trying to elevate the other person. Leaders with humility also do not use their status as a means of getting their own way and understand that their status does not make them a good leader.

Punctuality and respect

Punctuality and being early for meetings and appointments is a great show of respect for someone else's time and so is usually a likeable characteristic. President Barack Obama had a reputation for always being early and President Clinton had a reputation for always being late. It matters. If they are frequently late, a person may give the impression that they are being disrespectful and inconsiderate of their colleagues' time. Being late may also suggest that the person is self-centred in that they are prepared to keep people waiting, implying that their time is more important than the other person's. This type of person may have good intentions, ending up being late because they have poor time-management habits but their colleagues are inevitably going to judge on appearances. If the first impression is that a person cannot be bothered to plan to show up on time, their likeability will decrease.

6. Positive approach

Optimism

We tend to like and follow leaders who have a positive attitude. It is important that leaders try to promote an optimistic outlook, approaching issues with the belief that a solution can be found and seeing the opportunity ahead of the problems. People are more likeable if they have an optimistic demeanour and if they use positive language and positive body language. Positive language tends to focus on what can be achieved, making helpful suggestions about options that may be available, encouraging people to overcome problems and taking action to achieve their objectives.

Open-mindedness

Likeable people tend not to offer unqualified dogmatic opinions about different subjects, particularly if they do not have the facts or any knowledge or experience of a particular matter.

Opinionated people who speak with a great deal of conviction will simultaneously convey the message that they are not open-minded or keen to listen to alternative points of view, and this is not a likeable characteristic. Open-mindedness means being able to listen to new ideas even if they do not conform to one's usual way of thinking. Good leaders are able to suspend judgement while listening to others' ideas and able to accept new ways of doing things that may have been someone else's idea.

Balance and accuracy

Many people enjoy telling good-news stories and so may, often with good intentions, present an overly positive, glossed version of events. They may have a tendency to be unrealistically positive and upbeat. Unfortunately, if a person is known as someone who tends to put a positive gloss on their interpretation of what has happened, others will tend to discount what they are hearing from them. At worst, a person may lose respect if others feel that there is a lack of balance in their judgements or that what they say lacks credibility. It is not likeable to be a 'good news messenger' or make excessive use of hyperbole if others doubt the veracity or accuracy of what they are being told.

7. Genuineness

Authenticity

The idea that leaders must first of all be true to themselves is hardly new. Authenticity has two components: personal authenticity and moral authenticity. Personal authenticity is about a lack of pretence and trying to be yourself, but moral authenticity is about the choices you make and what you are prepared to act upon. At a deeper level, authenticity is about figuring out who you are and who you want to be as a leader. Authentic leaders tend to be genuine, transparent and trustworthy; they display a strong moral code and can be counted on to keep their word – except that one cannot always be honest and open if there are organisational confidential issues. Authenticity is an on-going process by which leaders gain self-awareness and establish open, transparent, genuine and trusting relationships in appropriate circumstances.

Avoid over-promising

As a follow on to the 'good news messenger' type of person, some people habitually make promises that they are unable to fulfil. Perhaps they have a tendency to make a number of invitations to people that they do not keep or have no intention of keeping or they may be overly optimistic about the speed and quality of delivery on a particular topic. In either case, it is not likeable to overpromise when over time colleagues will doubt their capacity to deliver and have a negative impression when plans are discussed in the future.

Integrity

It probably goes without saying that a likeable person is someone who tells the truth. However, it is ironic that most people probably stretch the truth on a regular basis to make an impression, avoid blame or embellish a story for entertainment value or to make them look good. These examples may include white lies but it is important not to have a regular pattern of telling stories with the aim of self-aggrandisement or one's likeability will decrease very quickly.

Avoid chameleon-like tendencies

A chameleon character is the type of person who changes their beliefs or behaviour in order to please others, attract personal acclaim from others or just to gain some personal advantage. Some people are known as 'political chameleons' because they are known to change their beliefs and arguments for personal gain and self-interest. As a strategy, a person may sometimes adopt a position because they do not think that their real ambition will be achievable and because they have a fear of failure in not being accepted, but then they may change their position as

CHAPTER 6: THE FUNDAMENTAL FOUR INSIDE-OUT REPUTATION WINNERS

circumstances change. In any of these situations, it is not likeable to be seen as an inconstant person who is likely to change frequently without a cogent reason.

Avoid insincerity and pretentiousness

Insincerity is not a likeable characteristic and is linked to chameleon-like tendencies but it also refers to saying things to flatter or criticise when these feelings are not genuinely felt. Some people have a pretentiousness, in that they choose to 'big themselves up' and perhaps talk about material activities in a way that is designed to promote their self-importance or in an attempt to indicate their relative levels of success in comparison to others.

8. Acting the part

Dress and appearance

Likeable people tend not to make clothes an issue. In other words, a stylish dress code is not necessary to enhance likeability but it can be important to ensure that dress and appearance do not become an issue by dressing appropriately for a particular context or occasion. In most organisations or at most social events, there is an informal dress code and if someone chooses to rebel against or step outside the typical dress code or make a particular individual statement about their appearance, then they need to have good reasons for deviating from normal codes of practice. However, as a general rule, it is unlikely to increase the chances of appearing more likeable unless there is a purpose to appear 'innovative' or 'left-field' in attitude.

Likeability key summary points

- It is important to be likeable as it will help to make you successful. Likeable people are more likely to be hired, promoted, to get others to help them to be successful, to influence and to get others to offer useful information. Likeable people are also more likely to have their mistakes

- and errors tolerated and to be given more time to make a success of a particular role.
- Likeability is a relative concept. It is a long spectrum with very few people at the top but it does give those highly likeable individuals a career advantage.
- Likeability is learned. A number of development strategies and behaviours are discussed including the following:
  1. *Reaching out and engaging* by showing interest and curiosity, and using multiple cognitive and non-cognitive questions
  2. *Giving behaviours* like active listening, compliments, smiling, lightness of demeanour, humour, kindness, polite manners, generosity of spirit, compassion
  3. *Connecting strategies* like handshaking, eye contact, name contact, remembering personal information, sharing personal information
  4. *Conversational connections* like using matching language, regulating conversational ratios and mastering small talk
  5. *Respectful attitudes* like displaying humility, punctuality and respect
  6. *Positive approach* like displaying optimism, open-mindedness, focusing on balance and accuracy
  7. *Genuineness* like authenticity, sincerity, avoiding chameleon-like tendencies, avoiding insincerity and pretentiousness
  8. *Acting the part* like demonstrating appropriate dress and appearance.

6.3: How to Win a Reputation for Making Wise Judgements

Why is the ability to make wise judgements important for developing a strong reputation?

The ability to make wise judgements is important for developing a strong reputation because successful leaders need to be balanced, objective, credible and wise in the judgements they make. They also need the skill to dig beneath the surface of issues and engage in root-cause analysis of problems and performance indicators rather than just reacting to the symptoms of a problem. The capacity to cut through to the core of problems and an ability to arrive at a persuasive 'net judgement' about complex problems is a highly valued skill. Most of us instinctively avoid ambiguity and gravitate toward certainty, which means that there is a human tendency to embrace simplistic black-and-white polarised thinking and avoid uncertainty or ambiguity. This is known as attribute substitution where we redefine a complex problem into more simple terms in order to make the problem more manageable and easier to answer.

The difference between intelligence and wisdom

In assessing a leader's capacity to make good judgements, it is important to differentiate between intelligence and wisdom. Intellectual smartness is vital for success but it appears increasingly insufficient for the top job. Moreover, there is a difference between intelligence or cleverness and wisdom. Intelligent leaders may impress us with their cleverness and intellectual horsepower in order to find solutions to problems but intelligent, clever people usually excel in finding a solution to a factual, linear problem or in finding a finite solution to a binary problem.

Intelligence alone may be insufficient to achieve success in our increasingly complex and uncertain world and, in making judgements, wisdom is something a little different from intelligence. Wisdom typically involves more breadth and depth than intelligence, in that wisdom requires the capacity to embrace many ill-defined variables with the capacity to hold two opposing premises in mind simultaneously. Wisdom also requires the factoring in of a moral, social or contextual element in that a wise judgement needs to be appropriate for the moral, social, psychological, economic or practical context in which the judgement is made. Unfortunately, our educational and political systems encourage individuals to polarise issues and simplify complex multi-variable problems.

Leaders with agile minds stand out for their ability to combine information from different sources and are comfortable working 'in the grey'. There are many clever guys who are not wise or who do not have good judgement because they insist on reducing everything to black-and-white alternatives. Certain leaders also confuse wisdom with knowledge, failing to see that it is possible to be knowledgeable and informed but poor at reaching wise judgements that depend on the collation and conflation of different perspectives and the patience to analyse the data in a balanced manner. The challenge to achieve sound judgements is to generate a range of options and ideas, to appreciate that there are layers of analysis and to maintain an open mind over time to allow multiple solutions to be generated or uncovered.

Wise judgements are a process not an event

Effective leaders not only make better wise judgements but are able to discern the really important decisions to be made and get a higher percentage of them right. They are better at the whole process that runs from seeing the need to make a judgement call, to framing issues in an appropriate way by asking the right questions, and to deciding what are the most critical variables in seeking to reach a solution. According to Noel Tichy and Warren Bennis [5] there is a framework of three critical domains within which all decisions are made. Tichy and Bennis stress that good judgement calls are a process not an event.

Tichy and Bennis propose that each judgement process begins when a leader recognises the need to make a judgement. The leader then frames the decision to be made by laying out the various factors and options, and then continues the process towards the execution and implementation of the judgement. Tichy and Bennis also stress the importance of possessing good self-knowledge in making a judgement because making a judgement call is usually not a solo performance – it may require the support of a team and need other colleagues to fill knowledge gaps, and it involves an awareness of our own perceptual filters that may bias the outcome.

We all tend to have a perspective on life shaped by our perceptual filters that is relatively narrow, shaped by our predispositions, assumptions and experiences. The longer we wear our perceptual filters without challenging them, the more we tend to get attached to our limited perspective. We can end up seeing only what we want to see, rarely observing anything that is outside our zone of interest and thus unwittingly developing tunnel vision.

Context sensitivity is a key element of wisdom

Wise leaders are sensitive to the context they operate in and fine tune their judgments accordingly. In his book *Smart to Wise*, Mike Clayton [6] identified some pillars on which wisdom rests. In particular, wise leaders need to develop their ability to see past the surface layers of a situation. Whatever is being considered, it is important to get into the habit of examining the problem or issue from a series of different perspectives before one tries to make an assessment. The judgement or practical wisdom of knowing what should be done in a given situation requires the ability to understand the context to determine what is a good thing to do in a specific time and situation, and to understand the best actions at those times to serve the common good.

How can wise judgement be developed to improve a reputation?

The capability to make wise judgments can be developed to improve a reputation by focusing on the following nine strategies and behaviours:
1. Investigation process
2. Moral considerations
3. Clarify assumptions
4. Managing ambiguity
5. Questions
6. Reason and consequences
7. Falsification
8. Critical-thinking skills
9. Multiple perspectives.

1. Investigation process

It is important to realise that the serious study of thinking is rare. It is not a subject taught in most schools, colleges or universities, but everything we do or want or feel is influenced by our thinking. To improve our ability to make wise judgements and enhance our reputation, we should approach the decision-making process like an investigative process and not as an exercise in advocacy. Advocates tend to project and communicate a single perspective of a decision or judgement but the challenge is to evaluate all the available information in as unbiased manner as possible, so as to be able to detect the flawed argument among all the options. Wise judgement makers or decision-makers engage in an open-minded decision-making process that is enquiry led rather than advocacy led. Wise decision-making steps, therefore, involve the gathering of a genuine variety of options that can significantly enhance the quality of judgements made. The better the quality of information available, the more likely we are to make a high-quality judgement.

The ability to reach a wise judgement can be helped by adopting three values:
- Scepticism, the willingness to question everything with an open mind
- Discipline, the ability to assess all of the evidence on its merits by weighing up evidence for and against and avoiding dangerous shortcuts in the reasoning process
- Having the courage to change the judgement quickly in the light of new evidence, regardless of the perceived loss of face.

2. Moral considerations

Wise judgements require leaders to make judgements based on sound values and ethics so that there is clarity about the common good, and what judgement will lead to a 'good' and 'appropriate' outcome from a moral, just and fair perspective. Wise judgements may require the ability to exercise political judgement by understanding the emotions and viewpoints of others; when to consider making judgements; and how the judgement or decision will impact on others from a logical, practical, political, economic, social, geographical, psychological and emotional perspective.

3. Clarify assumptions

Wise judgments require a good understanding of the assumptions behind a particular situation and problem so it is important to try to understand the real meaning of what people are saying and look beneath the surface. Write down or verbalise your assumptions to explain your understanding of an issue and clarify your own mind and practise summarising in your own words what others say. If we are to develop the ability to think wisely, we must learn the art of clarifying assumptions.

4. Managing ambiguity

Wise judgements often require the ability to hold two opposing ideas in the mind at the same time. We must avoid leaping to premature judgement and replacing or redefining a complex problem with a simpler problem, and so avoid attribute substitution. We can be faced with paradoxes where two different courses of action appear to be correct in certain circumstances, without polarising or reducing the problem to a binary issue. There are some tools available such as the forced-field analysis approach that enables a weighting of different factors impacting for and against a judgement. Thinking that leaps about with no logical connections is usually poor-quality thinking. When you are working through a problem, make sure that you stay focused on what sheds light on the matter in hand and do not let your mind wander to unrelated matters.

5. Questions

Wise thinkers focus on looking for opportunities to use questions that look beneath the surface of issues and help to uncover more information. Listen to how skilled interrogators use questions and *when* they question. Most people are not skilled questioners and most accept the world as it is presented to them. If they do question, the questions are often superficial or loaded. Wise thinkers routinely ask questions in order to understand the world around them and to query the status quo.

6. Reason and consequences

One of the hallmarks of a wise thinker is the preparedness and disposition to change one's mind when given good reason to change. Wise thinkers will tend to change their thinking when they discover better thinking and they can be moved by reason and the consequences of a particular decision. Wise thinkers will also try to anticipate and think through the possible consequences of a course of action. This is a massive differentiator when comparing those who make sound or unsound judgements.

7. Falsification

The Falsification Principle is at the heart of Karl Popper's philosophy of science. Essentially, it states that a judgement can only be considered sound if an attempt is also made to explore whether it can be proved to be unsound or false. Popper argued that no amount of evidence in favour of a judgement can prove the judgement to be sound unless one also tries to prove the judgement false or inappropriate.

8. Critical-thinking skills

Wise thinkers also have good critical-thinking skills. Critical thinking is reflective thinking in which a person reasons about relevant evidence to draw a sound or good conclusion. In addition to good critical-thinking skills, it is important for a wise thinker to have a critical-thinking disposition, including open-mindedness, intellectual curiosity, tolerance of ambiguity, scepticism, the patience to think laterally and consider alternative options, a preparedness to evaluate alternative options systematically, a comfort with paradoxes and an appetite for making quality judgements.

6-P Critical Thinking Model

Critical-thinking skills can be developed by following the author's 6-P Critical Thinking Model. The model advocates following the six steps outlined below.
- *Purpose/Problem*: Strive for clarity about the situation or problem by describing assumptions.
- *Position*: Understand the context about the current position and situation, and the consequences of acting or not acting.
- *Possibilities*: Look for alternative options to explain or resolve the problem or situation, and search for data both for and against each option.
- *Probe*: Be challenging about the quality of evidence and look for data triangulation, which is a powerful technique to validate data through cross-verification from two or more sources.
- *Proposal*: Evaluate the alternative options by weighing up arguments for and against each option, and make a proposal for a plan of action.
- *Postscript*: Review the critical-thinking process and look for feedback on the quality of your thinking so that you can look for ways to improve the quality of your thinking on a future occasion.

9. Multiple perspectives

Wise judgements often benefit from gathering a broad range of different views and perspectives so that as many minds as possible can be applied to a situation. A technique to improve the quality of a judgement is to use the 'three perspective' methodology as follows:

Perspective 1: Make a strong positive case for the judgement you hold.
Perspective 2: Make a strong negative case against the judgement you hold.
Perspective 3: Ask a colleague or friend to give you a different perspective from their own viewpoint on the merits of the judgement you hold.

Wise judgement key summary points

- The ability to arrive at a persuasive net judgement about complex problems is a highly valued skill. Wise judgement is the ability to think widely and deeply about a situation, and to find a solution that is appropriate for the social, economic, geographical, social, psychological or emotional context. Context sensitivity is a key element of demonstrating wise judgement calls.
- Wisdom is different from intelligence. Intelligence or cleverness is usually demonstrated when individuals are good at solving finite problems and where problems require binary, linear and logical thinking processes.
- Wise judgement calls are the result of an investigative process not an event. We have to be careful that our perceptual filters do not colour our perspective and judgement.
- Wise judgement can be developed by adopting the values of scepticism (to question and show curiosity), discipline (to explore all the variables) and courage (to change a judgement in the light of new information).
- Wise judgement calls will be enhanced by focusing on moral considerations, clarifying assumptions, managing ambiguity, using questions to uncover more information, using reason and consequences, falsification, critical thinking and multiple perspectives.

6.4: How to Win a Reputation for Perceptiveness

Why is the capability to be perceptive important for developing a strong reputation?

Perceptiveness is important for developing a reputation because perceptiveness and the ability to accurately 'read' people and their interactions with others have a huge impact on our professional success. Perceptiveness is often more important than cognitive intelligence or other competencies in getting to the top of an organisation. The ability to manage people and relationships is fundamental to success as a leader so one of the key characteristics required for modern leadership is the ability to understand why people behave in the way they do. Perceptiveness refers to our ability to pick up on cues from other people, to understand what is going on, why things are happening, and anticipate possible consequences. Perceptive people tend to be good at spotting patterns in other people's behaviour and what they say, and they pick up on tone of voice and body language. It is often estimated that 70–90% of all information is transmitted through our body language but whatever the percentage, this is a significant part of the way we communicate and so perceptive people need to be skilled in reading body language.

However, there are other concepts that overlap with perceptiveness, such as emotional intelligence and psychological-mindedness. Perceptiveness and emotional intelligence are very similar concepts but they are not identical. Emotional intelligence is both self-oriented and other-oriented, and it has been defined as demonstrating an awareness of our own and other people's emotions. Perceptiveness, on the other hand, is used here as being other-oriented and is concerned with understanding how other people behave, think and feel.

Psychological-mindedness is another similar concept and is typically defined as referring to someone who is interested in the inner needs, motives and experiences of others – someone who is a good judge of how people might behave, think and feel about things. However, although psychological-mindedness is a very similar concept to perceptiveness, it is perhaps a less user-friendly term than perceptiveness.

Perceptiveness involves accurately reading people and predicting their behaviour by connecting the dots and linking the cause and effect of the behaviour. Individuals with high levels of perceptiveness are interested in the complexities of people's motives and feelings, and they notice what people are thinking and feeling. Individuals with low levels of perceptiveness are uninterested in the complexities of people's motives and feelings, take others at face value, tend not to notice subtle changes in people's behaviour and fail to understand what is expected from them by other people.

A successful leader needs to be able to use their perceptiveness in a number of different areas such as the following eight:

1. Judgement:
   The perceptive person will know who to consult in order to gather different views to widen their perspective, and improve the breadth and depth of their thinking, and hence the quality of their judgments and decision making.
2. Team selection:
   The perceptive person will have the behavioural insight to identify the right person for the right job, so they will make a higher percentage of good hiring decisions and appointments.
3. Performance management:
   The perceptive person will be quick to identify behaviour issues that might interfere with optimum performance.
4. Coaching:
   The perceptive person will be skilled at one-to-one coaching and able to see how individuals can be coached and developed to optimise their performance.
5. Success profiling:
   The perceptive person will recognise the importance of identifying how successful people differ from less successful people in the way that they do their jobs, and introduce an objective assessment methodology to uncover stand-out performers and define what success looks like in specific roles.
6. Managing others' expectations:
   The perceptive person will understand the expectations and needs of senior managers and be proactive, taking the initiative to update senior managers and leaders in a timely fashion about organisational and personal development progress.

7. Managing conflict:
   The perceptive person will know how to read the situation and use questions to diffuse potentially difficult confrontations.
8. Adapting influencing style:
   The perceptive person will know how and when to adapt and tailor their communication style to match the needs and expectations of different groups.

How can perceptiveness be developed to improve a reputation?

Perceptiveness can be developed to improve a reputation by focusing on the following seven strategies and behaviours:
1. Empathy
2. Body language
3. Use of language
4. Reading people
5. Headlining
6. Managing conflict
7. How to be a good judge of character.

1. Empathy

It can be a slow and difficult process to develop and improve perceptiveness. Perceptive people will have good social awareness in terms of their empathy and awareness of their impact on people, and good relationship-management skills in their ability to build connections with other people. However, the ability to see the link between thoughts and emotions and subsequent behaviour is clearly a critical step in improving one's ability to be perceptive. Progress will not be made unless the perceptive person is sufficiently interested and curious to explore how and why others behave, think and feel as they do.

A person with a high level of perceptiveness about others will typically have a high level of empathy and will usually know what to say, how to say it and when to say it. Empathy means seeing and feeling the world from the perspective of other different people and so empathic people are good at asking questions to uncover emotions and feelings. For example, good questions might include "how does that make you feel?" or empathic statements like "it sounds like you are feeling..." in an effort to check one's interpretation of events. Demonstrating empathy also requires good use of non-judgemental verbal reinforcements to encourage the other person to talk, statements such as "I understand", "that must have been upsetting", "that is a lot for anyone to manage", "it must have been very hurtful" or "It must have been very difficult". In these examples, the highly perceptive person uses questions or comments to identify with someone's feelings without judgement or interpretation. Empathy is the capacity to imagine oneself as another person and to try to feel what the other person feels and to understand the way that he or she thinks.

Empathy requires one to move perceptual positions, something that is not an innate skill. NLP philosophies describe three perceptual positions: our own perception; trying to perceive the world from another person's position; and thirdly, taking a neutral, impartial, bird's eye view perspective.

Building rapport

Highly empathic people are also usually good at building rapport. Building rapport with someone can be achieved by using good questions to make the other person feel that they are the centre of attention and by trying to match them by using similar vocabulary, tone and pace of speech. Developing empathy in a relationship involves the ability to listen and understand in order to develop a deeper relationship.

Building rapport may also involve doing things for someone else that they value. The purpose of rapport building is to establish mutual trust and confidence by focusing on what two people have in common and doing things that will resonate with and be valued by the other person. When you are able to do something for the other person that they value and appreciate, you build the foundations for a strong and lasting sense of rapport between two individuals.

Building rapport means going beyond the superficial relationship and trying to establish a level of comfort so each person can speak openly without fear of interruption or judgement. However, good rapport also means that the other person is free and comfortable to give feedback or suggest when they think that you may be taking a wrong or mistaken course of action.

Use of open questions

At one level, the quickest and simplest way to build empathy is to become a high-quality question asker: ask what a person is thinking about an issue and how they feel about it; listen to the answer, suspend judgement and avoid the temptation to jump in with a response. The best response may be to summarise what you have heard to demonstrate understanding, and try to share and identify with the feelings that may have been experienced by the other person. A perceptive person will try to use questions frequently in their everyday language, to help them better understand other people, and will tend to use open questions that do not assume a particular response.

Avoid use of inappropriate questions

An unperceptive person will typically use the wrong questions and ask closed questions that can only produce one type of obvious answer. This is not going to uncover any real feelings or insights about the other person. The challenge here is for the highly perceptive person to make a judgement call as to when it is appropriate to use questions in a particular way to explore the feelings of the other person. Learning this process may take time and practice. Check with others: how would they have behaved and what questions would they have asked?

Listening

Listening well is essential for empathy. Very good listeners recognise the need to invest a great deal in being attentive and concentrating on assimilating all the verbal and non-verbal information being emitted. Good listeners make mental notes of both what is and what is not being said – it is often remarked that the most important thing about listening is tuning in to what is *not* being said. Listening well involves using open questions to encourage people to talk. For example: "tell me more about what it was like. How did it make you feel? What else did you think about when you had that experience?" It is also important to use silence to encourage others to talk. Silence offers the other person space to reflect and speak freely without interruption, and without expressing views that may be seen as judgmental to a certain extent. Listening skills may also involve summarising to show that you have understood and checking back to ensure that you have taken away the correct message.

2. Body language

Highly perceptive people have the ability to read body language relatively accurately. The ability to read people's facial expressions and body language, and sense the temperature or atmosphere in meetings or relationships, is a key quality of the highly perceptive person. However, much of the popular information about body language is oversimplified and sometimes trivialised. It is commonplace to hear comments with unfounded observations like "you should have seen his face", "he turned white with shock", "her face turned grey" and "you should have seen the expression on his face". Many of these observational assessments are so prone to personal bias that they are usually worthless.

Learn about body language

- Eye contact, posture, crossed arms, tone of voice and hand gestures are easy indicators as to whether someone is interested or not interested in what is being said. If someone leans in, they are engaged; if they back-up, look down or turn away, they are not relating to what you are saying.

- If someone is answering in monosyllables or with very few words, they are most likely uninterested, bored or keen for you to finish speaking. If they look at you when you speak and move closer, they are obviously finding value in what you are saying.
- The absence of reinforcing verbal comments and non-verbal nods and acknowledgements is usually an indicator that the person has lost interest in your communication or conversation.
- Active listeners maintain eye contact and will offer positive verbal reinforcements like nodding or smiling. They will encourage you to continue speaking if they are interested in what you are saying.

Learn about eye movements

- Lack of eye contact is a good indicator that someone has lost interest in your communication or conversation, or they may be choosing to send a signal that you should stop speaking and give someone else a turn. Eye movements in any direction increase when a person is recalling information but excessive eye movements in the listener indicate disinterest.
- Excessive eye contact may appear to be staring, which is obviously a rather intimidating or aggressive gesture. In order to build good rapport with another person, the gaze should be held for about 60–70% of the time.

Learn about facial expressions

- We all touch our face from time to time during conversations but research has shown that the number of times face-touching occurs increases during moments of deception.
- When people get restless, there is a tendency to increase mouth movements, such as pursing the lips or curving the corners of the mouth down.

3. Use of language

Conciseness

A perceptive person will aim for linguistic conciseness as they are sensitive to the need to speak in short bursts and then check with the other person as to whether the other person wants them to continue. An unperceptive person will typically speak for too long because they are not picking up on the non-verbal messages.

Avoid excessive use of hyperbole

A perceptive person will avoid excessive use of hyperbole and superlatives. Language that is laced with superlatives is not the language of a wise and intellectually discerning person. Hyperbolic figures of speech tend to over-state feelings and send a message that may lead others to conclude that you do not understand the subtle nuances of what is being experienced or that you are intellectually unsophisticated. The highly perceptive person uses language designed to reflect the individual nature of the person and situation involved, tempered by balanced, realistic and discerning comments that appreciate that feelings about people and events are relative and incremental.

Someone who makes excessive use of hyperbole distorts reality, as this strays too far from the facts. To exaggerate the depth and intensity of their feelings may also come across as inauthentic and lacking in the sincerity they may be trying so hard to convey. A perceptive person will also use language that is relatively accurate and discriminating. The highly perceptive person tends to use moderate language that aims to reflect the reality of a situation rather than the aspirational idealism of an imagined situation.

Colour, shade and differentiation

Colour, shade and differentiation in verbal expression are symptoms of an agile, perceptive mind. Someone who uses a similar type of language to describe different situations by saying that everything is 'great' or 'wonderful' or 'lovely' may identify themselves as unperceptive, in that they appear to be failing to appreciate the colour, shades and differentiation of different people and events. Such blandness in the use of language can come across as underpowered or lacking a critical edge in one's thinking processes. Someone who attributes a feeling to another person without checking may appear to polarise issues, misinterpret a situation and merely be making a statement that reflects their own personal biases and perceptual filters. This can appear judgemental and lacking in emotional insight.

4. Reading people

Reading people is about the ability to notice cues appropriately, in that two different people can observe the same circumstances and draw completely different conclusions. There are two basic processes in reading people. Firstly, there is the process of behavioural observation and of gathering data. Secondly, there is the process of interpreting the data, understanding how one's personal filters may distort the true and useful meaning of that data and then adjusting one's perceptions accordingly. We can all be surprised by the realisation that our first impression of a person turned out to be wrong because we misread the cues and clues gathered through our initial observation.

When seeking to report a perception of someone else, it is important to establish a baseline as to what may be their normal behaviour, recognising patterns in their behaviour. You then need to challenge and refine your assumptions and draw a conclusion. To put it simply, we get better and more accurate in reading people if we have a good understanding of our individual perceptual filtering processes and perceptual biases.

5. Headlining

The perceptive person is able to deliver information in headlines and then backfill with detail if necessary. Clarity will often mean being able to deliver the key point of the message in 10–20 words. Perceptive people do not deliver a long-drawn-out monologue or brain dump on their audience to show off how much they know. Rather, they focus on communicating key points in bundles of, say, three points so that it is easily digestible and intelligible.

Perceptive people have a particular way of speaking and communicating because they appreciate how to adapt and tailor their style to the needs of different audiences in order to increase their chances of being interesting and listened to. The perceptive person is usually identified by an ability to assimilate a lot of information and extract the key salient points. In other words, perceptive people are good at headlining and signposting, and making communications clear and memorable.

A verbose person has no chance of building a reputation as perceptive. It is also important to avoid speech mannerisms by repetitively using terms such as "like", "you know", "do you know what I mean" or "if you understand what I mean". Filler language like "um" and "so" should be avoided. Language like "sort of" or "this may not be a good idea but" does not convey authority or presence and will not accelerate the building of a good reputation.

6. Managing conflict

A perceptive person is usually skilled at managing differences of opinion and usually good at resolving confrontations. A perceptive person is more likely to manage a confrontation with carefully chosen questions rather than advocacy or assertive statements. Assertiveness can be expressed in different ways – it is often more powerful to manage confrontation by asking questions such as:

- Can you explain how you arrived at that opinion or point of view?
- Can you talk me through the pluses and minuses of that particular comment?
- What are the positive and negative consequences of that action or strategy?
- How do you think someone might criticise that point of view?
- In percentage terms, how confident are you that you are correct in that observation?

In a conflict situation, it is often more difficult for the other person to respond to this type of question because it puts them on the back foot. They have to pause and reflect to explain in a rational and reasonable manner how they arrived at their current position. It is often easier for the other person to reply when confronted with a diametrically opposed statement like "I don't agree" or "that's rubbish" rather than being asked to explain the thinking behind their own position.

7. How to be a good judge of character

Perceptiveness means possessing the ability to be insightful about assessing people, which includes assessing people for particular roles in an organisation, team or department. It is commonplace to see wrong or poor appointments where the leader appears to have made a wrong choice or poor selection decision, and very often they are not held to account. There is a common saying that people get "hired for what they know and fired for who they are" but senior executives should know better: before any appointment is made, they need to be sufficiently perceptive and insightful to know who these people are, whether they will fit into the culture of the organisation, whether they will fit into the team and whether they have the behavioural skills to leave a lasting legacy in a particular job.

A large element of perceptiveness is the use of information gathered through observation and conversation to help understand the causes of someone else's behaviour. Psychologists and others will attempt to understand the world around them, seeking reasons for an individual's particular behaviour and evidence to predict their future behaviour. However, assessing people is an extremely difficult task, even for psychologists who spend large amounts of time assessing people for specific roles. The best predictor of a person's behaviour is the way they think and interpret events, and although this is not an infallible rule, it is much more likely to be a better guide to predicting behaviour than any other assumption. Understanding a person's personal constructs, which they use to describe their world, is a sound way of helping to understand and explain their current and future behaviour.

Interview limitations

One of the fundamental problems of assessing people by interview is that the information is provided by verbal reports from the person themselves that may be inaccurate. Interviewees may speak inaccurately to create a favourable impression, or because they do not have accurate self-insight or an accurate memory of past events, or because they misread what is expected of them. It is always surprising how many people try to convey a 10/10 impression in an interview without admitting to any areas that require development. By so doing, they define themselves as lacking insight, integrity, honesty or credibility. Whichever way this is interpreted, the applicant will not convey the confidence or the maturity or the gravitas that they will adapt and grow in a new job and new culture.

The perceptive leader will know the limitations of their interviewing skills and the limitations caused by their perceptual biases and filters. The ability to observe other people in an informed, insightful and intelligent way is not an easy skill to master. Observers watch what people do and make judgements about others based on those observations. Skilled psychologists have usually developed expertise in making inferences about someone's likely future behaviour based on their knowledge of the person's thinking patterns, and previous and current behaviours. A skilled interviewer will avoid leaping to conclusions about other people's behaviours, intentions, emotions and beliefs, and try to take into account all of the relevant evidence and cross-validate information from different sources.

Perceptiveness key summary points

- Perceptiveness means being insightful and intuitive about other people, and being very good at noticing things about them that others may miss. It refers to the curiosity to explore how and why people think and feel in the way

CHAPTER 6: THE FUNDAMENTAL FOUR INSIDE-OUT REPUTATION WINNERS

  they do, and how their thoughts and feelings impact on their behaviour.
- There are several other terms that overlap with perceptiveness about others like emotional intelligence and psychological-mindedness. Perceptiveness is used here as referring to perceptiveness about other people.
- The perceptive person will stand out in the following areas by exercising good judgement: team selection, performance management, coaching, success profiling, managing others' expectations, managing conflict, and adapting and tailoring their influencing style.
- Perceptiveness about others can be developed by understanding more about empathy, body language, use of language, reading people, headlining, managing conflict, and how to be a good judge of character.

Chapter 7

Reputation Leakage and the Fundamental Five Reputation Losers

"Reputation is only a candle of wavering and uncertain flame, and easily blown out".

James Russell Lowell

Chapter 7 Key Points

- This chapter explores the difference between reputation leakage, which is short term and temporary, and reputation derailment, which is long term and may lead to career-threatening consequences.
- There are three behaviour patterns that lead to reputation leakage that will create short-term damage to a person's reputation but 'correcting behaviours' can be learned and recovered.
- The Fundamental Five Reputation Losers will create long-term damage to a person's reputation, and as they tend to be more 'hard-wired' aspects of a personality, they may lead to reputation and career derailment.

7.1: Reputation Derailers

There are more leaders who derail and lose their reputation than leaders who become great successes, yet most of the leadership literature focuses on the great leaders who succeed rather than those rising stars who are primed for greatness but lose their way and, usually, their jobs. Adrian Furnham [1] described the subject as the "elephant in the room": the potential negative or unhelpful behaviours of a senior leader are often seen as a taboo subject or an unspoken issue.

It is estimated by Adrian Furnham [2] that a surprisingly high number, between 40–60%, of senior leaders will derail and lose their reputation for varying reasons. The paradox is that most of these senior leaders will have been carefully recruited with impressive CVs and track records but it would appear that the selection procedures have not been sufficiently rigorous to identify potential problems or perhaps assessment psychologists have not been engaged to identify future potential damaging behavioural issues.

Let's start with some definitions. A leadership derailer is a behaviour that gets in the way of our progress at a particular level and is sufficiently significant that it is not compensated for by other strengths. It is also important to make the distinction between leadership incompetence and derailment. The incompetent leader usually has a skill deficiency, a lack of intellectual horsepower perhaps, or a lack of learning ability. Derailment, on the other hand, tends to be a consequence of certain personality factors and behaviours that are unacceptable to the organisational hierarchy or that do not meet the expectations of other key stakeholders.

It is also the case that there is no direct linear relationship between certain competencies and derailment, so we need to adopt a more curvilinear approach. For example, self-esteem is good but over-confidence and arrogance are bad. It may be good to be a team-player but not so good if the leader hides from decision making and seeks to spread responsibility too much among other team members. It may be good to be very charming but not so good to appear manipulative. It may be good to be very single minded and determined but not so good if the leader appears closed minded and suffering from tunnel vision. It may be good to be affable and eager to please but not so good if the leader is too keen to be liked and appears indecisive and conflict avoidant. An experienced leader is also attractive unless they appear rigid and inflexibly bound to tried-and-tested approaches.

In the last 30 years, Robert Hogan has worked in this field to identify and measure characteristics that may lead to failure and has referred to these behaviours as derailers. Hogan has developed a psychometric measure of the "dark side characteristics", called the Hogan Development Survey, and this test can be used as part of a selection assessment programme. Hogan has proposed that there are three different groups of derailing behaviours that individuals typically use when under stress. These groups are as follows:

> **Moving away from others:** These behaviours are associated with mistrust, hostility and negative feelings towards others.
>
> **Moving against others:** These behaviours are associated with hostile, autocratic, dominating, manipulative behaviours towards others.
>
> **Moving towards others:** These behaviours are associated with an extreme tendency to please others, agree with others' opinions and avoid making waves.

Although there are many factors that might indicate that a leader could derail, the purpose of this section is to identify the most common causes of career and reputational failure. Some of the factors that cause some reputation damage are short term, easily learned and recoverable. However, there are other factors that appear more important, significant and hard wired, and these can lead to long-term career and reputation derailment.

7.2: Reputation Leakage and Reputation Derailment

Reputation is lost in varying degrees but, as mentioned earlier, it is a career fact that half to two-thirds of senior leaders will be fired, demoted or plateau at some point of their senior career trajectory. Another very poignant finding from various studies suggests that those leaders who overstate their self-assessment of their abilities are about six times more likely to fail than those leaders with a more realistic and accurate self-awareness and self-assessment. It also seems likely that many leaders have a

CHAPTER 7: REPUTATION LEAKAGE AND THE FUNDAMENTAL FIVE REPUTATION LOSERS

reputation problem because they do not appreciate that their existing skills, which may well represent a strength, are not the skills their employing organisation needs or values at a more senior level or in a particular role or function. It may also be the case that some leaders will focus on their strengths and fail to see or identify a critical skill gap or personal behaviour blindspot.

Reputation damage will, of course, depend on context and the severity of the reputation-losing behaviours. Some such behaviours, which we call here 'reputation leakage', are temporary and recoverable while other types of reputation-losing behaviours will tend to lead to long term and often permanent reputation and career damage, which we call here 'reputation derailment'.

7.3: The Three Reputation Leakage Behaviour Patterns

'Reputation leakage' refers to the inability of people in senior-level roles to demonstrate positive changes in their competence or behaviour when they take on a new role. They are seen to continue to operate in their existing comfort zone or not to progress or develop at a sufficiently fast rate. Therefore, reputation leakage occurs when any progress or development of a potential leader is not visible to a senior stakeholder; and once senior stakeholders have formed a view about a person's strengths and weaknesses, they tend to place more emphasis on the data and observations that support their view. As a consequence, all individual leaders who fail to proactively demonstrate progress or movement in their ability to adapt and cope with new leadership positions will suffer from reputation leakage.

Reputation leakage is caused by three different behaviour patterns:
1. **Slowness to adapt and change:** Failure to adapt to the needs and demands of the new role.
2. **Slowness to recognise how expectations have changed:** Failure to recognise how specific abilities need to be developed and the different criteria being used to assess one's performance.

3. **Slowness to show political maturity** in understanding the way that senior relationships need to be managed: Failure to invest in building collaborative relationships and understanding the way that senior relationships need to be managed.

All the reputation-leakage factors are critical and important, and they are often seen during the leader's honeymoon period, when the leader is learning how to be an effective leader. However, all these behaviours are not necessarily fatal career-threatening liabilities as they can all be learned from, improved and developed with appropriate support. In a typical situation, a new leader is given time to address and develop these potential reputation-leakage areas in their performance. However, if these behaviours continue over a period of several months, they will cause longer-term damage when the honeymoon period is over, which may lead to reputation derailment.

Reputation leakage behaviours explained

Reputation Leakage Behaviour 1: Slowness to adapt and change to the needs and demands of the new role

A primary cause of reputation leakage is a failure to recognise the need to change priorities and to change how the leader uses their time, focus and energy in order to adapt to the new level and areas of responsibility. At various times in their career, people have to learn to change their existing ways of operation and acquire new skills, knowledge and approaches. The work at more senior levels becomes less tactical and more strategic, and the leader needs to get further removed from the operational end of the business and more responsible for the longer-term timetable. The complexity and importance of building and maintaining relationships, business models and sources of data increase exponentially. To transition successfully to more senior leadership roles, individuals must reinvent themselves in the new role, particularly with regard to how they distribute their time and attention and how they interact with stakeholders and set their priorities.

Learning agility is the ability to learn quickly, to apply the learning as soon as possible and to be proactive as well as responsive to the constantly changing work environment. However, some leaders are also threatened by change and seldom produce innovative approaches to new business conditions. Reputation leakage can occur if new leaders continue to work in their comfort zones and appear slow or unwilling to learn. Unfortunately many leaders move into senior roles with the implicit expectations of doing more of the same or believing that they will pick up what is expected as they go along. Leadership, however, requires a different mindset and different behaviours. Good leadership is driven by having the right attitudes, values and, most importantly, a well-informed understanding of the role. This requires a realistic assessment of what is expected and what gaps need to be closed in their specific situation.

Leaders know that when they are in their comfort zone, there is no anxiety, no pressure and no stress, and the leader may want to continue to have a hands-on involvement in the execution and delivery of tangible operational tasks. Unfortunately, the comfort zone places a ceiling on one's potential and limits the extent of one's likely achievements as no risks are taken. The other problem in living in a comfort zone is that there is a tendency to think that average is acceptable. The best leaders are courageous, unafraid of challenging the status quo and pushing boundaries to make things better.

Reputation leakage will also occur if leaders fail to show confidence beyond the boundaries of their personal comfort zone experience. People who are promoted to positions of leadership based on their subject-matter functional and technical expertise alone are often locked into their way of doing things as the basis of their own perceived value to the organisation. They may not be open to other approaches.

Reputation Leakage Behaviour 2: Slowness to recognise how specific abilities need to be developed and that different criteria are now being used to assess performance

Reputation leakage may occur if the leader does not demonstrate a self-awareness as to how they need to grow and develop in the role. Many people fail in a leadership role because they lack self-awareness and self-insight about why they got selected or promoted in the first place, and how their abilities need to be developed to cope with their new responsibilities. There is also a tendency for underperformers to be rather black-and-white in their self-assessments. They may not have grasped the incremental nature of a performance continuum or the concept of marginal gains. In other words, you will often hear senior leaders claiming to have a particular skill or attribute without demonstrating a recognition that we all have certain attributes to varying and different degrees, or that the skill, ability or attribute they possess may not have been developed to a level to meet the expectations of key colleagues. Many people have abilities in most relevant leadership areas to a certain extent, but high-potential leaders need to convey and present a development strategy on how they intend to close any gaps in their leadership performance and capability.

The key lesson for a new leader to learn is that the skills, abilities and behaviours that get individuals promoted are not necessarily the same skills and behaviours that will enable them to perform well in a more senior role. The rules of the game change at senior leadership levels. There is a different set of performance-assessment criteria and expectations for leaders and potential leaders. There is a dramatic change from being a manager who focuses on delivery and execution to a leader who focuses on setting direction, managing at a distance, careful delegation, monitoring and measuring performance, leading teams and influencing across different functions. All these requirements place hitherto unknown challenges on an individual's attitude and behavioural skills as a leader.

The key change for all new leaders requires an increased focus on the soft behavioural relationship skills required to lead and work through colleagues, team members and direct reports. These soft skills mean learning the skills of delegation, having empathy for people, being able to talk effectively with them and actually motivating them to achieve a common purpose. These soft behavioural skills are also the foundation for influencing, for negotiating, for managing different people, for communicating and so on. Unfortunately, many successful experienced managers and leaders are often seen to lack soft behavioural skills. When managers get promoted, the key transition is from managing things to managing through others.

Reputation Leakage Behaviour 3: Slowness to show political maturity in collaborating and understanding the way that senior relationships need to be managed

Reputation leakage can occur if a leader displays a lack of political maturity, failing to recognise that they can only optimise their performance by understanding how to navigate the organisation and the specific gatekeepers at different stages of the operational or strategic process. Leaders who think that they are being true to themselves often find the process of investing time to leverage relationships and to get buy-in from their colleagues to be distasteful. It feels artificial and political. It is, of course, no such thing. The recognition of the need to collaborate, influence and align colleagues to a particular common purpose is part of the leadership maturation process. When people are told to step up and do the 'networking thing', it can appear like valuing form over substance. If the 'string pulling' is too obvious, some leaders cannot make themselves do it.

However, it is important that newly appointed leaders are aware of the political landscape in the organisation, which individuals have influence and how things get done in that specific organisation and in different specific functions. If leaders are indifferent to politics or unaware of organisational politics then they may be slow to exercise influence in the organisation and so marginalise their impact.

However, if an aspiring leader cannot craft an emotional message to influence and inspire others because they feel less authentic than when relying on facts, figures and spreadsheets, their career in a top leadership role will be short lived. Many leaders know that their good ideas and their potential will go unnoticed if they do not do a better job of selling themselves but they struggle to bring themselves to do it. Outstanding leaders recognise that they will be more successful if they are able to extend their reach and increase their impact on the organisation by giving colleagues the confidence that they are on top of the job. It is an obvious win–win scenario when you can reassure senior managers that you are performing well and on top of the job, and it also conveys political maturity if you are able to present evidence-based data on what you have learned and how you are planning to maintain progress and take your performance to the next level. However, some potential leaders find it particularly hard to sell themselves to senior management when they most need to do so in order to build the confidence of senior executives that they are up to the job.

Reputation leakage key summary points

- Reputation leakage or the weakening of a person's reputation is caused by three different behavioural patterns:
  - *Slowness to adapt and change:* Failure to adapt to the needs and demands of the new role.
  - *Slowness to recognise how expectations have changed:* Failure to recognise how specific abilities need to be developed and the different criteria being used to assess performance.
  - *Slowness to demonstrate political maturity:* Failure to show political maturity and understanding of how senior relationships need to be managed.

7.4: The Fundamental Five Reputation Losers

As described earlier, reputation leakage behaviours are usually short term and temporary and an individual's reputation can typically be restored as new leaders learn on the job. However, although there may be many factors that might indicate that a leader may fail and lose their reputation, the Fundamental Five Reputation Losers are proposed as the most significant and important derailers because their effects are potentially longer lasting and more difficult to change. The Fundamental Five Reputation Losers that will probably lead to career derailment if not arrested to some degree are:

- **Untrustworthiness:** Inconsistent principles and values, and failure to build and maintain trust.
- **Narcissism:** Excessive self-regard and self-importance, and failure to build a positive work environment where talent is nurtured so that people can contribute, add value and feel valued.
- **Myopia:** Narrow perspective and failure to focus on the bigger picture and common purpose.
- **Dogmatism:** Narrow tunnel-vision thinking and failure to exercise open, unbiased judgements.
- **Emotional detachment:** The inability to recognise personal emotions in oneself or others or to share personal emotions. This leads to an impaired capacity for empathy and for building personal and work relationships.

7.5: Reputation Loser 1 – Untrustworthiness

Building and maintaining trust are essential for leading. As trust is the foundation of all really strong relationships, the perception that someone has an untrustworthy reputation is a blemish on the relationship landscape that is difficult to ever overcome. In a team situation, team members need to be able to trust their leader and trust their judgement and decisions; they have to trust their word and trust that they are trying to do their best for the team and the organisation. People assess a leader's trustworthiness based on how they act and behave and whether they seem to be acting in the best interests of others. The trustworthy person will be straight in their language, push back respectfully, make a point of ironing out differences in private and show a willingness to compromise.

In many ways, trust, unlike many other personal attributes, is usually a binary concept in that we either trust someone or we don't. However, we occasionally have a continuum of trust in which we trust someone to a certain extent, we don't trust them when the going gets tough or we don't trust them if there is an opportunity for personal gain. Trustworthiness clearly enhances a person's reputation and untrustworthiness clearly damages a person's reputation irreparably.

Behaviours that create trust include integrity, honesty, transparency, reliability, consistency, inclusiveness and appearing to be concerned about the best interests of others. People also have to know you to trust you, so people will want to know what you believe, your values, how you like to work, what they can expect of you and what you expect of them. To be a leader you need followers and followers are increasingly demanding and selective about who they trust and who they will be prepared to follow. Essentially, if leaders are untrustworthy, people working for them will usually be unmotivated, disenchanted and alienated. They will become less productive and, at worst, they may become potentially subversive.

The following seven indicators suggest that a leader will be perceived as untrustworthy if they are:
- Prone to corporate dishonesty and a lack of integrity
- Prone to treating employees in an unequal manner
- Prone to blaming others
- Failing to act transparently and openly
- Prone to break promises
- Inclined to act out of self-interest
- Prone to rudeness and incivility.

Corporate dishonesty

A leader will be perceived as untrustworthy if the employees believe the leader to be prone to corporate dishonesty, lying and making unsubstantiated statements about the organisation and its policies with regard to career development, career opportunities, pay and rewards and so on. We can all be guilty of making over-generalisations and making unsubstantiated statements from time to time, and all organisations talk about their mission, vision, culture, values and integrity. However, if some of these statements are blatantly untrue, employees will be severely alienated from their leader and their organisation.

Perceived inequalities

A perception of untrustworthiness will result if some people in the organisation are perceived as being treated differently from others – 'one law for the rich, another for the poor'. One of the most important words at work is 'fairness'. People should be fairly assessed, fairly promoted and fairly rewarded, yet it can seem to some that who you know, how you look or how you speak in meetings may be more important than loyalty, hard work and productivity.

Blaming and finger-pointing

Leaders will lose trust with their employees if the employees believe that the leader is uncaring and prone to finger-pointing and blaming other people for mistakes. It is to be expected that the leaders who use this finger-pointing strategy will be seen as self-serving and potentially bullying if specific employees are made to feel like scapegoats for any lack of success or performance.

If excuse-led leaders keep looking for someone to blame then others will begin to question their integrity, loyalty and dependability. Great leaders take responsibility for their actions. As the saying goes, the best leaders use 'I' when admitting to mistakes and 'we' when talking of success. Excuse-led leaders may also like to consult widely with colleagues as in this way they can spread the risk and share and diffuse responsibility to avoid any personal blame sticking to them. This process can make them appear democratic and participative but in effect stops anything significant happening because they are conservative, risk avoidant, indecisive and lacking courage.

Failing to act transparently and openly

A lack of transparency and openness in the communication of organisational goals or problems can lead to a clear sense that the organisation does not fully trust its employees. This makes it likely that employees will not trust their leaders or the organisation. While top management may demand loyalty from staff, it may not always be clear why that loyalty should be given.

Broken promises

A sense of untrustworthiness will also be a consequence of broken promises, unmet expectations or contradictory statements by leaders. Hopefully, during the selection interview process and induction period, new employees are told about what is expected of them, what the company stands for, how things work and their role. However, all too often an employee does not have their expectations clarified and there is a lack of clarity about criteria for promotion, salary increases and so on. This accelerates the creation of a lack of trust in the organisation and its leaders.

Self-interest

Leaders will be perceived as untrustworthy if they are seen to act out of self-interest and put their own welfare, interests and personal gain above those of their immediate team and the wider organisation. When leaders give themselves disproportionate rewards, take all the accolades for good performance or make decisions that result in personal gain, they are seen to disrespect and undervalue those colleagues who may believe that their contribution is not being recognised.

Incivility

Incivility is another form of untrustworthiness. If leaders are inconsistent and cannot be trusted to behave in a decent and respectful manner, their reputation will suffer. However, discourteous behaviour, treating employees with a lack of respect and consideration, and even rudeness are surprisingly common. Incivility may manifest itself as brusqueness or directness, but it can also take much more subtle forms. It is often prompted by thoughtlessness rather than actual malice – for example, sending texts or emails during a meeting or presentation, public teasing of direct reports by a boss, the team leader who takes credit for good news, the team leader who is always late for meetings or the leader who is unresponsive or slow to respond to emails and phone calls. Such relatively minor acts can be even more insidious than overt bullying because they are less obvious and easy to overlook yet they result in the erosion of organisational engagement and morale.

7.6: Reputation Loser 2 – Narcissism

Narcissists are frequently encountered in senior executive roles but their success is frequently short lived. Narcissism is characterised by an extreme arrogance, self-regard, self-absorption and self-admiration. Narcissists suffer from a bad reputation because of their perceived failure to build a positive, collaborative work culture as they are unable to work well with others. Narcissists are primarily driven by the need to get the admiration of others. They can be unreliable and unreceptive to contrary views or any helpful, well-intentioned feedback that differs from their own perspective.

Self-absorbed

Narcissistic leaders like to be the centre of attention, are intensely self-focused people and have an inflated sense of self-importance and a deep need for admiration. They have a tendency to focus excessively on their own accomplishments and to exaggerate their achievements as proof of how well they have done. Narcissistic people may appear infatuated with their own abilities and tend to have an overly optimistic view of their talents and believe that they are special. Narcissists are overly confident about the correctness of their own judgement, are more likely to bend the rules and tend to reward loyalty to themselves as a leader and an individual over valuing expertise or honesty or contribution to the wider team or organisation.

Poor social interaction

Narcissists usually lack empathy and the narcissistic leader tends to be poor at interacting with others as they are overly self-centred and lack curiosity or the inclination to question others to hear another perspective. Narcissists are prone to belittle the achievements of others, appear to disrespect others by not valuing their input and, as a consequence, are poor social and interpersonal performers. Narcissistic leaders tend to have shallow uncommitted relationships, they tend not to make close, supportive friendships, and they tend to exploit and use others for their personal gain and personal self-interest. Narcissists can only establish superficial relationships with colleagues because it is often difficult to have a balanced conversation with them. This is because they are invariably driven by self-interest and pay little attention to what the other person is saying, usually trying to direct conversations back to themselves.

Unreliable and unreceptive to feedback

Narcissistic leaders are often unreliable, they fail to learn from experience and they can act on whims. They want immediate gratification and can be seen as manipulative in the way that they use people. Narcissists have a tendency to discount negative feedback so they remain oblivious to any correcting feedback from well-intentioned colleagues. Narcissists are also thin-skinned and hostile when challenged and they also often use defence mechanisms to avoid any criticism or negative perceptions of themselves. As a consequence, any personal attack or criticism of a narcissistic leader may compel the leader to tell everyone how well they have done as they are never likely to admit mistakes or errors or show remorse.

There are two other characteristics closely associated with narcissism: hubris and Machiavellianism.

Hubris

Although closely related, the hubris syndrome differs from narcissism in that it is an acquired personality change involving people in positions of power who develop autocratic and tyrannical behaviour. The distinguishing feature of hubris syndrome is that it is confined to people who could be said to have normal personalities in a social or non-work context. It is typical of hubristic behaviour that there is a gross overconfidence, overestimation of a person's likely achievement and a gross underestimation of the risks and likelihood of failures.

Hubris is defined as excessive pride, arrogance or self-confidence. A hubristic act is one in which a powerful figure with overpowering self-confidence acts without fully considering the consequences. At a certain level, hubris can indicate a shift in the behavioural pattern of a leader. Hubris syndrome is important because the people who develop it hold powerful positions, so the effects of their hubris can be widespread and in some cases extremely damaging.

David Owen [3] proposed that hubris syndrome is evident when a leader has too much self-confidence and does not worry about the detail of a decision or judgement. The leader displaying signs of hubris syndrome tends to have a disproportionately high concern with image and presentation, and a propensity to see their world primarily as an arena in which to exercise power and seek recognition. They tend to demonstrate exaggerated self-belief bordering on a sense of omnipotence. Owen argued that other character attributes of hubris syndrome include excessive belief in the individual's own judgement and a tendency to dismiss or undervalue the advice or criticism of others, bordering on a sense of omnipotence in what they personally can achieve.

Many leaders display confidence in the rightness of their own decisions and their powers of persuasion that borders on hubris. However, a leader whose rhetoric becomes increasingly focused on self-promotion and attention-seeking behaviours is likely to fail because if someone values self-interest above anything else, they don't understand that leadership is about something beyond the leader and leading others to a better place.

Machiavellianism

Machiavellianism is also closely associated with narcissism because it refers to a personality trait that describes a person so focused on their own interests that they will manipulate, deceive and exploit others to achieve their goals. Machiavellian personalities usually have a cynical disregard for morality. Traits associated with Machiavellianism include duplicity, manipulation, self-interest and a lack of emotion. Machiavellianism is considered as part of the Dark Triad. This is a subject in psychology that focuses on three personality traits that includes Machiavellianism, narcissism (described above) and sociopathy or psychopathy, which usually refers to personality traits associated with a lack of empathy, antisocial behaviour, impulsiveness, emotional volatility and lack of remorse.

A leader with the trait of Machiavellianism will tend to focus on their own ambition and interests, and possibly prioritise money and power over the success of different relationships or the success of the whole organisation. They will have a tendency to exploit and manipulate others to get ahead, they may lie and deceive when required and they are generally lacking in principles and values. Machiavellian leaders may often lack warmth in social interactions and they can be excessively cynical in their assessment of what is right and wrong.

The problem with malevolent personality traits like Machiavellianism is that those who have such traits are unlikely to recognise them or want to change. Many leaders may have a degree of darkness in their personality but in order to ensure that it does not impact substantially on their performance, it is important to acknowledge and accept that it is there and to know when the behaviour pattern may be at work.

7.7: Reputation Loser 3 – Myopia

A key challenge for a new leader is to focus their time and energy on the most appropriate and relevant issues. Myopia or a myopic perspective will derail a leader's reputation if he or she is seen to have a disproportionately narrow perspective, a short-term focus and an apparent lack of concern for strategy, long-term vision, broader implications, and the consequences and ramifications of specific decisions, judgements and plans. If a myopic leader fails to focus on the big picture and fails to convince their followers that they have the capability to develop a future vision and common purpose for the team and the organisation, they will lose their credibility as leader. The myopic leader will lose their reputation because they will be seen to focus excessively on the small detail, and fail to appreciate the wider context and consequences of their actions. The myopic leader will also focus on short-term task execution and implementation without stepping back to see the broader and bigger picture.

There are at least three key indicators of a myopic reputation derailment:
- Working at a level below their pay grade
- Failing to think ahead
- Failing to apply relevant metrics and milestones.

Working below one's pay grade

Leaders and potential leaders will fail if they use their time in the wrong way and focus on inappropriate issues or issues at the wrong level. Most commonly, ineffective leaders focus on short-term issues and operational processes and tasks in their comfort zone. Many executives get to senior positions because they have been 'successful doers' and they have had a good track record of positive results. However, when moved into senior leadership roles, some leaders continue to micro-manage and engage in excessive 'doing' behaviour. In running around and trying to do everything, unbeknownst to themselves they are often exhibiting the kind of behaviour that undermines their leadership reputation. If a leader is seen as a micro-manager and overly controlling in their management style, and if they do not empower others with the freedom and latitude to do their best work, they will quickly lose reputation as a successful leader.

Failure to think ahead

The myopic leader may be seen to be constantly rowing the boat rather than steering the boat. The inevitable conclusion will be that the leader is an accident waiting to happen as he or she is not looking where they are going. The perpetually busy myopic leader may think that they are sending the right messages but they may struggle to achieve what is really important because they do not have enough time to think and reflect and look ahead at the bigger picture issues. This can often represent a major blindspot for myopic leaders as there can be a tendency to justify what they are doing expending a huge amount of energy and effort in trying to make their team and organisation a success.

However, the myopic leaders who are not focused on the bigger picture are probably not looking for the most effective way of directing and allocating their resources to achieve a common goal. Leaders must be able to create a vision for the business but they must also direct that vision by channelling the existing resources of people towards a common goal and create an environment in which people can flourish. If the myopic leader is preoccupied with the here-and-now issues, they are unlikely to be investing sufficient time in building the necessary relationships, aligning different groups to a common purpose and thinking about how to plan and shape the future.

Failure to apply relevant metrics and milestones

Myopic leaders will also tend to avoid introducing success metrics or milestones and will tend not to set clear measureable targets or agree objective criteria of success by which their performance can be assessed. Many myopic leaders and managers get immersed in reporting and recording information rather than analysing, evaluating and interpreting what has been done in the pursuit of a particular objective. However, this tactic is insufficient and misleading as recording progress is not an absolute concept. Outstanding leaders try to interpret and evaluate what has been achieved in order to undertake a relative analysis on how these figures might have been different or might have been improved.

7.8: Reputation Loser 4 – Dogmatism

Dogmatism is a way of thinking that is stubborn, closed-minded and narrow-minded often as a consequence of prejudice and bigotry. Dogmatism is a tendency to believe something is true without consideration of evidence or the opinion of others and not accepting anyone else's opinions. Successful leaders are open-minded, curious and self-driven in the pursuit of their own personal development. If leaders are prone to dogmatism, closed-thinking processes, subjective bias, poorly thought out decisions and non-evidence-based decisions, employees will begin to lose hope and belief, morale problems will develop and the leader's reputation will be permanently derailed.

Unconscious bias is responsible for a number of dogmatic judgements and it can have a negative impact on our decisions and eventual outcomes. This is largely due to the process of self-deception. This can be described as true information being preferentially excluded from our consciousness and replaced by false information that better suits our needs and plans at a particular point in time. As a consequence, this self-deception tendency can impact on a dogmatic leader's ability to process facts objectively, accept advice and incorporate the views and opinions of others.

Leaders who appear excessively dogmatic are often defensive about their behaviour and their judgements. Such leaders will soon suffer from reputational damage if they are not seeking a broad evidence-based perspective. Dogmatism can destroy relationships. It creates a climate of contention that eventually leads to a loss of trust and goodwill. Dogmatic behaviour in a leader may create a reciprocal cycle, in that one party may act dogmatically, which then causes the other party to respond dogmatically, which in turn causes the first party to be even more

dogmatic and so on. The opposite of dogmatism is open-mindedness, which creates an atmosphere of mutual respect. It is always better to respond to an impasse, confrontation or conflict with a question rather than a direct opposing statement. For example:
- Why do you think that?
- What have you seen to make you conclude that?
- What example would support that statement?

There are at least three indicators for a reputation derailment as a result of dogmatism:
- Polarised black-and-white thinking
- Lack of curiosity and learning agility
- Over-generalisations and lazy thinking.

Polarised black-and-white thinking

Dogmatic leaders tend to exhibit some form of polarised, black-and-white thinking that involves artificially making complex issues into a black-or-white bipolar issue, statement or decision. Black-and-white thinkers can be good linear thinkers in solving problems with a finite solution but they are less able to deal with ill-defined ambiguous data or hold two or three competing options or possibilities in their mind simultaneously. Dogmatic leaders fail to appreciate shades of grey and therefore fail to cope with the ambiguities surrounding many top-level decisions and courses of action. These are inevitable at senior levels, so the dogmatic leader's reputation will dramatically suffer as he or she is seen to be not up to the job.

Lack of curiosity and learning agility

Dogmatic bias leads individuals to see situations in overly rigid, inflexible ways. The ability to cope with change and ambiguity in an organisational world that is constantly changing is an essential requirement for successful leaders. However, dogmatic leaders tend to display a lack of curiosity, which is very common with self-confident, single-minded leaders who choose not to make the time to see and understand issues from different and varied perspectives. It can be a positive attribute to be single minded and determined but if this attribute develops into a tendency to be rigid and inflexible then the leader will probably lack the learning agility required to be a successful leader. Learning agility is the ability to assimilate new information quickly and to apply the new learning in a proactive way. However, if the leader is slow to seek out and understand diverse groups and teams or seek out different points of view then their capacity for widening their perspective and improving their judgement will be severely limited.

Over-generalisations and lazy thinking

Dogmatic leadership is in some ways evidence of lazy thinking in that lazy thinkers tend to have an over-reliance on tried-and-tested solutions or thought processes, and they often come to big conclusions based on minimal evidence. Laziness and the failure to check facts, challenge assumptions or to gather the additional input from colleagues are evident when dogmatic leaders just rely on experience and expect the future to be a mirror of the past. Dogmatic leaders may also fail to anticipate consequences, to make the time to consider what might go wrong or to do their due diligence.

7.9: Reputation Loser 5 – Emotional Detachment

'Emotional detachment' refers to a person's inability to recognise personal emotions in themselves or others or to share personal emotions. It leads to an impaired capacity for empathy and for building constructive personal and work relationships. Emotional expression and emotional experience are the very things that makes us human, so when that feeling is missing it can be very hard to connect with others.

Leadership is primarily about connecting with and influencing other people. It is a relationship between leaders and followers based on a common understanding that they are members of the same team, that they have the same goals and aspirations, and that the leader is looking out for the interests of the group. The key to leadership relationships is communication. Any leader who connects at a superficial level and does not invest in building and developing meaningful relationships with colleagues and direct reports will suffer long-term reputation damage and derailment. The primary task of leadership is to promote a sense of shared identity and to cultivate the recognition that the leader and the team have different but equally important roles. The reciprocal nature of this relationship must be seen as a key value in an organisation. A leader needs to be able to build positive supportive relationships, treat people with respect and fairness, and embrace opportunities to influence and align disparate groups. Any lack of competence in this area will make it extremely difficult for a leader to succeed in his or her leadership role.

When there is a failure to recognise that the interconnected nature of leadership involves building a wide range of connections to influence and align different groups to get things done, relationships will become dysfunctional. The leader who has difficulty sharing or recognising emotions will be severely handicapped as they will not be able to empathise or understand how to make meaningful connections. There are at least four indicators of the leader who appears to have emotional detachment issues and that will lead to reputation derailment:

- Difficulty recognising and sharing emotions
- Failure to invest time in people
- Difficulty in making connections to build teams
- Lack of interest in networking to broaden one's sphere of influence.

Difficulty recognising and sharing emotions

Any leader or potential leader who has difficulty recognising or sharing emotions is not going to last long in a senior position. 'Alexithymia' is the term used to describe the inability of someone to recognise personal emotions in themselves or others, or to share personal emotions. The word derives from Greek words that literally mean "no words for emotions" and it is estimated that the condition is prevalent in about 10% of the UK population.

Typical characteristics of alexithymic individuals are that they tend to lack an understanding of the feelings of others, to have a dependence on logical, concrete, factual thinking and to ignore any emotional responses or feelings about a situation or a problem. Alexithymic individuals are unable to elaborate on inner feelings and emotions, which leads to an apparent insensitivity to the feelings of others, an apparent lack of empathy. They rarely compliment others and they struggle to make meaningful social connections. Alexithymic individuals also lack the capacity for significant self-awareness and, when asked how they feel, will tend to revert to a description of an external factual event. Alexithymic individuals are also noted for being direct with their opinions in a way that, to a non-alexithymic individual, can often seem overly direct, rude or hostile.

Alexithymic individuals can be intellectually bright and capable, knowledgeable and able to relate to colleagues at a surface cognitive, task-related or issue-related conversational level. Alexithymic individuals can often be good at direct communication, good on detail, possess an excellent memory for facts, have strong perseverance and focus in areas of interest, and tend to be dependable and loyal. They can function successfully at work but their impaired capacity for empathy means there is an absence of the 'human quality' in their personal and work relationships. In the longer term, they will have limited success and, very probably, the inability to relate to colleagues at an emotional non-factual level will lead to reputation derailment. It is also important to note that alexithymic individuals can express emotions verbally and use a vocabulary relating to emotions, but are unable to elaborate beyond a few words or adjectives in describing these feelings. This can suggest to people that they have no depth of understanding, leading to the impression that they are emotionally detached or emotionally shallow.

Many leaders who are alexithymic may come across as polite people who may make all the right noises but they show little interest in others and are incapable of asking meaningful questions about the other person's life. They will usually come across as superficial and so will suffer in any culture that values the ability to network and build collaborative, positive relationships.

Failure to invest time in people

Many leaders do not invest in relationships as they believe that leadership is a rational, logical task rather than a relational task. In other words, these leaders believe that leadership deals with the manipulation of overt resources and mechanistic, predictable, factual and easy-to-understand processes rather than an exercise in building relationships to galvanise, motivate, influence and align people to a common goal and purpose. However, leadership is not a rational activity performed by rational people with rational direct reports aiming to achieve goals in some rational work environment. Leadership needs to be understood in terms of ill-defined and complex interpersonal dynamics, group and intergroup processes, and the consequent and accompanying conflicts, anxieties, tensions, cultural and organisational political issues. Unsuccessful leaders never seem to understand the limits of rational thought and processes, and fail to understand the hidden dynamics that cause reputations to be formed or the psychologically informed perspective that is the first step towards becoming an effective leader.

Leaders will not succeed if they fail to recognise the interconnected nature of leadership at senior levels, which involves building a wide range of connections in order to influence and align different groups to get things done. Leaders are only ever as effective as their ability to engage followers (for example, see Bennis [4]). If leaders fail to establish meaningful relationships with followers at an emotional level, they will suffer extensive reputation damage. The task of leaders, therefore, is not to impose what they want but to shape what followers want to do for the common objective. Leaders cannot succeed by only stating what they themselves believe. They must try to make emotional connections with others and convince others that it is in their collective interest to pursue a particular strategy or achieve a particular objective.

Difficulty in making connections to build teams

It is highly important for a leader to spend a significant amount of time building and developing team relationships. A leader who stays at their desk ("my door is always open") and works hard will be overtaken by competitors who have demonstrated their ability to proactively build relationships with colleagues. The core problem of leaders with relationship skill gaps is a failure to reach out to other team members because they do not ask questions or show curiosity about what other team members think and feel. Or if they do ask a question, it may be a closed one requiring a 'yes' or 'no' answer. There is also a tendency to want to give their ideas before hearing another's and a tendency to match the other person's points or conversation, using statements like "yes, I had something like that happen to me. It all started when…" to take over the conversation, turning it into an opportunity to talk about themselves. It is self-evident that such individuals will be poor at building relationships with other team members and will suffer long-term reputational damage.

Lack of interest in networking to broaden one's sphere of influence

Leaders will also suffer reputational damage if they fail to invest time to broaden their network to expand their sphere of influence, and to widen their perspective and information base so that they can strengthen their judgement and decision making. A successful leader needs to demonstrate that he or she can manage a broad network and confidently communicate. The emotionally detached individual who fails to show curiosity or ask questions, or who gives their own views before hearing another person's, will weaken their opportunities to develop a wide network.

Many leaders fail to adjust how they spend their time and focus more on doing rather than the broader more critical issues relating to strategic development and relationship development, and coaching their direct reports to take on increasing levels of responsibility and accountability. If the emotionally detached leader fails to establish new networks, they will not be able to uncover hidden dynamics and agendas. This may lead to isolation, disconnection from key sources of information and a reliance on old data sources that causes narrow decision making and oversimplifies the complexity of the issues at more senior levels.

Chapter 7 Key Summary Points

- Reputation leakage is short term and temporary; reputation derailment is long term and may lead to career-threatening consequences.
- There are three behaviour patterns that lead to reputation leakage that will create short-term damage to a person's reputation but which can be recovered from: slowness to adapt and change; slowness to recognise how expectations have changed; and slowness to demonstrate political maturity in building collaborative relationships.
- The Fundamental Five Reputation Losers that create long-term damage to a person's reputation and may lead to reputation and career derailment are: untrustworthiness, narcissism, myopia, dogmatism and emotional detachment.

Chapter 8

Taking the First Steps to Manage One's Reputation

"It takes 20 years to build a reputation and five minutes to ruin it. If you think about that, you'll do things differently".

Warren Buffet

Chapter 8 Key Points

- Learning to understand how you behave and how you are perceived
- Cultivating self-awareness:
  - Stage 1: Self-Assessment
  - Stage 2: Soliciting Informal Feedback from Senior Managers
  - Stage 3: Stakeholder Feedback Survey
  - Stage 4: Writing Progress Reports
  - Stage 5: Quarterly Reviews

8.1: Building a Stronger Reputation

The key theme of this book is that a person's reputational legacy is primarily determined by the consequences of their behaviour (the 'how'). Taking the first steps to build and manage a reputation thus needs to begin with a strategy for improving your understanding of how you behave and how you are perceived. Many talented executives have high intelligence and high levels of knowledge, and are often expert in their function, technical or professional field. However, a common issue in leadership development is that high fliers often reach a senior position where their lack of relationship skills hampers their performance and proves a barrier to their on-going career progression.

Learning to appreciate what others need to know about what you can offer

These talented individuals are often unable to leverage their assets to progress their career because they do not know how to promote their skills and behaviours in a genuine and authentic manner that is not inappropriately self-promoting. This is not about the manipulation of other people's perceptions. It is about personal sensitivity and sound judgement as to what others expect, need to know and want to see, to give them reassurance and confidence that the person can be expected to fulfil a role with no problems or negative consequences. Just being aware of the need to engage in this process combined with an understanding of what works and what does not work will help to make this type of individual stand out from their peers.

8.2: Cultivating Self-Awareness

In order to build a reputational legacy, it is very important for individuals to increase their self-awareness and understand how they can interact better with others. No-one believes someone who makes out that they score 10 out of 10 in all aspects of their job, so it is important to understand the principle of relative incremental progression. Every person should always be prepared to list their top three characteristics and top three areas of stretch, development plans or personal development work in progress that will convey credibility, maturity and gravitas. Self-awareness as an attribute is highly valued as we know that people who understand themselves will be able to develop and close their performance gaps, work better in teams, build long-term valuable relationships and tend to be more authentic, credible and adaptable leaders.

CHAPTER 8: TAKING THE FIRST STEPS TO MANAGE ONE'S REPUTATION

The importance of having access to a good-quality database on how we are perceived

Since our reputation is controlled by the perception of stakeholders, the smartest approach is to manage our reputation in a planned, controlled way, and this process starts from being well prepared. This means we need to have access to a good-quality database on how we are perceived. The only real way to manage reputation is to understand what is going on as early as possible, and that means monitoring and listening to what the on-line and off-line world has to say about you, analysing the data and watching the trends. Perhaps most importantly, it is about gaining deep knowledge about colleague feedback and taking pre-emptive action.

The process of gaining self-awareness incorporates the following five stages:
  Stage 1: Self-Assessment
  Stage 2: Soliciting Informal Feedback from Senior Managers
  Stage 3: Stakeholder Feedback Survey
  Stage 4: Writing Progress Reports
  Stage 5: Quarterly Reviews

Stage 1: Self-Assessment

Our political capital refers to our USPs (unique selling points or propositions) and to an amalgamation of many intangible variables that reflect an individual's value in an organisation. Political capital tends to be an amalgamation of the personal-attribute reputation bestowed by the perceptions of many colleagues. The following questions are a good starting point to increase self-awareness as to what you bring to an organisation.

1. **Signature strengths**
    - What do you feel you are very good at and why?
    - In which aspects of your job are you most competent and why?
    - What is your favourite activity and why do you like it so much?

2. **Development challenges**
   - What do you feel you are not so good at and why?
   - In which aspects of your job are you less competent and why?
   - What is your least favourite activity and why do you dislike it so much?
   - In what area do you want to improve and what do you feel is holding you back?
   - What types of activity do you intend to avoid?
3. **Job satisfaction**
   - How satisfied are you with your current job on a scale of 1–10? What would need to happen to get you to the next level?
4. **Career satisfaction**
   - How satisfied are you with your career progress on a scale of 1–10? What would need to happen to get you to the next level?
   - How confident are you in your ability to make career progress in the next 12 months on a scale of 1–10? What would need to happen to get you to the next level?
5. **Relationships at work**
   - Which relationships at work would you describe as the strongest?
   - Which relationships at work have pleased you most?
   - Which relationships at work have concerned or troubled you most?
6. **Judgement and decision making**
   - Which work-related judgements or decisions have turned out well?
   - Which work-related judgements or decisions have turned out less well?
   - Which opportunities did you do well to take?
   - Which opportunities have you missed, avoided or regretted not taking action on?

Stage 2: Soliciting Informal Feedback from Senior Managers

It is also true that building a strong reputation requires an openness to feedback and a willingness to question before reaching judgements. If colleagues can see that you have a high level of self-awareness, they will believe that you will be the type of person who will continually grow, develop and adapt to cope with different situations and circumstances in the future.

It is advisable to start with an informal process of gathering feedback from senior colleagues. As an introduction to these informal meetings with colleagues, you could say that you would like to meet regularly to discuss and explore how your work relationships can be further strengthened. Ask the following four questions:
- Have you any thoughts on how we can work together more effectively?
- In your view, what two or three things can I do to build and develop our working relationship?
- What comes to mind when you think of anything that I should stop, start or continue doing?
- How do you feel that I can best support you and your business/organisation/function?

There is a huge positive impact from just being open and non-defensive about how to improve

You will be amazed at the positive impact just arranging these informal meetings with senior colleagues and asking these open questions will have. It sends a message to colleagues that you are self-aware, open to change, non-defensive and serious about stretching your personal performance. Following these meetings, it is a good idea to 'informally contract' with these colleagues and career sponsors, and undertake to meet with them at regular quarterly intervals to demonstrate what you have been doing to address any identified areas for further progression. At these subsequent meetings, you have the opportunity to seek further on-going feedback from them, which is helpful as progress will be incremental.

The power of writing

At these follow-up meetings, it is important to prepare in the same way as for any other business meeting and write down evidence of progress. Writing down plans and goals is the first step to making them a reality. Writing down plans commits you to action and is an excellent method to help you reflect and consider. When you have collected this feedback data from the key stakeholders, it is suggested that you prepare another action plan to discuss with your senior manager, then take responsibility for demonstrating progress to your senior manager on a quarterly basis.

Another strategy is to use a trusted colleague to explore the following types of question about how you have demonstrated particular behavioural skills.

1. Identify differences between yourself and others at your level or at a senior level on the basis of specific behavioural attributes.
2. Identify when and why there may have been a gap between your intentions and the impact you had on others. In other words, what behaviours have been difficult to implement?
3. Identify any specific good or bad examples of the impact of your emotions and behaviour on others, and your reactions to others' behaviour.
4. Keep a journal to describe important meetings and discuss your emotional reactions to these meetings.
5. Connect the idea of specific behaviours that may have been responsible for successes at work and may have enabled a successful outcome, making a note of any examples.
6. Practise using open questions in different relationship scenarios. Consider and evaluate the impact and power of using open questions in managing confrontations, in motivating and persuading others, and attracting followership from others.

Stage 3: Feedback Survey

A more formal feedback process involves setting up a 360-degree feedback survey. The process for the feedback survey usually involves up to 12 participants, the majority being at a more senior level but also including some peers and some direct reports or junior colleagues, depending on the nature of the issues to be explored. The individual is advised to take ownership of the process by sending an introductory email to the participants asking for their support, stating the reason for asking for feedback and what the person plans to do with the findings, as well as assuring participants that their feedback will be anonymous. The feedback interviews are usually done on the phone by a colleague or an independent consultant and usually take about 20–30 minutes. The feedback interviews will focus on what is going well, what is going less well and what advice the respondents would offer to the individual to help them to be more effective in their current role and to continue their career progression. Occasionally, the feedback survey can be 'competency focused' if, for example, the individual wants to target the 'talent differentiators' for a more senior role. The feedback report prepared by the consultant is typically only shared with the individual who is the subject of the feedback.

Sharing the key takeaways

As part of the process, it is strongly recommended that the individual manages the expectations of the key stakeholders by sharing the key takeaways from the feedback survey, identifying which issues will be addressed and then publicly committing in writing to meet again in about three months to update the senior stakeholders on what progress has been made and what has been learned. This offer of an update is an easy quick win to build the confidence of stakeholders that the feedback has been heard and understood, and that the individual will attempt to address their concerns.

Typical underestimation of the extent and importance of the feedback

Many individuals have some general idea of the 'feedback buckets' or areas into which the feedback might fall but most are unaware of the significance of the feedback or underestimate it. So the huge value of the interview-led feedback survey is that it will solicit data to enable both a qualitative and quantitative assessment, and provide an evaluation of the degree of importance of specific feedback. The individual will gain a better understanding of 'what good looks like'. Moreover, as there is a tendency to polarise behaviour issues ("I do that" or "I don't do that"), the survey will also help the individual acquire a better understanding of the relative incremental nature of performance and the different levels or gradations of performance or behavioural impact expected. They will gain a clearer understanding of what a below-average, average or above-average performance might look like with regard to specific attributes.

Emotionally bruising

The feedback survey can be difficult and potentially emotionally bruising but avoiding the feedback will not help as it won't change the way people think. Unfortunately, we often think that we are doing better as leaders than other people think that we are doing and our self-ratings tend to be higher than those by our colleagues. The feedback process will ensure that the leader faces reality and acknowledges potential shortcomings. Successful people can be delusional about their abilities, many research studies suggesting that over 90% of successful people believe that they perform in the top 20% of their work group at their level. Although this is statistically impossible, it is psychologically real and so leaders can be shocked and defensive when confronted by feedback.

CHAPTER 8: TAKING THE FIRST STEPS TO MANAGE ONE'S REPUTATION

Uncover the soundbites 'on the street'

The second major advantage of the feedback survey is to uncover the soundbites or 'word on the street' and what people say about us when we are not in the room. Each of us has to be able to uncover these if we are going to be able to manage our reputation. The colourful soundbites and narratives on the street that might resonate strongly with the individual can often provide the motivational triggers and drivers for change. The feedback will often provide the phrase, expression or metaphor that can be a life-changing, never-to-be-forgotten moment that changes people's lives.

Increase awareness of blindspots

A third advantage of the survey is to increase levels of self-awareness and awareness of blindspots, which is usually poor for most of us as the correlation between our own self-assessment of our behavioural attributes tends not to correlate highly with colleagues' perceptions of our attributes. Increased self-awareness and increased self-insight are the most important ingredients for leadership development as they give others confidence that the individual can identify and see personal gaps. This suggests that, consequently, they will be better equipped to structure a plan to close gaps and to continue to incrementally improve what they bring to the organisation.

The feedback survey process is emotionally challenging for all those individuals who commit to it but, as feedback is based on perceptions and subjective data, it is an opportunity for the individual to get a better understanding of their reputation and political capital and how they are valued in the organisation. They do not necessarily have to agree with all the feedback but it does provide an opportunity to reassure some colleagues that some perceptions may not be well-founded and to give others confidence that the individual has understood the feedback and plans to address the issues.

Opportunity to shape your reputation

The stakeholder feedback process will give you a very real sense of how you are perceived by others and is an opportunity for you to shape your own professional reputation. Accepting feedback takes a tremendous amount of objectivity and discipline, and requires an introspective view into the values and priorities that are most important to you. It also requires the ability to understand and respond to any discrepancy between your values and your priorities. After identifying the experiences that have shaped your character and considering feedback about how you are perceived by others, you may begin to notice some significant themes emerge.

Stage 4: Writing Progress Reports

I have consistently been surprised at the slowness of many clients to grasp the following reputation-building strategy. The plan is as follows. You highlight to a senior stakeholder the gaps that have been identified in your performance then you informally contract with your boss or other senior stakeholders or sponsors to meet up at agreed intervals. You also commit to updating your boss with written evidence on how you have made progress on the gaps identified. The perception that you are making progress then becomes a self-fulfilling prophesy.

Public commitment is an easy quick win

By making a public commitment to implementing behavioural action plans, you have already scored a quick win, as your boss will assume that you are serious about making progress and will, as a consequence, assume that progress is being made. The proposal to put progress evidence in writing is also essential if you want to create the impression that you are tackling your personal assignment in a professional way. If you attempt to talk about progress without written back-up, you are not building the written trail that can be tracked and reviewed and monitored at future dates. You may also come across as not fully committed, disingenuous or insincere in your attempts to make progress.

CHAPTER 8: TAKING THE FIRST STEPS TO MANAGE ONE'S REPUTATION

The intellectual challenge of finding authentic words and expressions

However, many people find this process extremely challenging and daunting. It requires much intellectual rigour to find words and expressions that are authentic and credible to demonstrate progress and avoid sounding as if the words have been lifted from a management textbook. So what evidence does it make sense to use in this situation?

Focus on what you have learned rather than what you have done

There is a need to compile evidence on not just what you have done but also on what you have learned, and how you and the organisation have benefited. The insight and ability to describe what you have learned is the key point that will give others confidence that any progress or change will be long lasting. In summary, measuring progress and writing notes on progress for each objective will require a 'compare and contrast' analysis between a person's behaviour a few months ago and their current behaviour. This reflective process will require the person to reflect upon the following questions:

- How does your current behaviour compare and contrast with your behaviour six months ago?
- What have you done differently?
- What evidence conveys that other stakeholders will have noticed that you are doing things differently?
- What have you learned?
- How have you benefited as an individual performer?
- How has the organisation or team benefited?
- What will you do to ensure that progress is sustained?
- How do you propose to measure and evaluate future progress?

Stage 5: Quarterly Reviews

Marshall Goldsmith and Howard Morgan [1] have researched the process of measuring improvements in leadership effectiveness. One variable that emerged as crucial to the perception of long-term change was the extent and level of on-going interaction and follow-up with colleagues and stakeholders. A natural leader will grasp the issues and develop an action plan, and go back to stakeholders on a regular basis to tell them what they are doing about the flagged issues. This will build the confidence of senior managers that work is in progress and improvements are being made.

Those leaders who made the effort to report on progress and discussed their own personal development priorities with colleagues on a regular on-going basis, then regularly followed up with them, showed a reported significant improvement. This is perhaps unsurprising. Leaders who did not have on-going dialogue with colleagues showed improvement that barely exceeded random chance. This was true irrespective of whether the leader had an internal or external coach, had no coach, had been on a one- or five-day programme, or had not experienced any intervention at all. What appears to be happening here is a form of cognitive dissonance in that, if a person appears to be working hard on identified areas for development, it is assumed that progress has been made whether or not there is evidence to confirm this.

It is not self-ingratiating to arrange progress meetings

Finally, it is not self-ingratiating to arrange quarterly review meetings with a senior manager if it is arranged as part of an on-going agreement and not undertaken on an ad hoc basis. If the meetings are also supported with business-like written evidence, it would be very strange if the senior manager did not feel enthused about the effort made and did not feel increased confidence in the person's capacity to grow and develop their capability for more senior roles.

Chapter 8 Key Summary Points

- Learn to appreciate what others need to know about what you can offer and learn to do this in an authentic and credible way.
- The process of demonstrating self-awareness is highly important to convey credibility, gravitas, maturity and authenticity. Your reputation needs to be managed in a planned, controlled way and the starting point is to have access to a good-quality database on how you are perceived.
- Cultivating self-awareness needs to start with personal self-reflection on signature strengths, challenges, and job and career satisfaction.
- Soliciting informal feedback from senior managers is vitally important as there is a huge positive impact in being open, proactive and non-defensive about your desire to improve.
- A more formal feedback survey with colleagues or senior stakeholders will provide more quality data about the importance of specific feedback of which you might already be aware. The process enables you to uncover the soundbites used about you 'on the street' and makes you more aware of the incremental nature of your performance in specific areas.
- Progress reports and public commitment to an action plan are an easy quick win. The habit of providing written evidence on progress is crucial if you want to appear professional, serious and motivated about a desire to improve. The intellectual challenge is to find authentic words and expressions to describe progress. The key point is to focus on what you have learned rather than what you have done.
- Quarterly reviews are not self-ingratiating but they need to be arranged as part of an on-going agreement rather than taking place on an ad hoc basis. Not surprisingly, if a person overtly demonstrates how they are planning to

progress specific areas, they will be assessed and evaluated more favourably than those who don't bother to initiate review meetings.

PART 3

BUILDING AND MAINTAINING A PERSONAL BRAND

Chapter 9

Developing a Personal Brand

"Your brand is what people say about you when you are not in the room".

Jeff Bezos (Amazon Founder and CEO)

"Personal branding is distinctively marketing your uniqueness. Without differentiation you have no brand. It's your duty to build your brand daily and not in a day".

Bernard Kelvin Clive

"If you don't build a personal brand, someone else will brand you with the wrong label".

Richie Norton

"I am the master of my fate, I am the captain of my soul".

William Ernest Henley (from the poem 'Invictus')

Chapter 9 Key Points

- Creating a personal brand
- Learning how to stand out
- The value proposition
- Planning to manage your personal brand
- Eight key steps to building a personal brand

CHAPTER 9: DEVELOPING A PERSONAL BRAND

9.1: Creating a Personal Brand

There is frequent confusion about whether reputation and personal brand are the same thing but, although they are tightly linked, reputation and personal brand are not the same concept. Personal brand is a term that may mean different things to different people, but what it means and why you actually need a personal brand are not things that get discussed often enough.

A reputation is past-oriented and a personal brand is future-oriented

It is not unusual to talk about having a reputation but it is more unusual to talk about having a personal brand. In simple terms, a person's reputation is retrospective and past-orientated, in that it is the sum total of a person's track record based on how they have previously behaved, an accumulation of our actions to date as usually recorded on a CV. A personal brand is future-oriented, a proactive strategy to hopefully differentiate the person from others in terms of what they can offer a future employing organisation. So while a person's reputation is the accumulation of their actions and behaviours to date, a personal brand is developed to define a person's aspirations, to describe what they bring to an organisation as a leader, professional or executive, and what they can offer in a future role. A personal brand is how you would like to be perceived, so understanding your brand allows you to act to change those perceptions in a positive, authentic way. A personal brand is thus an aspirational set of leadership traits, behaviours, attitudes and values, and should identify your strengths, communicate them to others and make explicit that which may have been implicit.

However, a strong personal brand does not necessarily equate with a good reputation and a solid reputation does not always result in a strong personal brand. You can build a solid reputation on what you have done but you cannot build a reputation on what you are going to do. Reputation is positioned more accurately as an *acknowledgement* of what a person is known and respected for. A personal brand, on the other hand, is an *impression* that outsiders may have of an individual because a personal brand is a direct *expression* of future plans and intentions.

Taking ownership of what you can offer

Many people, of course, do not consciously manage their personal brand. Many people will work hard, take pride in their job and trust that their performance and word-of-mouth will promote their achievements and their successes. However, it rarely works like this in practice. Many talented colleagues will not achieve their potential and will go unrecognised because they have not invested the time and effort to develop their personal brand.

One way to approach the process of personal branding is to think of yourself as an organisation in which you are the chief executive. This means being very aware of everything you present to the way you conduct yourself on the job. The first rule of branding is to be proactive in controlling the way you are perceived so that you do not allow other people to define you. The secret to branding is to distinguish and differentiate yourself from others in a way that best serves your interests. What makes you different? What makes you special? In what ways are you different from colleagues at a similar level? What have you to offer that others may not offer? In what way do your characteristics, personality and approach differ from those of others? For what reasons would you be selected or preferred to another candidate?

You have a choice. You can either let other people form their own opinion of what you are about and what you have to offer in a future role or you can make it easy for the target audience to understand what you are about and what you have to offer in a future role. This is not a dichotomy of form over substance – it is about taking ownership of your responsibility to ensure that a future organisation can use your skills and knowledge to the best advantage of the organisation.

In addition, those who prefer to 'keep their head down' and beaver away at the task-centred day job are also not demonstrating the political awareness, political judgement, organisational or emotional maturity to appreciate that senior managers have busy jobs and cannot always be expected to have the time or insight to recognise how individual talents can be used to optimal effect.

So how do we differentiate ourselves?

Many of the products we buy on a day-to-day basis are difficult to differentiate but we make buying decisions based on our perception of brands. This is also a problem for leaders: how do we differentiate between leaders when we perceive them to be of similar competence? The way that leaders need to differentiate themselves is by the story they create about themselves to demonstrate their particular talents. Many modern careers entail numerous shifts in direction and periods of reinvention. Without a personal brand, it is easy for the business world to lose sight of who you are and what you can do. People get stuck on several historical versions of how they are perceived based on previous job history and achievements, which is what is referred to as your reputation, but the personal brand is the perception that people have about your future capabilities and what you can contribute in the future to any given role.

Create your own narrative

In 2010, two business writers, Joshua Glenn and Rob Walker [1] demonstrated how everyday products rose in perceived value as the result of the story created about them. They were able to show that the value of bland, undifferentiated products could be increased by telling a story about the product. In the same way, a senior executive can be more successful in securing future positions by creating a story about themselves that covers the questions:
- Who am I?
- Where am I going?
- How will I get there?

9.2: The Value Proposition

A personal brand is a value proposition that tells the story of a person's individual characteristics and how they can be differentiated and distinguished from others. However, although the idea of a personal brand is gaining in popularity, what a personal brand means is perhaps not well understood, nor how a carefully constructed personal brand can be highly instrumental in helping a person shape their future career direction.

A strong reputation may get you into the consideration for specific roles but it is the personal brand that provides a compelling reason to select a person over a competitor who may have a similar background experience and reputation. The personal brand reveals what you have to offer and is used to determine a person's total perceived value to the organisation. In this sense, being clear about your personal brand requires excellent self-awareness so that you can squeeze every ounce of equity out of what makes you unique.

Specialisation is important

In creating a personal brand, specialisation is important if a person wants to stand out from the crowd. In order to do that, each person needs to develop a specific area of competence. If a person tries to be a generalist, they will miss out on opportunities. Each person needs to think about a small number of skills or things that they are good at and passionate about. If these attributes can be used by the organisation and meet its needs then the person needs to put their energy into developing and messaging them.

Personal branding is the process of defining an identity that describes what the person stands for in terms of their values, beliefs, philosophies and behaviours and what they can offer and contribute to an organisation in the future. However, whether or not an employer is attracted to what the person can offer depends on a combination of personal brand and reputation. A strong personal brand may clarify what a person has to offer the organisation in the future and what a person can do for the organisation,

CHAPTER 9: DEVELOPING A PERSONAL BRAND

but a person's reputation is about their legacy and whether they have been able to deliver in the past.

9.3: Planning to Manage your Personal Brand

The first step in the process of taking control of a personal brand is to acknowledge the importance of this personal brand. It is each person's choice whether or not they actively manage their brand but, if it is unmanaged, a person's personal brand will almost certainly have less impact. Therefore, the first decision is for each person to acknowledge their preparedness to take control of their personal brand.

Taking control of managing your personal brand is in itself a differentiating factor

The process involved in taking control of a personal brand will in itself be seen as a factor differentiating you from other colleagues at a similar level who choose not to take control of managing their own brands. Taking control of the process shows leadership and political maturity. If taking control of one's own personal brand means taking control of one's career and one's future, then each person needs to ask themselves the basic question: do they want someone else to define their future or do they want to do it for themselves? In building the personal brand, it is obviously very important to set one's goals appropriately and to be realistic about one's leadership brand qualities. Depending on how well this process is managed, the outcome can be either extremely positive or, if done with a poor level of self-awareness, extremely negative.

The personal brand must always be evident in your behaviour

A personal brand is a clear statement about what each person wants to be known for by colleagues, customers and clients. Most successful brands establish an emotional connection with their customers and the value of the brand is obviously damaged as soon as the individual fails to deliver on their brand promise.

Therefore, each interaction that a person has with colleagues and clients has three possible outcomes. It reinforces the brand, damages the brand or misses an opportunity to build the brand. The personal brand, therefore, must always be evident in the behaviour exhibited by the person towards their colleagues and towards their clients.

9.4: Eight Key Steps to Building a Personal Brand

The process of creating and disseminating a personal brand can be loosely divided into eight types of activity as follows:

Step 1: Discovering your existing personal brand
Step 2: Developing a brand strategy
Step 3: Defining your destination
Step 4: Leveraging your points of difference
Step 5: Creating a personal brand statement narrative
Step 6: Finding the language to promote the personal brand narrative
Step 7: Marketing the personal brand
Step 8: Maintaining the personal brand.

Step 1: Discovering your Existing Personal Brand

Firstly, discovering your existing personal brand and how you are perceived is the first stage in the process. A person needs to find out about how others perceive them and what they need to do to make progress to grow and further develop. Most personal brands are described in five-to-six traits or adjectives, so when trying to assess your personal brand start by writing down the six key signature traits and characteristics that distinguish you from others. Then, check your list with a colleague to find out whether they agree and how accurate you are in making these types of assessments.

Many people are completely out of touch with how others perceive them. They are either extremely ignorant or in a state of denial about how others perceive their existing personal brand. Therefore, it is very important to ask for feedback and advice about primary strengths, blindspots and the areas that need to be strengthened in order to make you more competitive. In many ways, the most difficult part of the personal branding process is that it involves confronting perceptions that may not be comfortable or pleasant to hear.

Step 2: Developing a Brand Strategy

The next stage is to develop a personal brand strategy based on an identifiable set of desirable behaviours that you want to use to promote the personal brand. There needs to be a strategy to create the personal brand and convey it to the external world. In other words, in establishing a personal brand, it is important to focus on what you can and want to do in the future. Most people are not taught how to understand themselves fully, how to identify their talents, how to understand their values, how that affects their work or how to develop talents with appropriate skills. Purkiss and Royston-Lee [2] suggest that there are a number of elements that can help define and build a personal brand such as:

- Talents: those things that you do naturally well
- Values: those things that you believe are important
- Purpose: those things that demonstrate that you have a sense of direction
- Mission: those things that reflect how you want to live your life.

Most people make very little conscious effort to build their personal brand. They get on with their work, hoping that someone will notice them. Then they become upset when they find out "why others didn't notice me". However, being proactive in building a personal brand message is an attempt to communicate personal capital in order to position oneself for future roles and opportunities. Core beliefs and core values should permeate a personal brand and the personal messages that are sent via behaviour and spoken words.

Step 3: Defining Your Destination

The personal brand should ideally be conveying messages about a future direction, role or career path to which a person aspires. The process of building a personal brand will also help one to focus on longer-term goals. Moreover, if the person is seen to be managing the process, they will also appear to others as more strategic, serious and focused than others who manage their careers in a more opportunistic, passive or reactive manner. If a person is looking to change jobs or position, or move to a more senior role, then a basic understanding must be that there is a fundamental need to possess or demonstrate skills over and above technical competencies.

Purkiss and Royston-Lee [2] suggest producing a personal mission statement to help shape the personal brand narrative. Personal brand stories demand a careful use of words and a positive vocabulary. Positive aspirational language includes: challenge, aims, goals, opportunities, direction, change, passion, self-fulfilment, talent development, pride, achievements and so on.

Step 4: Leveraging Your Points of Difference

The key challenge is to understand what key attributes or attitudes differentiate a person from other colleagues at their level. What is the unique value proposition? What are your signature strengths? Are there different 'value-adds' that a person can convey as a result of a different perspective, attitude, characteristics or experience? Each of us needs to think about any distinguishing or differentiating characteristics that we can use to our advantage. A key facet of determining a personal brand is to decide what differentiates us from others and what are our unique selling points or proposition (USP). This competitive advantage is crucial in establishing one's difference. Remember that many colleagues may share the same attributes or characteristics but will possess them to different degrees, so one challenge is to explain why you may have developed a more polished skill in a particular area.

Only select USPs on which you can deliver!

However, when choosing the USPs that we choose to highlight, we need to ensure that we can actually deliver on our promise or point of difference. Many individuals make claims about the superiority of their differences, which they are unable to validate, confirm or deliver. If you don't deliver, it will make matters worse. This can critically damage any work you have put into your personal brand strategy. Secondly, each person needs to ensure that their edge or area of difference is something that will be meaningful to their organisation or senior managers. For example, people do not care if a car brand has the best-sounding horn so, when shaping one's competitive advantage, choose wisely: make sure it is relevant to what other key stakeholders need. Otherwise, you are wasting your time.

The behaviours that should be included in a personal brand statement or narrative will vary considerably from one person to another but there are a number of foundation behaviours that typically characterise individuals with a successful personal brand. For example, some key behaviours to promote might include those that demonstrate credibility, trustworthiness, rapport-building, relationship skills, being a team player, innovation, consistency, optimism, perseverance and resilience, among many others.

This is not an exhaustive list of behaviours for the personal brand narrative. Other desirable behaviours will need to be developed in line with the needs and expectations of the organisation. However, the personal brand framework must be realistic. An effective personal brand should complement and enhance the individual's personal history, reflect the expectations of senior managers and must also be lived and breathed by the individual concerned. This is no easy task so any personal branding exercise will need to focus on identifying and bringing to life the specific behaviours that can reinforce and confirm the personal brand.

Measuring success to reinforce the brand

The personal brand should be characterised by a consistent set of behaviours driven by a desire to support the personal brand statements. Once the personal brand framework has been established, it is important to put in place robust ways of measuring success. These are likely to involve analysing behaviour to see what impact the person has on the organisation and other colleagues, and then seeking feedback on whether the perceptions of colleagues have changed. However, there is often very little correlation between the words we use about ourselves and our behaviour. Every company wants integrity, respect for people, quality, customer satisfaction and innovations but since the big messages are all basically the same, the words quickly lose their real meaning.

Step 5: Creating a Personal Brand Statement Narrative

At some stage it is necessary to create a written narrative that reflects your personal brand message. It is important to be able to develop a narrative to explain a personal brand and how it has been developed. Advertising is about having an idea that captures the imagination and makes an emotional connection, compelling other people to change their attitudes or their behaviour. A personal brand narrative should be based on the same principle. Those individuals who have a compelling narrative are more likely to attract interest and attention.

As a starting point, it may be useful to reflect on the following structure and think about your career goals and how you can optimally contribute in the ways that will help a future organisation and provide personal satisfaction.

- Personal background: What has influenced and shaped you to be the person you are today?
- Experience: How would you describe your key areas of experience in terms of your technical/functional, professional, management, leadership and life perspectives?

- Expertise: How would you describe your key areas of expertise and how would you evaluate your expertise relative to others?
- Achievements: What are the achievements of which you are most proud from a personal and professional perspective?
- Talents: What are the things that you do well relative to others? What are your signature strengths?
- Credibility: What less-desirable characteristics or less-well-developed attributes or skills are you prepared to admit to and discuss? I make this point because trying to create a 10/10 impression does not work, actually detracting from the authenticity and credibility of your message. You therefore need to be prepared to balance the positive messages with an acknowledgement of and insight into things that could be further improved.
- Values and philosophy: What are the beliefs and values that are important to you and that guide and shape your personal and professional behaviours and attitudes? What is your philosophy about the ideal forms of leadership and how leaders should be expected to behave with particular emphasis on the soft skill behaviours?
- Career direction and ambitions: What are you striving to achieve in the next five-to-ten years? Do you have a mission in terms of what you would like to achieve in your life or what legacy you would like to create?
- Differentiators: What is different about you from your colleagues in the way that you think, act or relate? What insights, learning, knowledge, characteristics, attitudes, beliefs and values do you have that may differentiate you from others from cognitive, emotional, interpersonal, personal and professional perspectives?

Don't give false, over-generalised or embellished information

The problem is that most people lack the self-insight to write meaningfully about themselves. Instead, people tend to give false, over-generalised or embellished information. This behaviour is broken down by psychologists into two types. Firstly, *impression management* is where people attempt to create a good impression by leaving out information, adding untrue information or giving unsolicited and not strictly correct information that they hope will create a good impression. Secondly, *self-deception* occurs when people, in their own view, answer honestly, but what they say is untrue because they lack self-awareness. Therefore, someone might honestly believe that he is a good listener whereas all the evidence shows that this is not true.

Create a narrative with yourself as hero

In order to create a personal brand, a person needs to draft a narrative with themselves as the hero. No-one really wants to know about your job description or your day-to-day activities, and so you need to be able to tell a story of how you have made a difference to your organisation or your clients. The person needs to be the main character but the narrative or story should be about learning and overcoming difficulties and set-backs. They must manage to develop a storyline or plan to explain a personal career journey that should ideally have a clear sense of integration and direction. It is also important to talk about your motivation, what gets you excited about your work and where your passions lie. Most leaders are not necessarily looking for the smartest people but they are looking for people with passion, high motivation, good culture-fit, good team players with political savviness and authenticity. This means that you will need to be able to showcase the qualities you choose to describe yourself.

CHAPTER 9: DEVELOPING A PERSONAL BRAND

Develop an integrated, coherent narrative that ties past events

Although it is human nature to have many interests and many experiences, other people may view an unstructured career path and diverse skills as a sign of being a dilettante. Or conversely, they may view a structured career path and a very clear sense of direction as being inflexible. Many positions in the past may have come about by chance as a result of unplanned opportunities. However, in order to protect a personal brand, a person needs to develop a coherent narrative that explains how their past fits to their present, and how the past and the present may have prepared them for the future.

The narrative must be authentic but one can use a number of techniques to make the narrative more interesting and compelling. For example, anecdotes may tend to spice up a story and are often used to generate emotion. It is a common characteristic to use an anecdote in conversations and in making an argument. For example, some storylines may include some description of the answers to the following:

- Who are you as a person? What is the DNA of your personal brand?
- How do you present to the world in terms of your values, aspirations and philosophy?
- What are the signature characteristics of your personality?
- How will your personal contribution enable the organisation to achieve a common purpose?
- Where is your capacity to grow and change, and how do you meet the particular demands and expectations of the job?
- How will your leadership enable the team, group or organisation to achieve a common purpose?

Step 6: Use of Language in Writing the Personal Brand Narrative

> "If you talk to a man in a language he understands, that goes to his head. If you talk to him in his own language, that goes to his heart".
>
> Nelson Mandela

Language and storytelling are a very important strategy for creating a personal brand. Many attempts at storytelling fail because the language used lacks credibility and gravitas – if we do not believe or trust what we hear then there is no prospect for creating impact and influence or a longer-term relationship. In relatively recent times, President Trump has used language poorly to damage his reputation by excessive use of superlatives and hyperbole and by ignoring the use of softening comparative adjectives to add colour and differentiation; by a lack of balance or credibility in language used; and by a storytelling technique that always presents himself in a positive light. He thus manages to have zero credibility with the non-populist electorate.

Writing about oneself – one of the most elusive skills

Writing about oneself in a succinct, clear, clever, persuasive and credible manner is one of the most important and yet most elusive skills. One of the challenges that even the most articulate struggle with is to find appropriate language to describe their abilities in order to differentiate themselves from others. It is also important to recognise that part of the challenge of creating a personal brand statement is to avoid the textbook, baggage-laden language that may seem tired and over-used, and to avoid those 'motherhood generalisation statements' and try to introduce more credible or original language that might convey more authenticity.

It is crucial to find and invent a new lexicon

It is vitally important to shift the lexicon to new ways of describing behaviours that allow for a mind shift and avoid the pre-conditioned response to words that have a tried-and-tested meaning. The challenge is to describe how you behave differently from other leaders and managers: it is important that you try to come up with some meaningful narrative to tell the story of your career. A major part of the challenge is to be detailed and authentic about how you write the story of your personal brand. It is not enough to say that you are 'creative' or a 'good problem-solver' as such general statements do not distinguish or differentiate you from many other types of people who use the same generic terms. You need to be more detailed in terms of the narrative to describe what types of problems you are particularly adept at solving or the particular creative activities at which you tend to excel.

Compare and contrast

You can build your credibility by writing and talking about how your behaviour has changed, in comparing and contrasting your behaviour to others or to yourself when you were younger or less experienced. You can write and talk about what you have done differently, what others have noticed and what you have learned. You can write and talk about how you have grown, how the business has benefited and how you as an individual have progressed as a performer. Describe the next step for you to continue to develop your behaviour and skills in specific areas.

Break down behaviours and skills into meaningful segments

More sincerity and authenticity can be achieved by breaking down skills and behaviours into more meaningful segments to illustrate that you understand what has been learned, in what areas you excel and where gaps continue to exist. Many people claim to have 'good communication skills' but the term is more or less meaningless because it is such a relative concept. There is more credibility if you talk about the nature of the concept, the different forms of communication and those areas of communication that you enjoy more. Describe where you think you have developed skills and how you have developed them, and where you can focus in order to take your communication skills to a higher level in certain areas.

Credibility can be introduced by breaking down communication skills into different segments relating perhaps to formal presentations, informal peer and senior manager group meetings, informal one-to-one meetings, first impression meetings, 'elevator pitch' speech-making skills, rapport-building, networking, use of language, writing skills, article writing skills, creative writing skills, use of words to influence, data-reduction communication skills tailored to the needs of different audiences, summarising ability and your challenges with succinctness and adaptable styles. It will also be found that the very process of breaking down a skill into these different roles and opportunities will go a very long way in making any claims appear credible because it appears that one's skill profile has been analysed and thought through. This means so much more than just referring to 'communication skills'.

Choose your words carefully

Words make our world but the basis of human communication is whether the meaning behind the words matches the picture in your mind when other people say it. So some words should be banned from the process of crafting a personal brand narrative. By changing the words we use, we provide ourselves with a new playing field on which to start a conversation. It is also true that most descriptive concepts are relative, so their use needs to be qualified to show some understanding of the range of the skill spectrum. Here are some personal brand statement words that you need to be careful to use or that you might prefer to avoid:
- **Innovative**: It is a fact that most people are not highly creative and the word no longer has much meaning. So if you *are* innovative, you will need to be able to prove it and demonstrate how you have differed from the norm.

- **Thought leader:** If you use this term about yourself, you will need to demonstrate your expertise or ideally have some articles published to support your claim.
- **Results-orientated:** Another term with dubious meaning, particularly if you have just focused on doing what you are paid to do. Everyone probably says this about themselves, so it is not a differentiator. Using this, at best, ambiguous term may also demonstrate a lack of awareness or a lack of integrity.
- **Influential:** Most people are not as influential as they might imagine. You would have to demonstrate some understanding of the strategy by which you think that you are more than averagely influential.
- **Dynamic**: This is another term that often appears in CVs and personal brand statements but what does it mean? Is it just that you are enthusiastic or hard working?
- **Guru:** Never, never refer to yourself as a 'guru'. It is highly pretentious and often refers to those people who try to be clever for the sake of being clever.
- **Passionate:** This term can sound over the top and may thus diminish your credibility. Are you just highly interested or highly motivated to work in some specific area? Try to explain why these interests have developed if you want to be believed.
- **Unique**: You may be unique but your business contribution is almost certainly not.
- **Visionary**: There are very few visionaries. Perhaps you are a strategist who is able to look at the present, identify a new path and develop approaches to make change or new goals a reality.
- **Collaborative:** Another ambiguous term – everyone is cooperative to some extent. However, most people are also driven by self-interest so how do you demonstrate that you are more than usually collaborative or cooperative?

Don't try to be too smart

There is a theory that we tend to place more value on written words if we are forced to work hard to understand them and that, occasionally, obscure writing can have benefits because the reader has to do so much work to get any meaning out of it. When they have to work hard for something, they tend to value it more. This conclusion is based on 'effort justification', an idea stemming from Festinger's theory of cognitive dissonance. There is also some evidence to suggest that writing that uses superficially sophisticated language may enhance a leader's impact. This has been dubbed the 'guru effect' by the cognitive scientist Dan Sperber [3] who found that less confident people can describe as profound those communications that they have failed to grasp because obscurity may inspire a sense of awe. There is also some evidence that less confident people are prone to avoid the use of simple, clear language in case they risk appearing inadequate and less well educated.

However, Daniel Oppenheimer [4] challenged the prevailing wisdom that complicated language increases the perception of someone's presence and intelligence. Oppenheimer adjusted student dissertations by switching words of nine letters or more with the second-shortest entry in a thesaurus. The simplified abstracts he produced were rated as more intelligent than the original versions. In Oppenheimer's acceptance speech for his Nobel Prize for this research, he summed up his findings by saying "My research shows that conciseness is interpreted as intelligence. So thank you".

If readers have to reach for a dictionary to find the meaning of a term, our ideas risk getting lost. This clearly will not help the impact of a leader. Conversely, reading a well-written email or article can bring great pleasure and an eloquent author may convince us of their point of view even though the evidence may be poor. To some people, good writing is simple writing but simple writing is not fast writing. It is usually the case that good writing is often the result of a great deal of hard work in rewriting and editing.

Even if you have to delete what has taken lots of time to write, it is not necessarily a waste of effort because it is part of the process in filtering and fine tuning how you propose to communicate. When writing, it is amazing how the necessary ingredients and elements are only revealed when you have put in some unnecessary ones, so you can then appreciate which points are more important than others.

How does the language make us feel?

It is often the case that when we listen to the leader's words and weigh up their explanations, we then forget most of it. Cold hard facts tend not to inspire people and straightforward analysis will not get people excited about a goal. Successful leaders have always understood that the stories they tell are what make people interested and excited. What is not so easily forgotten is how listening to or reading a specific communication made us feel.

Step 7: Marketing the Personal Brand

Once the essential elements of the personal brand have been drafted, it is time to market it to the world. In the real world, one of the toughest tasks is to convince people about any reinvention: there are often gatekeepers to the networks that produce job leads and client referrals, and these people must buy into the personal brand. For example, part of the strategy to demonstrate expertise is through knowledge and membership of professional associations, coupled with on-line activities such as writing articles.

Creating an on-line presence

Networking is clearly important in building a personal brand, as is embracing the digital and social-media universe. It is inevitable that some people will Google you, so it is ideal if they discover a personal website that demonstrates a personal brand, displays a person's knowledge and expertise, and shows that the person is aware of the latest industry trends.

The promotion of a new personal brand will involve a range of connection strategies through email, phone calls or even LinkedIn, and also getting involved in projects that will showcase particular skills, interests and characteristics. Although someone may have a wide range of contacts, the vast majority of our contacts are not paying much attention to our career. This means that perception is probably a few years out of date, so it is important that a person recognises how information can be used to shape and direct their personal brand.

Step 8: Maintaining the Personal Brand

Finally, a personal brand needs on-going maintenance that reflects the on-going process of staying current and contemporary. Individuals who are career-focused 'reinvent' themselves on a regular basis to stay fresh and to stay ahead of the competition.

What do you want to learn and what do you want to achieve next year?

It seems to be worthwhile on an annual basis to ask yourself what you want to learn and what you want to achieve this year. In the modern world, it is important to invest time in reflecting on your personal brand as the only way to remain competitive in today's economy is to be agile and flexible in one's thinking and behaviour. It is no longer solely about what university degree you have or the job knowledge and experience that you have gained, but about the things that you know how to do and the ways that you can apply ideas or strategies innovatively.

Build a portfolio of evidence

In maintaining a personal brand, it is important to start to build up a portfolio of evidence or examples to demonstrate the skills and value-add that a person claims to be able to bring or contribute in a future role.

Gain credibility by sharing self-development work in progress

As previously mentioned, it is clear that trying to convey a 10/10 impression is a point-losing strategy because it is not credible. Others will not trust what is being claimed and may draw conclusions about a person's credibility and integrity. It may sound counterintuitive but when a person discloses insights about work in progress in a personal development sense, their credibility goes sky high because their colleagues are not used to that level of openness or self-insight.

However, it is, of course, common sense to choose your work-in-progress areas carefully. You do not want to give others ammunition to hold against you so be careful about the insights shared as research suggests that we do not see ourselves as others see us. As mentioned elsewhere, the correlation between people's ratings of their own personal attributes and other people's ratings of them tends to be rather low. However, the extent of the correlation can depend on the trait: there is more likely to be agreement about personality traits like extroversion and introversion but less agreement on personality traits like social skills, warmth, friendliness, altruism, collaboration, cooperation, helpfulness, agreeableness, likeability, kindness, generosity, planning, organisation, focus, conscientiousness and so on.

And finally...

In summary, the challenge is to be strategic about identifying how you wish to be perceived, to develop a compelling story that explains your evolution in carefully processed language, and then to spread that message. People need to remember who you are, what you do and what makes you different. The more connections you make, and the more value and content you regularly add to the brand, the more likely it is that your new brand will be known, recognised and sought after.

Chapter 9 Key Summary Points

- A person's reputation is retrospective and past-orientated, in that it is the sum total of a person's track record based on how they have previously behaved and is an accumulation of our actions to date as usually recorded on a CV. A personal brand is future-oriented and is a proactive strategy to differentiate the person from others in terms of what they can offer a future employing organisation.
- A personal brand is a value proposition that tells the story of a person's individual characteristics, how they can differentiate themselves from others and how they can offer something different in the future.
- It is important to take ownership of defining what you can offer rather than passively waiting for others to define you.
- Failing to be proactive in building a personal brand will only show a lack of maturity, and a lack of political and emotional intelligence to appreciate that senior managers do not have the time to recognise how your talents can be used to optimal effect.
- The challenge to differentiate yourself from others is to create your own narrative to demonstrate who you are, what you can do and what you can offer in the future.
- Choosing to manage your personal brand proactively and taking control of the process will in itself be seen as a differentiating factor demonstrating maturity, credibility and emotional intelligence.
- There are eight key steps in building a personal brand: discover your existing brand; develop a brand strategy; define your destination; leverage your points of difference; prepare a personal brand statement narrative; learn to create a new and interesting language to describe the brand narrative; market the personal brand; and maintain the personal brand.

- The narrative needs to be well crafted using information that can be verified. You must develop an integrated, coherent narrative that ties together past events.
- Finding the language to write the personal brand narrative is the biggest challenge. Learn to use language strategies like compare and contrast, breaking down behaviours to convey meaning and credibility, avoidance of over-generalised terms and choosing words carefully.
- Marketing the personal brand will involve networking and developing an on-line presence.
- Maintaining the personal brand may involve an annual review describing what you want to learn and what you want to achieve in the next 12 months. This can in turn involve compiling a portfolio of written evidence on what has been achieved and being prepared to share work in progress and what behaviours you are seeking to develop incrementally in order to gain credibility and trust.

Chapter 10

Managing Expectations

"Reputation is fine but you have to keep justifying it. In a sense, it makes it harder because people's expectations of you are higher. So, you have to fulfil those expectations but it becomes more difficult as time goes on".

Derek Jacobi

"Winners make a habit of manufacturing their own positive expectations in advance of the event".

Brian Tracy

Chapter 10 Key Points

- The importance of managing upwards
- The first 100 days plan
- Understanding what your boss thinks of you
- How to improve the relationship and communication with your boss
- Attitude change towards your boss
- How to manage different boss profiles
- Career management strategies

10.1: The Importance of Managing Upwards

Managing the boss is an essential part of being successful in building and maintaining one's personal brand. The best bosses clearly express their expectations for their employees' behaviour and performance but many individuals don't work for great bosses. A boss is fundamental to your welfare at work because he

CHAPTER 10: MANAGING EXPECTATIONS

has the power to hire or fire, promote or increase salary, empower or micro-manage. However, not all senior managers are wired to be successful or good at doing the job. Each person can only focus on what they can control, so the key challenge is to understand your boss: what he/she wants and what he/she expects, in terms of both tasks and your behaviour. You cannot easily change your boss so the onus is on you to adapt your style to make the relationship work.

Learn to ask the right kind of questions

You need to take responsibility for managing your relationship with the boss by asking the right kind of questions. Individuals can survive for long periods because of good upward management (excellent relations with senior management and the board), good lateral management (maintaining the support of colleagues, sponsors and other supporters) and good downward management (never undermining direct reports or teams in public).

If a person has made a number of enemies on his way to a successful leadership role then the support is not always there when things go wrong. As a consequence, certain leaders cannot deliver sustained success for one organisation because, having been contemptuous or disrespectful of people or abusive in their language, others will not support them when times get tough.

Damaged by association

The bottom line is that your boss's reputation can help you or hurt you. Once you have an accurate description of your boss's personal brand, you may need to be defending him more – or perhaps you should start defending him less. It may be important for you to start your own networking efforts in order to raise your visibility across the organisation so that other colleagues become familiar with your skills and expertise.

It is a truism that when other people respect your boss, you benefit from their positive reputation but if other colleagues do not respect your boss, you suffer personally too. This is the consequence of cognitive dissonance: if you like the boss but not their direct report this creates a tension that you have to reduce by liking the boss less or by liking the direct report more. If your boss is not highly valued and respected, you may not be in the conversation for certain roles, issues or jobs because other colleagues do not wish to involve your boss's team or department; or you may not be appointed because others do not respect your boss's nomination or assessment of your potential.

Who does your boss respect?

'Respect' is a strong word in business. It means that there is something about you that others appreciate, admire or want to emulate, and it really is the highest form of corporate flattery. Your boss is likely to be transparent about whom they respect in the company and this knowledge is important to you for several reasons. If your boss has respect for someone, it is an insight into what they value in terms of personal attributes, skills, experience or work ethic. For example, if they respect people who build a broad network, they are sending a signal that they would like you to develop cross-functional relationships. If they respect people who challenge the status quo, they are giving you licence to push back on some of their ideas. If they value a wide range of past experiences, that is a sign that you can reference your previous companies' best practices and successes.

Make a list of the qualities your boss respects because this is their set of 'people values' and you need to know in what way your boss interprets other people. Secondly, you also need to know who your boss thinks is worthy of their time and attention and whose opinion they value. The boss's relationships are based on the foundation of respect so study their relationships and alliances throughout the company as it is unlikely that they are going to be close to someone whom they do not respect. One of the most critical things you can know about your boss is what they think about office colleagues. Armed with this information, you can more accurately predict what they want from you when it comes to building or leveraging relationships. Who does the boss think is talented? Who does the boss go to for advice? Who

CHAPTER 10: MANAGING EXPECTATIONS

does the boss confide in or admire? Who does the boss form coalitions with to get work done?

Create a roadmap to navigate the organisation

A useful exercise in order to bring a network of relationships to life is to prepare a relationship map on which you plot the quality of a boss's relationships across the company using a simple five-point scale with anchors of excellent, very good, ok, needs improvement and poor. The act of plotting this network reveals a lot, from how the boss gets work done to where they have blindspots across the company. By analysing their relationships, you will get an idea of how the boss works the system and where the boss is positioned on the leadership path of the organisation. Also, knowing what and whom your boss respects gives you a roadmap to navigate the organisation. Knowing the boss's network is critical to your own relationship-building efforts.

Where does your boss have influence?

In understanding your boss's brand, it is also important to understand where your boss has influence. It might seem that studying your boss's reputation and level of influence would yield the same insights but actually they can be quite different. The boss might have a reputation as a difficult colleague to work with but that doesn't mean they cannot have impact and influence across the organisation. Reputation has to do with people's perceptions but influence has to do with getting things done. Influence is gained by demonstrating a track record of success, having great ideas and being able to execute.

10.2: The First 100 Days Plan

Managing upwards often starts with an introduction into a new role or a new job. In any new role, it is important to make a good start and first impression. The starting point is to create a plan for your 'First 100 Days'. It is important that this plan is a blend of purpose, success measures, strategy, focus and value propositions.

Purpose: Why have you been appointed? What is the purpose of your role and why does the organisation benefit from it? What impact do your activities have on your colleagues, the organisation and your customers? There is a story told by Benjamin Zander, conductor of the Boston Philharmonic Orchestra, who awards an A-grade to each student at the start of the year rather than at the end of the year. However, the grade is on the condition that the students write a letter to him within the first two weeks of starting the course that must be dated next May. He asks the students to state in this letter what they did to achieve an A and to write about the person they will have become by the end of the course. The whole point of the approach is to challenge people to start a journey that is as important as the destination. This encourages them to think about their unfulfilled potential and who they could be, and consciously identify the specific actions they need to take. This is a challenge to start working towards a courageous goal with the belief that anything is possible. This approach also challenges people to think about possibilities, to stop questioning whether they are good enough and to avoid self-limiting beliefs.

Success measures: What are you setting out to achieve? How will you measure or monitor your progress or success? When will you know whether you have been successful? You must define what good looks like if you are to be successful but recognise that good is a relative concept: in a broader role, good will look and feel different from how success was measured in the past. Write down a clear set of objectives with defined metrics and milestones to provide evidence of how well you have performed.

Strategy: What is your plan to get there? What are you required to do to achieve your ambition and success? What shorter-term tactics are required to deliver on the longer-term strategic goals?

CHAPTER 10: MANAGING EXPECTATIONS

Focus: How do you plan to use your time to best effect? You need to be selective about where you commit your time so select high-value networking opportunities, project groups, strategic committees and external groups that are open to new ways of thinking about the business and prepared to break old models and introduce new models.

Value proposition: Within your competitive landscape, how do you express what makes you special and unique? What is your value proposition? How do you differentiate yourself from others at your level?

100-day action checklist

In more specific detail, here is a checklist of possible actions in the first 100 days.

1. Understand the organisation's vision and mission. Why does it exist?
2. Meet all stakeholders to find out their expectations. You will find that each key senior manager probably has different expectations and weight different outcomes with differing levels of importance.
3. List three major changes you would like to implement to improve company/team performance and share them with colleagues.
4. Be transparent and open about your concerns and plans to build trust among stakeholders.
5. Do not necessarily follow the strategies of a predecessor. What worked for them might not work for you.
6. Conduct an organisational assessment of structure and personnel. Create a scoring grid to assess all team members against both task and behavioural criteria.
7. Craft your own vision of your role and use diversified communication vehicles like emails, memos, conference calls and meetings.
8. Identify priority areas for improving performance. Create an action plan and clear priorities.

9. Assess and identify how to build a strong team in which team members have a clear understanding of their role.
10. Make sure people are in the right roles and identify which poor or below-average performers need to be replaced.
11. Encourage innovative ideas and encourage the team to challenge the status quo.
12. Provide inputs to employees regularly to guide, coach and inspire.
13. Do a SWOT (strengths, weaknesses, opportunities, threats) analysis and anticipate internal and external threats.
14. Do not be in a hurry to cut costs as this may give clues as to where real problems lie.
15. Be flexible. Adapt and tailor your leadership style to different team members.
16. Seek early quick wins to build momentum.
17. Decide how you want to be remembered and what you would like your legacy to be.

Create a compelling narrative of what you hope to achieve

Telling a compelling story of what you plan to do is one of the most important things that a new leader can do in their first 100 days. It demands a degree of humility and self-criticism, and leaders who admit to their frailties and need for help will find that they are trusted more by their contemporaries and bosses. Too many people in new roles adopt an attitude that they will 'wait and see how things go' before making any decisions but no good leader would waste so much time without an active plan on how they proposed to add value. A starting point for the compelling story is to think about the headline that you would like to see attached to your name or the epitaph that would fit on your tombstone at the end of the appointment. It is also important to build 'learning from mistakes' into your story. Tell your story and repeat your story and make sure that people remember the best stories about you – as long as the message is conveyed in a way that will *not* be interpreted as self-promoting or self-congratulating.

CHAPTER 10: MANAGING EXPECTATIONS

Giving managers confidence that you are on top of the job

At its simplest level, managing upwards is finding a vehicle to reassure your senior manager that you are covering all the right bases, and giving your senior manager insight into your thinking and planning processes so that he has confidence that future objectives will be achieved. The roadmap concept, introduced elsewhere, is an example of such a vehicle. In it, you share with your senior manager on a single page your interpretation of the key focus or priorities for different tasks, the key challenges or difficulties to interfere with progress, your planned next steps and potential success measures.

Adding value to your boss's thinking

Managing upwards also means adding value to the thinking of your senior manager, acting in a way in which he sees you as an equal partner and confidante, and giving him or her reason to respect your judgement and decision making. It is important to understand your senior manager's agenda so that you can selectively contribute to their thinking, help them achieve their objectives and demonstrate an ability to work outside your narrow functional role.

Trust enablers

Building trust is essential in any new position. It comes from the confidence others feel about your capacity to listen and how you are able to make a difference. There are some obvious strategies for building and enabling trust, like sharing information about who you are and what you believe. It is important to seek colleagues out and listen attentively to what others are saying. You need to learn how to ask open questions and seek clarity when you do not understand.

It is also important to acknowledge the need for personal improvement and show that you are willing to change your mind when someone has a good idea. When you have meaningful discussions with colleagues, you should be able to understand what the other person wants and then maintain regular and consistent contact, having on-going discussions about what you did right and what you can do better.

10.3: Understanding What Your Boss Thinks of You

This section explores the following six questions that you should consider when examining the quality of the relationship with your boss.
1. How does your boss describe your reputation?
2. What does your boss value about you?
3. How important are you to your boss's success?
4. What does your boss think you need to improve?
5. How does your boss talk about you when you are not present?
6. What is the history of the relationship between you and your boss?

1. How does your boss describe your reputation?

By analysing yourself through your boss's eyes, you will need to look objectively at your skills, personal attributes, experience and attitude. You will have to put away your ego or cognitive biases to build an impartial view of how he or she really sees you. Does the boss feel that you are a star or merely an average performer? Does the boss see you as supportive or a pain in the neck? How does the boss compare you to other direct reports? Does the boss believe you have minor development challenges and opportunities, or major skill gaps? Does the boss have any grievances with you with regard to past behaviour?

2. What does your boss value about you?

The starting point is to make a list of your strengths: what are you good at and what skills stand out? Now check the strengths that fit your current role and check whether these are something that your boss truly values and leverages. Your first list may include 10–12 capabilities but the strengths that your boss values may shrink to 4–6 capabilities. Your boss may view your contribution through a very narrow lens and actually want you to maintain that level of impact. A boss may place your skills and expertise in one compartment and may not use your ideas and abilities to solve problems in another compartment. For example, you may have been given an individual contributor role because your boss does not value your people-management skills.

In some cases, your boss may want you in a box where you deliver specific results and nothing more. He may want you to use certain skills from your toolbox but not all of them. In other cases, your boss may recognise your talent but choose not to use it. This may be true of the insecure boss who is afraid that you may be more talented than he or she is. If you are good at building relationships, you may not get appropriate credit for it, if your boss is not good at building relationships. So which skills does your boss appreciate and what skills is he or she ignoring? Pick out a skill that your boss is not leveraging and look for ways to demonstrate your capability. Tell stories in your one-to-one with your boss about talents that you have used in the past. In other words, take responsibility for how your boss sees you. Don't let him/her dictate how his/her organisation views your skill set. Look for opportunities to get involved in a project outside your normal scope of work so that you can demonstrate different talents. If you can change the perception of your capabilities, you may change what the boss wants from you.

3. How important are you to your boss's success?

With regard to all the things that your boss is trying to deliver, how critical are you to his success? Are you thought of as one of the key resources for your boss to carry out his objectives? You cannot expect your priorities to be exactly the same as those of your boss but do you recognise the major themes of your boss's objectives? Do you see where he is taking the department or organisation and are you part of these plans? Do your skills, experience, attributes and attitude fit his agenda? Do you know how important you are personally to the objectives of your boss?

How indispensable are you? Has anything happened recently to change your value as a direct report? Has the value equation changed and have you acted too late to do anything about it?

Take a hard look at your contribution and what you are working on. Be objective about your value because the chances are that you are over-estimating it. Don't assume that because you got on with your boss six months ago, you are still seen as a must-have part of his team. The business may have changed, the group may have changed or the group may have lost or gained stature in the organisation. If you judge your value correctly, it should provide some useful insights. Analyse what your bosses focus on and how involved you are in those priorities. Look at your full range of capabilities and evaluate how they fit with your boss's agenda. Give your boss a reason to see you as part of the future and not the past.

4. What does your boss think that you need to improve?

It is almost certain that your boss believes that your skills could use a little polish. When your manager seems to be frustrated or critical about your work, don't think "what's wrong with him/her?" but ask "how am I not meeting their expectations?" Since we all have development opportunities, what does your boss think you should be working on? This question cannot be fully answered by looking at your performance review or development plan. You may have both agreed upon some growth areas in your most recent review but what else does your boss want you to work on? Think about your boss's motives and preferences – is there anything your boss is not telling you? What types of behaviour have caused your boss frustration, possibly anger or upset, and what does this tell you about the areas in which you need to improve? Typically, there are many unspoken development suggestions and it is important to get ahead of what may well become a 'career derailer' if the boss's perceptions do not change.

CHAPTER 10: MANAGING EXPECTATIONS

What skills can I develop that would add more value for the boss?

It is not helpful if the boss tells you that you need to gain more polish or generally improve but you will only get better quality data if you ask more specific questions like "what one or two things could I do that would make me more competitive in this area or stretch my skills in this area?" Uncovering the insight about what your boss really wants you to work on is an important piece of the relationship contract. In your next development discussion, listen carefully to the suggestions made by your boss but also listen to what is not being said. A great question is "what can I work on that would improve our relationship?" Or "what skills can I develop that would add more value for you?" Your job is to take the guesswork out of what your boss wants you to improve. By sharpening your insight into their motives and preferences, you should be able to deduce what they want you to develop. Then ask for specific feedback about those skills or behaviours and you will create a clear picture about what your boss wants from you. Ultimately, you may choose not to work on those skill areas but at least you will drive the discussion and get the resulting insights out into the open.

5. How does your boss talk about you when you are not present?

One of your boss's responsibilities involves evaluating your performance and potential, and sharing this assessment with other leaders in the company. In a large company, this will be part of a formal talent and performance review process; in a smaller company, it is probably a more informal process. So how is your boss describing your performance, attributes, attitude and work ethic? Does your boss support your potential to advance in the company?

This may be a hard insight to read and validate but it is important that you have some idea of how you are being presented to the organisation. There are at least three comparative evaluations that your boss is making at all times and each has to do with what he wants from you.

What benchmark is used to evaluate your performance?

Firstly, your boss is comparing you to a standard or model of what he expects from a direct report. If your boss has been managing people for a while, the boss will have a strong sense of what they want from an employee at your level. As an exercise, write down the qualities of an ideal employee and compare yourself to this list. How well do you match up? Do you match the ideal profile of work ethic, attitude, passion, teamwork and so forth? Whether it is fair or not, your boss is talking to other managers about how you match this ideal-employee model and there may be cultural norms that make this prototype fairly common across the organisation.

How does your boss compare to your peers?

Secondly, it is a fact of life that your boss is comparing you to your peers. In conversations with their boss or other leaders, the boss is ranking their direct reports along a number of dimensions. Do you know your place in the pecking order? Do you know how the boss discusses this list with their peers and how they are representing you specifically? Has your boss ever said that you need to be more like Tim or Louise – if so, you can be sure the boss is comparing you to your peers. While the peer comparison may feel unfair, it is one way that senior leaders discuss and score your contribution. Are you better than Tim or Louise? From your boss's perspective, can you rank their direct reports from favourite to least favourite and where you are on the list? More importantly, what are the people above you doing that you're not doing? Now write out their behaviours and compare them to your own. Are there any adjustments that you are willing to make in your approach? Many people find this a useful exercise to help them pinpoint exactly what Tim or Louise or Jane are doing that works well for the boss and that unlocks the insights they need to plot the next course of action.

Thirdly, when your boss represents you to the organisation, are they comparing you to people in other teams or departments? Think back to the people the boss respects in the whole

CHAPTER 10: MANAGING EXPECTATIONS

organisation – how do you stack up in comparison with people from other functions or departments? Are these fair comparisons and are these people worth emulating? The only way to really know is to ask your boss directly and hope the boss tells the truth. If your boss says "I told you that you are doing fine" then the boss is not giving you the full story. What positives is the boss highlighting to colleagues and what is the boss mentioning that is not so positive?

6. What is the history of the relationship between you and your boss?

The final step is to consider how the relationship has evolved from your boss's perspective. Has it improved lately or declined? Have there been specific incidents that have caused the relationship to fluctuate? Did the boss appoint you? Did the boss join the team after you? Was the boss a peer before becoming your boss? Did you get a clear sense of the boss's objectives and mission? You may have forgotten the original selection interview but the chances are that your boss has not forgotten what he communicated. If you were already on the team when the boss joined, how was the assimilation of the boss into the team? Did you quickly adapt to their style? Did you ask questions about what the boss wanted from you?

If your boss was previously your peer, you are talking about the most challenging transition of all. From their perspective, did you make it easy for them or did you make it difficult? Were you supportive from the beginning or did you hold back your full commitment to see how the relationship evolved? If you put yourself in their shoes, can you see how your behaviour may have coloured their views? How has the relationship evolved, has the relationship been consistent or are you on a rollercoaster ride?

An exercise to assess your working relationship

Try this personal exercise: draw a horizontal line across the middle of a piece of paper and, working from left to right, record the general date and description of any critical episodes that impacted on your relationship. Positive events go above the line and negative events go below the line. The challenge is to do this from your boss's perspective. How would your boss characterise these experiences? Are you looking at these events in the same way? Did you consider the perspective of your boss at the time and how would they remember the event? Some bosses forgive and forget but many don't – you may be missing what has been filed away over the years about your behaviour or attitude.

The evolution of your relationship says a lot about its current state. Can you pinpoint the exact event where things started to change between you and your boss? If so, is there anything you can do about it now? In looking at the here and now, if you could somehow get inside your boss's head, how would they describe your relationship? Consider the question from their perspective. What does he get from you? Can the boss count on you and do you have their back? Are you a team player? Are you high maintenance? Does your boss look forward to meeting with you? The bottom line is that you are not the only one in this relationship and your boss has a perception of you that is just as legitimate as the one you have of him. You may not agree with their view but you cannot deny their right to have one. Furthermore, your boss is human, which means that they have a long memory and everything about your work history gets wrapped up in their current perception of you. Don't count on your boss being the live-and-let-live type. The chances are that they have not forgotten anything that happened in the past. Looking at the relationship from your boss's perspective is an important step in the reflective process.

10.4: How to Improve the Relationship and Communication with your Boss

The following is a non-exhaustive list of suggestions on how to create a stronger impression with your boss. Communication is at the heart of all good relationships with your boss yet we know that many people repeatedly fail to make their communication count. The following rules for effective communication apply to anyone trying to build a close collaborative relationship with their boss.

Headlining and succinctness. Bosses don't have the time or the disposition to be lectured to or to be on the receiving end of a long, verbose chronological narrative or a 'brain dump'. They want insights that condense neatly into bullet points, so you need to become skilled at headlining and paraphrasing key information, and highlighting a few 'takeaway' points.

Synthesise information. Your job is to reduce data and present a summarised picture of a situation with a plus-and-minus analysis and some suggested or recommended next steps. The real value is to help your boss work through the data to understand the implications, real-world opportunities and/or threats to the organisation. If you brain dump and expand the database, you have failed in the communication process and you are likely to be seen as an extra burden to bear.

Understand how the boss processes information. Study your boss's cognitive processes and their way of thinking, then tailor your communications to suit your boss's style. Different bosses will also prefer different presentation formats. Some like detail, others like graphic models and visual flowcharts.

Use the boss's vocabulary. Just as bosses have preferred methods for processing information, they also have their own vocabulary, speaking and conceptual styles. It's a good idea to match your language to the language of the boss and to be familiar enough with their areas of expertise that you can understand their references. And avoid jargon, just be clear and direct.

Be an idea generator. The easy way to raise your value is to be a constant source of new ideas. Read widely and network widely to source new ideas, and think about how you can add value by generating options and alternatives.

Be a heavyweight thinker. Always be prepared to substantiate your views and always be prepared to discuss the relative strength of ideas. Lightweight thinkers polarise issues too simplistically, tend to be black-and-white in their thinking, struggle with option generation or rely too much on unsubstantiated intuition, and focus on just reporting results. Heavyweight thinkers engage in analysis, evaluation and interpretation.

Be newsworthy. Make yourself valuable by being a source of up-to-date news and information about company, departmental, industry or organisational events. If you widen the boss's information base, you are widening their perspective and strengthening their ability to make sound judgements.

Talk to the boss as you would to a colleague. You are not the boss's peer, but be direct, relaxed and respectful without being deferential. If you talk and act like a subordinate, you will be treated as a subordinate but if you talk and act like a peer you will assume more gravitas and presence as if you are a future leader-in-waiting.

Don't create surprises. If you need the boss to look at some information, make sure he/she has the material in good time. The term 'last minute' should not exist in your vocabulary.

Just listen. Everyone needs a confidante and particularly the boss. Many words they say in public are analysed for meaning; every expression of doubt, frustration or depression is construed as a sign of weakness. And while friends and family may offer sympathetic ears, sometimes these leaders need to unload on someone who also understands the organisation or business. Be that person. Be the audience with whom they can safely be themselves.

10.5: Attitude Change towards your Boss

Any progress you make with your boss has to be rooted in looking at the role of the boss from their perspective. When we look at our relationship with a boss, the main tendency is to portray ourselves as a victim. We may pay very little attention to the boss and their agenda, or their experiences and frustrations in dealing with us. Therefore, the most important adjustment you may need to make in manging your boss effectively is to your own attitude. Your attitude serves as the mental foundation for your behaviour so, if you can change the way in which you think about your relationship with your boss, then anything is possible in terms of shaping the future relationship.

What does your body language convey to your boss?

Your attitude can be seen and felt by others through body language, tone of voice and facial expressions that are the physical manifestation of your emotions. Here is an important exercise: describe or write every emotion, thought and feeling you have about your boss. Explain why you feel this way and write notes to explain your attitude. This may include your boss's motives, the history of the relationship, critical decisions and so on. In order to manage your attitude, you first have to clarify whether you have a specific attitude towards your boss and if you are going to change or maintain the relationship as it is. You must determine whether you need to make any modifications to your current attitude.

Modify your historical narrative with your boss and communicate new insights

So how do you manage your attitude towards the boss? There are three things you need to consider:
- Gain an accurate perspective on the relationship
- Review or modify your stories about your boss
- Communicate your attitude.

In order to create a fresh attitude towards your boss, you have to see your relationship through the eyes of the boss. The second step involves modifying your story about your boss. We are all living in a story, a story we have created from a single perspective, and this is a story of our view of our boss. It might be a story of great support, of lost trust or missed opportunities, or of being held back, but in this story you may have cast yourself as the hero and your boss as the villain. You may have convinced yourself that you are right and the boss is wrong in many instances. Your story may be very powerful but it may present a distorted reality that you have invented and rationalised to justify your behaviours. Even if much of the story is true, in your mind you have probably pushed it beyond the limits of credibility. Next time you talk about your boss to a colleague or spouse, listen to what you are saying because it probably portrays you as the victim. However, there are two sides to every story and regardless of how you feel about your boss, they will feel differently about you.

Freshen your attitude towards your boss

The old story about the boss, for example, may be that they withhold information but the new story may be that you need to ask more questions to encourage the boss to share the full picture. Modifying the story is a necessary part of freshening your attitude towards your boss. Take a hard look at your story and really strive to understand how you are representing the relationship. Once you have admitted to yourself the true nature of the story, you should start to modify it. Take every element and restate the story in the most objective terms possible, using all your insight to rewrite the script from the perspective of the boss. It's amazing how different the two stories may be: where the first story is generally a victim tale, the second story is an impartial view of the relationship that takes into account different motives, perspectives and circumstances.

Communicate your new story

The final step is to communicate your story and fresh attitude about your boss. If your peers and boss do not hear a fresh point of view then you have not made any real progress. There are two ways to do this. Firstly, you have to tell your colleagues a different or fresh story, literally. Your colleagues and direct reports need to hear you talk differently about the boss and they have to feel like you are taking responsibility for the relationship. Modifying your story involves stopping any negativity or complaining about your boss or replacing sarcastic comments with benefit-of-the-doubt statements. Try to stop talking about your boss negatively and start talking objectively. By eliminating the victim mentality from your story, you are more likely to appear positive and constructive, balanced and professional. That is the personal brand that you are aspiring to promote with this new and fresh attitude.

In developing a modified story about your relationship with your boss, it is often very important to lean on a trusted colleague to help you with the process. It is recognised that some things are still going to irritate and frustrate you about your boss but the difference is how you let those behaviours affect you and how you choose to act or react. Your perceived attitude has to evolve from being a victim to being in control.

Change the way you behave around your boss

The second way you need to communicate your modified story is by changing the way you behave around your boss or colleagues. You cannot just 'talk the talk' – you have to show that you have adjusted or modified your attitude, and you do this by adopting new behaviours or stopping unproductive ones and taking responsibility for the relationship. This means that you have to go more than half-way when it comes to improving the boss relationship. It's not a 50–50 proposition and you have to be more committed to the objective than your boss. In other words, you have to do most of the work in moving this relationship forward.

Make visible behaviour adjustments

Visible behaviour adjustments come in four types: actions to stop, start, emphasise or deemphasise. Some of these changes are subtle and some are very deliberate. As a starting point, you can make a list of any behaviours that annoy your boss, trying to be honest. Think back to their preferences and how they view you. Now, which of these behaviours could you stop doing immediately? And at what cost? For example, drawing the boss into uncomfortable discussions, meeting with colleagues without their knowledge, arguing over report or written style preferences, resisting their preferred work schedule, pushing a point of view that may frustrate the boss and so on.

How do successful colleagues behave?

With regard to adopting new behaviours, look at your most successful colleagues. What are they doing that you can copy? So what behaviours do you need to adapt? Where do you need to change your approach? What do you need to start doing differently? For example, you could give the boss more lead time to review materials or create and send an agenda in advance of your one-to-one meetings. Here are some more examples of common behaviour starts: talking positively about colleagues, volunteering for difficult assignments, providing more background in data than requested, anticipating issues by providing information prior to the event and using the word 'opportunity' instead of 'problem'.

At other times, all you have to do is to increase or decrease something and examine what you could do more and do less. For example, some people tend to check in with the boss too much and, although it may be the right behaviour, they simply need to do it less often. People that tend to check in frequently often worry about making a mistake, which ironically, can make your boss doubt you more or lose confidence in you. For example, here are some instances when more-or-less behaviour changes may be required. You might remember to give a heads-up on sensitive issues, asking for his perspective more often on tough decisions, bringing more than one possible solution to the discussion and monitoring your speaking frequency in staff meetings, disagreeing in public less and possibly making fewer drop-in interruptions into their office.

CHAPTER 10: MANAGING EXPECTATIONS

Draft a boss-relationship development plan

Adopting new behaviours will feed into your modified attitude and you will clearly win more confidence from your boss if you document both adjustments in a formal development plan. In the left column capture the two or three areas of the boss relationship you want to focus on. In the middle column, write the attitude adjustments you are committed to making. On the far right column, make a note of any new behaviours that you will start, stop or fine tune.

Always put development plans in writing

You will make more progress if your ideas are written as a formal development plan. This is a non-negotiable strategy and a no-brainer idea! The act of writing a development plan serves to cement your intentions. So write it out, keep the plan with you and refer to it often. Update the plan as you experience progress with your boss. Also, ask a trusted colleague to provide feedback on any progress. Ask your colleague: what are you noticing? What is working? How was the boss responding? The act of documenting your strategy in seeking feedback serves as a catalyst for your ultimate goal, which is taking responsibility for improving the relationship.

10.6: How to Manage Different Boss Profiles

Although all boss relationships may be unique, there are some common boss profile patterns that might be worth considering when looking for ways to build a personal brand and protect your reputation.

The insecure boss

The boss may be insecure about their standing in the organisation and may be avoiding rocking the boat. Perhaps they won't take risks and are not generating innovative ideas. They may be afraid or intimidated by their own boss. The insecure boss may just want you to lie low and not make waves, preferring that you just do your job and don't ask many questions.

The optimum management strategy with this type of boss is to help them to take calculated risks. Look for places to push and gently take actions, showing the boss that they have support from other groups to take this action. Inevitably, your reputation is linked to the reputation of your boss when it comes to innovation and challenging the status quo, so to become the best PR agent of your boss is important. Also try to gain the confidence of the boss as a sounding board so that the more they can talk to you about their feelings and concerns, the better chance you will have of helping them gain confidence. If none of this works with your boss, the best advice is to get away from them by talking to HR about your situation because, if the style of the insecure boss persists, it will do nothing for your career development.

The ego-driven boss

This style of boss is usually motivated by wanting to be recognised for success and they are usually keen to be proven right in their decision making most of the time. This type of boss tends to be convinced that their ideas are best, that they have the only clear perspective and that they are the smartest person in the room. The boss may listen to your ideas but is not going to implement them. The boss does not host brainstorming sessions because he or she does not need them – they have already decided what to do. The self-worth of this boss is tied up in always having the right answer and always making the right decision. The boss does not want to share the spotlight and their ego will not usually allow one of their direct reports to get much credit for anything. This type of boss wants acclamation for their wisdom and expertise, and they often want gratitude and appreciation from their team. The boss mainly wants you to execute, to do and not to think.

The optimum management strategy with this boss is to suggest ideas to them and ask them just to think about it overnight. Then follow up with the boss on the following day. By deferring the outright rejection of an idea, you are more likely to get an idea accepted. The idea might be adapted and taken over

CHAPTER 10: MANAGING EXPECTATIONS

by the boss but you may get your ideas accepted more easily. A smart boss will normally respect and value good ideas, so try to prepare evidence-based arguments and think about strategic contributions. Although the boss may have a huge ego, if they are bright, you may still learn a lot from them, and they may also be right about a number of things so that is good for your reputation and valuable for your career. So while you may not enjoy their style, the end result may be better than working for a less-competent manager.

The control-driven boss

This type of boss tends to be motivated by having complete control. They may not be the smartest person on the team and may even be a little insecure, which is why they want to control most of the detailed aspects of each task. This boss may be a micro-manager who needs to know everything that's going on so that every idea must be screened, every presentation approved and every step in the process examined. The boss tends to behave this way because they feel that it is the only way that work will get done right. This type of boss does not inspire or coach but wants you to follow their direction without challenging it. The boss does not want you to stray from their directions, and they probably do not want you to think outside of the box or draw attention to yourself.

The optimum management strategy with this type of boss is to stay patient. The challenge is to give the boss confidence that you are capable and competent to do things on your own without the need for them to micro-manage and check all aspects of the process. Another approach is to try the direct approach of talking to them about their style, and how it is making you feel under-valued and disrespected. You might want to clarify your experience and competence, and suggest a trial period in which you are given more responsibility to prove your worth with accountability measures agreed to monitor progress. It is interesting that many people never try the direct approach even though, more often than not, it usually works to some extent. It may take courage initially but this approach will send very many positive messages about your competence and maturity as a colleague.

The career-driven boss

This type of boss is motivated by career advancement and career progression. They are usually focused on their next promotion and spend a great deal of time in managing upwards. This type of boss may be competitive and preoccupied with power and politics, and may openly compare themselves favourably to other colleagues. This boss basically wants your help to make him look good and wants your help to get his next promotion; he probably does not want you to steal the limelight or to get more attention than him, so he wants you to keep a low profile. This type of boss tends not to provide a lot of coaching and development but does want you to work hard because the boss wants you to be successful. The boss also wants your best ideas as more good ideas generated will tend to make him look good.

The optimum management strategy with this type of boss is to recognise their motives and help them to get where they want to go. The chances are that they will remember you when they are finally in the role that they have been chasing. Another important point is to find a way to give your opinion about the boss because your judgement may be at stake. If your opinion of the boss is not known, you may be seen as approving and supporting his behaviour and attitude but it is also important that you do not appear disloyal or overly critical. It may be possible to craft a story so that people recognise that you understand and recognise how your boss is behaving without appearing overly critical. For example, it may be possible to say "Fred has been Fred for a very long time" or "It is what it is. I recognise that Fred is managing up and is primarily concerned with his career progression." Finally, focus on your own relationship-building skills. This type of boss will often make enemies up and down and across the organisation because most people resent others who appear to act primarily from self-interest. This is also the type of situation in which you need other career sponsors outside your immediate functional area who will look after you if the situation becomes difficult. It is important that you do not tie yourself to the boss's career too closely.

These may be the four boss types that are most common but there are many variations out there in the workplace. So what is your boss's particular combination of preferences, values and behaviours? How would you describe their motives? Do you understand all of their motivational factors so you can optimise the strategy for managing the relationship with the boss?

10.7: Career Management Strategies

Today's market features flat organisations that offer little room for organised vertical progression, which presents critical career-management issues. In today's world, it is unrealistic to believe that you can plan career pathways over a few decades. It seems that every generation needs to craft its own distinctive career journey. There is an art to moving ahead but, in a less predictable work environment, career progression may involve sideways moves, useful attachments and secondments, and acquiring the right kind of experiences and roles. Passive career planning was once the default option but it is now a very weak one: careers and jobs need to be invented, shaped and pursued in a systematic and logical way.

Career plans are usually retrospective rather than prescriptive

Many people mistakenly believe that every successful person had a well-formulated career plan but this is usually a workplace myth. However, cultivating career awareness is a different model and it is important to ask yourself four core questions:
- What kind of work do you find stimulating, inspiring and a good fit for your talents?
- What organisational opportunities are available or open to you?
- How can you develop or exploit these opportunities or create opportunities if none exist?
- How do you plan to exit the organisation if no opportunities appear forthcoming in the near future?

Career conversations with senior managers

These kinds of conversations do not happen by chance. The individual needs to take control where possible and enter the conversation with a clear sense that they have shared responsibility for shaping their career. They need to be able to talk about where they have added value in the organisation, how they want their job to grow or change, and they should attempt to package their career development needs in activities that the organisation will find useful. People having regular career conversations need to spend at least one day a quarter cataloguing skills, successes, learning and contribution to the organisation. This will allow them to communicate a concise summary of what they have added to the role and what they propose to bring to the role within the next 12 months.

In all career conversations, astute individuals understand that they have to make a business case for a move or for increased opportunities or responsibilities. They need to understand the following:

- Their skills, knowledge, experiences, motivations and values
- Their impact, where they have added value in the last 12 months
- A win-win offer of a new project, job, role or role extension
- The first suggested steps that might enable the change to happen.

Here are also some questions to consider when composing a career discussion and thinking about what topics to raise and discuss:

- What skills and knowledge do you want to acquire in the future?
- Which teams and individuals would you like to work with?
- Which projects or clients would be good for your development?
- Which of your career drivers or career motivations are not being fully satisfied?

- What will motivate you to improve and progress your work performance?
- How might you be able to reduce, pass or delegate tasks you find demotivating?
- What specific changes or different areas of responsibility can you suggest to improve your job?
- How can you communicate the benefits of these changes to your boss or employer?
- Who else do you need to convince to make change happen? What is the value in speaking with HR to explore other options from their perspective and contacts?
- What quick wins can you offer your boss or employer that will benefit the performance of the organisation?

Driving Career Progress

From a straightforward logical perspective, taking control of your career is an iterative process: you keep repeating the cycle of delivering evidence on progress made against agreed action plans; seeking feedback from a senior manager; taking away the feedback to work on; then scheduling a catch-up meeting in another three months, so that you can let the person know what progress you have made, get their feedback again and so on. This approach is undoubtedly the most successful way to take control and drive career progress, but guess what: hardly anyone does it in such a systematic and planned way!

Let's be clear. This approach is certain to give senior managers confidence that you are on an upward learning curve and it promotes the idea that you have the leadership mindset and attitude to take responsibility for managing your own career progression. As a consequence, others will believe that you will be able to demonstrate future leadership behaviours. The ability to manage the process in this planned way also sends a very positive message about your strategic perspective and your ability to be systematic and planned in relation to development issues. As a consequence, others are more likely to assume or believe that you will be similarly strategic in the way that you approach your leadership and talent-development roles.

Chapter 10 Key Summary Points

- Managing upwards is an extremely important process. Individuals will benefit from goodwill for long periods as a consequence of good upward, lateral and downward management.
- Your relationship with your boss can either help or hurt you as your profile can be embellished by association but it can also be damaged by association.
- It is important to get to know and understand your boss by finding out who they respect, what they value, and what behaviours and people they admire. Discover your boss's alliances and relationships so that you can understand how they work and identify a roadmap to navigate the organisation and where your boss has most influence.
- In any new role, create a good first impression by drafting a plan for the first 100 days. This should be a blend of purpose, success measures, strategy, focus and value propositions. This chapter presents a 100-day action checklist.
- It is important to understand what your boss thinks of you, how your boss describes you, what your boss values about you, how important you are to your boss's success and what your boss thinks that you need to improve.
- It is important to review the strength of your relationship with your boss and how to improve your communication with your boss, including a focus on headlining, succinctness, newsworthiness, analysis, evaluation and interpretation skills.
- An attitude modification is often required to improve the relationship with your boss. You may need to review your body language and the messages it sends. You may need to create a fresh attitude, make visible behaviour adjustments and compare your behaviour to the successful behaviour of other colleagues.

CHAPTER 10: MANAGING EXPECTATIONS

- This chapter offers some suggestions on how to manage different boss profiles: the insecure boss, the ego-driven boss, the control-driven boss and the career-driven boss.
- Finally, the chapter concludes with some advice on career-management strategies, career planning, career conversations with your boss and how to drive career progress.

Chapter 11

Networks and Reputation

"The most important single ingredient in the formula of success is knowing how to get along with people".

Theodore Roosevelt

"If I was down to my last dollar, I'd spend it on public relations".

Bill Gates

Chapter 11 Key Points

- Investing in relationships
- Key principles of building successful network relationships
- Understanding how network rapport works
- A purposeful networking model
- Networking discussion topics: So what do we talk about?

11.1: The Importance of Investing in Relationships

The power in any organisation is all about who you know

The exercise of power can only be understood as being conducted through social relationships. Well-connected people who know each other mix in the same groups at work. This is not based on official or formal arrangements but rather on subtle social relationships. Power tends to be exercised through a diverse network of people who have influence, and the ability to exercise power is often a function of who you know.

CHAPTER 11: NETWORKS AND REPUTATION

Networking is a critical skill for anyone who aspires to be an effective leader

The ability to network plays an important role in the success of any senior leader or manager. It is really important that you do not just manage upwards or downwards, but that you invest in relationships in all directions and at all levels. Networking is a critical skill for anyone who aspires to be an effective leader because networking is about building mutually beneficial relationships. Networks and relationships, both formal and informal, are very significant and powerful vehicles in a number of ways. Each networking opportunity has the potential to achieve the following:
- Information exchange
- Idea sharing
- Influence reach.

In this context, networks will also provide very clear hard benefits. Information from the network will provide a broad information base on which to make judgements and hopefully a person's decision making will reflect an improved capacity to factor in all mitigating variables. The network will also hopefully be used to share and exchange ideas and allow others to build on their ideas and so enrich future possibilities. Networks can also be used as sounding boards to boost confidence in any particular ideas and strategies that are being considered. In the future, therefore, networks should also accelerate faster turnaround of communications and ideas because people tend to respond much more quickly to emails from people they know well than to emails from people who they do not know so well. Finally, people with strong relationships at work tend to be happier and more productive.

The importance of quality and depth of network connections

Strong personal relationships in any organisation are essential if career progression is to be maintained. However, a common mistake in building networks is to focus on the number rather than the quality and depth of the connections. Leaders who build wide networks with no substance are in danger of ruining their reputation by being seen as political and acting out of personal self-interest.

Many networks also focus on the wrong structure by concentrating too heavily on the organisation's official hierarchy and ignoring possible benefits from informal connections. The network can then become overloaded with too many contacts and excessive interactions, and so becomes a bottleneck to progress. Another problem is that the network focuses on the wrong relationships. The network may focus on people who concentrate on safe issues and strategies, relying on colleagues who come from similar backgrounds, who reinforce existing biases and who will provide limited, narrow perspectives. Finally, the network may focus on the wrong behaviours and contacts may engage in superficial, surface-level interactions with as many people as possible.

Demonstrate curiosity about other people's roles

A good starting point for building any individual relationships is to demonstrate strong personal interest in other people and a curiosity about their roles in the organisation, and to search for mutual benefit and organisational gain from on-going contact as a part of each other's network. The development of strong working relationships requires significant investment of time in asking questions, listening well, sharing ideas, showing willingness to help and adding value to the other person. All these investments can be seen as deposits that will generate 'relationship credit'. Relationships will obviously be damaged if you appear driven by self-interest, manipulative, opportunistic, defensive, uncooperative, uneven tempered, unnecessarily critical, pessimistic or negative in your tone and attitude. Another key point is that relationships need to be developed and grown well before you actually need something from another person. The relationships that work best are those based on an attitude of developing a mutually beneficial long-term relationship rather than what one person can get from another at a specific moment in time.

CHAPTER 11: NETWORKS AND REPUTATION

Networking and political savvy

Describing someone as 'political' is often an insult, in that it is associated with negative ideas like self-promotion, manipulation and scheming. However, it is possible to redefine 'political' as influential or, charmingly and more prosaically, as having savvy. Savvy is being streetwise, knowing how the organisation works and how to get things done.

Good and skilful networkers are politically savvy because savvy managers know who's who. They can work out the real structure within the organisation and those who truly hold power and influence. Among the organisational politicians, it is possible to distinguish between the good guys and the bad guys. The 'political good guys' tend to be open, ethical, well liked and to have an impact beyond their immediate functional area. The 'political bad guys' tend to be manipulative opportunists with short-term aims, driven by self-interest. The good guys who are politically savvy build bigger networks, develop strong bonds of trust with useful colleagues and share agendas. The savvy politicians map the organisation – they know that X can be persuaded through Y, they know what the real agendas are and they can see through the various smokescreens that exist in any organisation.

The political bad guys differ in a very big way. They tend to be narcissistic, egotistical, selfish self-promoters who may thrive in the short term but who are generally found out in the end. The corporate sociopaths tend to be self-centred and self-focused but they can often be well educated, suave and good looking. However, what characterises them is not so much their strategy as their motives, evidenced in the way they see, use and exploit others.

Finding the right level of conversation

In networking discussions with senior managers, an important point is to pitch the conversation at the right level. It is important to avoid any self-focused conversation or becoming too granular or too narrow about specific functional detail issues. Try to focus on more wide-ranging and cross-functional issues that may have more relevance for the senior management population.

Small talk with senior managers who are not well known to you can be difficult and so it may be helpful to consider the different responses generated from cognitive or emotional types of questions. For example, it is one thing to ask a senior manager about what they have been doing in relation to a specific objective, but it is another type of question to ask them how they feel about what they have been doing, how satisfied they are with the progress that has been made, how confident they are that future progress will be maintained or whether planned objectives will be achieved. If you are able to use a more meaningful question that generates a more authentic feeling-based response, then you have moved closer to being seen as a confidante and a trusted team member – one with whom it is worth investing time discussing organisational issues.

It is incontestable that an aspiring leader needs to be able to master small talk, to be comfortable giving short responses about what they have done and what they can offer, and to ask meaningful questions that will be of interest to someone at a senior level. The ability to have a give-and-take exchange of views will demonstrate a confidence and comfort with discussing issues at a senior level. This will provide opportunities to build rapport and create a positive and warm feeling about having future similar meetings or discussions.

11.2: Key Principles of Building Successful Network Relationships

There are five key aspects of building any successful networking relationship at work.

Genuine respect: It is important that you try to think the best of other people and recognise the value in them regardless of their position. You should try to treat people respectfully for the role they perform irrespective of their level of seniority.

Use of questions: It is important to learn how to ask multiple questions and to show curiosity and interest in the other person's work agenda. You must demonstrate that you value the other person's perspective and point of view. The focus here is the use of multiple questions: one or two questions can be asked as part of a formal routine and so it is only multiple, deeper, probing questions that will succeed in conveying real and genuine interest in the other person.

Understanding and empathy: It is always important to take the time to listen and understand what others are saying. It is important to show that you can walk in the shoes of other people and try to experience their challenges and their difficulties. Demonstrate listening by periodically attempting to summarise their point as an expression of showing that you have listened and understood.

Trust and candour: It is important to encourage others to talk openly and honestly about what they feel, as the strongest links are often found when people care enough to say what they really feel about an issue as opposed to sharing a logical account of events.

Positive intent: It is important to become a rewarding person to deal with by demonstrating an optimistic and positive outlook on events. If you can approach issues with the belief that a solution can be found, and if you can see the opportunity ahead of the problems, then people will want to spend time with you and will value your company more. People who network less efficiently may have a transactional approach to relationships, focussing on the immediate practical benefits of collaboration that serve their best interests in the short term rather than developing a long-term relationship that is looking for a win–win outcome of benefit to both parties.

11.3: Understanding Networking Rapport

In a networking context, 'rapport' usually refers to a harmonious relationship in which two people understand each other's feelings and ideas and can communicate well. However, despite good intentions, not everyone is good at building rapport and the lack of this skill will severely limit networking opportunities. Here are four common mistakes.

Trying to be too nice to people: This can be a problem if it leads to an avoidance of real and honest communication. In such circumstances, rapport can then actually break down, as the content of the message can lack weight, colour and authenticity. Under these circumstances, people will lose respect and stop paying attention to the other person's views and opinions.

An overuse of positive language: In order to build rapport, it is important to appear interesting and as someone to whom it is worth listening. However, whilst it is good to be positive, if everything is 'great' and 'lovely', then nothing is great or lovely. In order to introduce meaning and interest, language needs colour and differentiation.

Trying too hard: If someone is a little too pushy, wants to be liked too much or moves too quickly, we tend to back off. In order to avoid being seen as needy, the best tactic is to build some rapport then back off a little, then build a little more rapport and back off again. If you come across as a little desperate in trying to build the relationship, you trigger what is known as the 'law of reversed effect' in that, the harder you try to do something, the more likely it is that you will fail.

A lack of genuine interest: A lot of communication between people actually happens on a non-verbal, even unconscious level and so, if you appear bored or uninterested in another person's agenda, problems and issues, they are most likely to respond to your signals by shutting down, getting annoyed or just losing interest in the conversation. The solution is to use questions with follow-up back-up questions, convey genuine curiosity about the other person and demonstrate an unconditional respect for them.

11.4: A Purposeful Networking Model – Who Should be Included?

In summary, there are seven considerations to help you determine who should be included in your network.

1. **Be selective about network size:** An effective network group ideally ranges in size from around 12 people, all of whom should have a specific purpose for being included. It is a good idea to classify your relationships by the benefits that they provide, which typically fall into one of five basic categories:
    - Information suppliers to help with decision making
    - Opinion shapers who can accelerate and ensure the implementation of decisions
    - Broad strategic perspective to ensure appropriate focus
    - Political support from potential career sponsors
    - Personal support for personal development.
2. **Ensure a diversified group:** The network group should include diverse range of people from other functions, divisions or geographies who can share best practice, provide different perspectives and inspire new and innovative thinking.
3. **Look for reciprocal benefits:** In the network group, it is important to identify whether or not there are reciprocal benefits in having a network connection. It is important to assess whether the network connection has a positive,

energising effect and to ensure that the group includes those people who see opportunities, are prepared to challenge situations and are trustworthy and committed to principles larger than their self-interest. By contrast, de-energisers are quick to point out obstacles, criticise people rather than ideas, tend to be inflexible in their thinking, fail to create opportunities and don't show concern for others.

4. **Include people who can help to fast-track professional goals:** Think about how you can connect your network to your professional goals. Write down three specific organisational or personal results you hope to achieve over the next year and identify people who could help you with them, whether as a result of their expertise, control over resources or ability to provide political support and influence.
5. **Connect with potential career sponsors:** Connect with some powerful people who can provide informal mentoring, political support, potential career sponsorship, and influence and help in your career.
6. **Connect with people who can provide personal developmental feedback:** Connect with people who are able to give personal performance feedback, challenge your decisions and push you to be better.
7. **Connect with people who can be a sounding board and offer support:** Connect with colleagues who can provide support, energy and help to get you back on track when you are having a bad period.

11.5: Networking Discussion Topics – So What do we Talk About?

One of the great ways of using networks is to sample the opinion of different people and seek their views on specific issues. If you are then able to say that 80% of the people you have consulted share a particular view, it provides terrific credibility in any discussion in which you are trying to influence another party. In many ways, recording data from networking discussions is the most important element of managing the network.

Recording network conversations requires a great deal of self-discipline. However, if the views, opinions and perspectives offered by members of the network are recorded on different specific issues and topics, then it will be easier to use the data constructively to influence, broaden your perspective or act as a catalyst for new ideas. As an illustration, the following headings might be useful to keep in mind when having a discussion with senior colleagues in your network:

Performance satisfaction levels: To what extent are you satisfied with current performance levels from your function and team? Are expectations being met? To what extent are you confident about meeting future expectations? To what extent are there any team, performance or process issues that are causing concern?

Organisation priorities: What are the organisation priorities for you and what do you think is currently most important for the organisation?

Best practice ideas: What is working well for you in terms of quality, service, delivery, technical, performance or team issues? Are there any opportunities to share best-practice ideas?

New opportunities/threats: Are there any new ideas, opportunities or threats being discussed in relation to strategies, products, service, teams, delivery or feedback from competitors or customers that we should be addressing?

Reciprocal feedback: What is working well and what is not working so well between us and our teams? Where are the key opportunities to improve what we do? Can we share a couple of things to focus on?

Future meetings: What common ground exists between us and what shared interests, values or priorities have been uncovered that imply that on-going contact would be mutually beneficial?

Chapter 11 Key Summary Points

- It is very important to invest in relationships at all levels and in all directions as the power in any organisation is all about who you know.
- Networking is a critical skill for anyone who aspires to be an effective leader. Networking has clear hard benefits in terms of information exchange, sharing ideas, influence reach, aligning resources to a common purpose, and providing a broad perspective to improve the quality of judgements and decision making.
- It is highly important to focus on the quality, range and diversity of network connections rather than numbers.
- Successful networkers are able to demonstrate curiosity in other people's roles and will search for mutual benefit in the interests of both parties as well as the organisation.
- It is important to pitch conversations in network relationships at the right level for senior managers. Evaluative and analytical types of statement and question can be more impactful than routine fact-based statements and questions.
- The chapter describes five key principles for building successful network relationships: conveying genuine respect; using multiple questions; showing understanding and empathy; providing trust and candour; and demonstrating positive intent.
- Understanding the nature of rapport in a network relationship is crucial as people are prone to make a

CHAPTER 11: NETWORKS AND REPUTATION

number of mistakes, such as: trying to be too nice, overusing positive language, trying too hard and lacking genuine interest in the other person's agenda and issues.
- The chapter describes a purposeful networking model with seven considerations to help you decide who should be included in the network: restricting network size, ensuring a diversified group, establishing reciprocal benefits, identifying people who can help to fast-track professional goals, connecting with people who can provide potential career sponsorship, connecting with people who can provide personal development feedback, and connecting with people who can act as a sounding board and offer support in difficult times.
- Finally, the chapter offers some suggestions on discussion topics with the network group, and how to use and consult with your network to sample the opinion of different people to provide weight to any particular cause or strategy that you are seeking to promote or influence. Other discussion topics may include: performance satisfaction levels, organisation priorities, best-practice ideas, new opportunities and threats, reciprocal feedback on personal or team performance, and shared interests to justify future meetings.

Chapter 12

A Final Thought – Working with a Coach to Enhance Reputation and Personal Brand

"Let him who would move the world, first move himself".

Socrates

"If you are under the impression that you have already perfected yourself, you will never rise to the heights you are no doubt capable of".

Kazuo Ishiguro, *The Remains of the Day*

"Happy are they who can hear their detractions and put them to mending".

William Shakespeare, *Much Ado about Nothing*

Chapter 12 Key Points

- Working with a coach for marginal gains
- Key attributes of those who will benefit most from coaching
- Five benefits of working with a coach
- The five key ingredients of a successful coaching engagement

CHAPTER 12: A FINAL THOUGHT

12.1: Working with a Coach for Marginal Gains

I began this book with the objective of seeking to clarify how reputations are formed, how reputation can be enhanced and damaged, and how you can take control of your career by building a future-orientated personal brand. Throughout the book I have offered many tips, guidelines and suggestions on how we can act and behave in order to enhance our reputation and personal brand in the process. In concluding this book, it may be useful to consider how we can all benefit from working with an independent coach to help us raise our game, seeking the marginal gains that can differentiate us from other like-minded players in our professional or functional domain.

The power of making a coaching relationship public

Although it may initially seem counterintuitive, the great leaders or great players can significantly enhance their reputation by publicly demonstrating that they are continually looking for ways to strengthen and improve their performance. The idea of working with a coach sends a message to colleagues that the person who wants to be coached has a self-improvement mindset and that they are always seeking to learn and improve. So what you see today may not be what you see tomorrow and the assumption will be that the person is on a learning curve and will always be 'getting better'. When the author worked as a leadership coach with the CEO of a leading FTSE 100 company, the CEO made a point of publicising that he was working with a coach. He was sending the message that, whilst he might be the 'top man', he would only stay that way if he used the available resources of a coach to challenge his thinking, his relationships, his ways of managing people, his strategies and his use of time.

In the context of personal development, there are many different development methods to choose from. Historically, leadership development has involved a workshop, training course, business course or a specific event. However, the most potent and successful form of individual development is arguably about engaging in an on-going coaching relationship.

Helping leaders to stay at the top of their game

The key purpose of coaching is to help senior leaders play at the top of their game and to maximise their effectiveness. Coaching is essentially a journey of exploration aimed at unlocking a person's potential to optimise their performance and the coaching process is designed to ensure that an individual's energies are fully committed to achieving both personal and strategic goals. The holy grail of coaching is to help people to learn and uncover new insights about themselves in relation to their impact and to use these insights to guide, steer and drive their behaviour for the rest of their life. The essence of coaching, therefore, is to help individuals to learn about themselves, and to help them to learn new ways of thinking and behaving to achieve optimum success in their lives.

Key attributes for those who benefit most from coaching

There are three essential behavioural attributes required by those who will benefit most from coaching. Firstly, the individual needs to be open-minded, curious, willing to accept feedback and prepared not to put limits on what they can achieve. Secondly, the person must be improvement-orientated, and interested and stimulated in acquiring more knowledge, desiring to grow and looking for ways to do things better. Thirdly, the individual must enjoy the introspective and reflective process, and be motivated by the challenge to become increasingly self-aware about personal assets, attributes and opportunities to do things better or differently.

Psychologist or non-psychologist coach?

It should be noted that the coaching profession is still unregulated, which does mean, unfortunately, that there are no official requirements or qualifications to become a coach. Potential clients thus need to be very careful to establish that their coach is suitably qualified, competent and experienced. In considering whether to work with a psychologist or a non-psychologist coach,

CHAPTER 12: A FINAL THOUGHT

it is worth bearing in mind that most of the tools, techniques, strategies and theories underpinning a successful coaching intervention are drawn from the psychology discipline. Working with a coaching psychologist or leadership coaching psychologist, therefore, provides the reassurance that the science of psychology will be applied in a professional, compassionate and insightful way. The coaching psychologist will draw upon psychological knowledge, especially in the fields of intrapersonal states, interpersonal communication, social interactions, power dynamics, cognitive processes and emotional intelligence, and without conveying to the individuals concerned that they are involved in a psychological process.

Many coaching psychologists will have obtained a postgraduate master's or doctorate degree and will be able to offer an explanation and evidence for applying specific techniques and strategies in a coaching relationship. Using a specialised coaching psychologist will ensure that professional practices are delivered to an appropriate standard under the auspices of a regulated professional organisation.

12.2: Six Different Benefits of Working with a Coach

Coaching can offer six main benefits to help a potential leader realise their potential and become as good as possible in terms of what they want to do and what they want to achieve.

Self-awareness: Firstly, coaching will help to increase their level of self-awareness, uncover blindspots and identify the behaviours that need to increase, start, stop or change.

Skill acquisition: Secondly, the person being coached may want to learn new skills and behaviours, and to understand the meaning and expectations of leadership.

Leadership reputation: Thirdly, the person being coached may want to develop their leadership profile, gaining a better understanding of how their reputation has formed and how it can be further developed, as well as how they can shape a personal brand to better engineer the achievement of future goals.

Focus and prioritisation: Fourthly, the person being coached may want the coach to help to focus their thinking, time and energy on those things that optimally need and deserve their attention, and how they can maintain clarity of purpose and thinking in spite of the distraction of everyday work pressures.
Sounding board: Fifthly, the person being coached may want to use the coach as a reflective sounding board to enable the person to step back and take a wider and longer term view of an issue. They may want help to pause and reflect, without getting caught in the trap of spontaneous reaction or reactive busyness.

Psychological safe place: Sixthly, the person being coached may want a psychologically safe space in which they can confidentially share concerns. This can help them maintain their energy and focus in the face of day-to-day pressures, and confront and support their private struggles to gain the necessary growth through which to add value to the organisation. The coaching framework can enable the client to talk through their personal issues with someone who has no organisational or career-advancement agenda.

There are several reasons why coaching is such a powerful technique. Firstly, everyone has self-awareness and self-knowledge limitations and most people lack an accurate appreciation of the impact of their own behaviour, and of their reputation and personal legacy. Secondly, most people struggle to embrace the notion of incremental performance and marginal gains, and so there is limited understanding about the relative possibilities of incrementally improving their personal performance. Thirdly, most people lack awareness of what great or good looks like in specific situations or roles, and so their understanding of behavioural possibilities in different roles is usually limited. Fourthly, most people lack awareness in terms of how their performance will be evaluated and assessed when moving from a transactional producer or performer to a senior executive or senior-level leader.

12.3: The Five Key Ingredients of a Successful Coaching Engagement

If you plan to work with a coach, there are five things to understand to ensure that you get the best return on your investment:

1. **Purpose:** It is important to be clear as to the purpose of the coaching relationship and what you want to achieve. What differences would you like to see at the end of the coaching engagement and what consequences would you expect to see as a result? However, clear specific goals need not be set at the start of an assignment as coaching is essentially a journey of exploration to find the best ways in which an individual can improve their performance, progress their career, and find a more satisfying and fulfilling working life. Setting clear or over-defined goals at the outset can produce a narrow focus and blind people to other possibilities. The coaching assignment is the opportunity to challenge existing assumptions and models, and to think outside of the box about ways of doing things differently. The achievement of a tangible objective is a limited outcome unless some new learning or new insights have occurred that enable the individual to replicate the performance in other situations with other task challenges. The specific tangible goal achieved will become history very quickly; it is the new learned insight that is the most important long-lasting success indicator.
2. **Stakeholder engagement:** It is important to get key colleagues involved in the process as the best results are achieved when colleagues provide input at the beginning

and conclusion of the programme. This allows you to use colleagues to measure observed progress.
3. **Time investment:** It is important to be prepared to work outside of the meetings by implementing agreed action plans, researching ideas and issues discussed, and seeking to integrate new insights into your typical behavioural patterns, attitudes and philosophies.
4. **Coach feedback:** Coaching should be a dynamic relationship between two individuals, so it is also important to engage in regular dialogue with the coach to enable them to help you in the best possible way. As a consequence, it is important to give feedback to the coach if they are doing something helpful, if you would like them to change focus or if you prefer them to be engaged in different ways.
5. **Maintaining a progress journal:** Maintaining a written record and analysis of your personal performance and progress is very powerful to help you think through and assess behavioural changes in a structured and focused way. An unwritten goal is only a wish. Writing down goals cements our commitment to them. Written long-term goals and daily to-do lists cause us to be proactive and planning helps us to think ahead as to what we want to accomplish rather than going through each day in a reactive mode, responding to whatever comes along and getting distracted from our long-term goals. The chances of acting on something increase if we write down specific plans, and the chances of making progress will also increase if we share with others or make a public statement about what we intend to develop. If we do not write things down, they don't seem to have the same weight and importance.

And finally...

I hope that this book has helped you to gain some new ways of thinking about your career, about how so many psychological factors come together in the way that reputations are formed, and in the way that reputations are damaged. I also hope that some of the ideas discussed will help you to develop a powerful personal brand that in turn will help to create a more exciting future of learning and success in whatever career path you choose to follow.

Chapter 12 Key Summary Points

- In conclusion, the author advocates working with an independent coaching psychologist to enhance the prospect of building a positive reputation and personal brand that differentiates you from your colleagues or other candidates who may be aspiring to similar roles.
- The key attributes for those who will benefit most from coaching are to be open-minded, curious and improvement-orientated, and for those who enjoy the introspective process to search for marginal gains.
- Coaching offers six main benefits to help leaders realise their potential: increasing self-awareness; skill acquisition; building a powerful reputation; ensuring that there is focus and prioritisation on the key issues; acting as a sounding board to broaden their perspective and improve the quality of their decision making; and providing a psychologically safe place to discuss concerns, anxieties and any situations that dilute confidence.
- The nature of a successful coaching assignment is discussed with reference to five key principles: agreeing the purpose of coaching; inviting stakeholders to engage with the process by offering feedback; investing significant time to implement action plans and research ideas discussed; providing feedback to the coach on a regular basis; and maintaining a written record of action plans and achievements.

Chapter Notes

Chapter 1

1. Zukav, G. (2001) *Dancing Wu Li Masters: An Overview of the New Physics.* Bravo Ltd.
2. Sidney J. Harris (1917–1986) was born in London but lived most of his life in the USA as a journalist and drama critic for the *Chicago Daily News*. He made frequent use of aphorisms in his writing, like the quote in Chapter 1.
3. Wilson, T.D. (2002) *Strangers to Ourselves.* Harvard University Press.
4. Mabe, P.A., and West, S.G. (1982) 'Validity of Self-Evaluation of Ability: A Review and Meta-Analysis'. *Journal of Applied Psychology*, 67, 280–96.
5. Thornton, G.C. (1980) *Psychometric Properties of Self-Appraisals and Job Performance. Personnel Psychology.* Wiley Online Library.
6. Amiel, H.F. (1989) *Amiel's Journal.* Create Space Independent Publishing Platform.
7. Goldsmith, M. (2010) *The Success Delusion.* Available at www.marchall-goldsmithlibrary.com.
8. Dunning, D., and Kruger, J. (1999) 'Unskilled and Unaware of It. How Difficulties Recognising One's Own Incompetence Lead to Inflated Self-Assessment'. *Journal of Personality and Social Psychology*, 77(6), 1,121–34.
9. Dunning, D. (2005) *Self-insight: Roadblocks and Detours in the past to knowing thyself.* New York: Psychology Press.
10. Bartlett, F. (1932) *Remembering: A Study in Experimental and Social Psychology.* Cambridge University Press.
11. Conway, M., and Ross, M. (1984) 'Getting What You Want by Revising What You Had'. *Journal of Personality and Social Psychology*, 47(4), 738–48.

Chapter 2

1. Tetlock, P.E. (2002) *Social Functionalist Frameworks for Judgment and Choice: Intuitive Politicians, Theologians, and Prosecutors.* Psychological review, 109: 451–7.

CHAPTER NOTES

Chapter 3

1. Burns, R. (2011) *The Complete Poems and Songs of Robert Burns*. Waverley Books Ltd.
2. Ross, L., and Ward, A. (1996) *Naïve Realism in Everyday Life: Implications for Social Conflict and Misunderstanding*. In T. Brown, E. Reed and E. Turiel (eds), *Values and Knowledge* (pp.103–35). Hillsdale, NJ: Lawrence Erlbaum.
3. Loftus, E.F. (2003) 'Make Believe Memories'. *American Psychologist*, 58, 864–73.
4. Festinger, L. (1957) *A Theory of Cognitive Dissonance*. Stanford, CA: Stanford University Press.
5. Heider, F. (1958) *The Psychology of Interpersonal Rel*ations. Wiley. New York.
6. Kelly, G.A. (1957) *The Psychology of Personal Constructs*. W.W. Norton New York.
7. Tversky, A., and Kahneman, D. (1974) 'Judgement under Uncertainty: Heuristics and Biases'. *Science*, 1,124–31.
8. Kahneman, D. (2011) *Thinking Fast and Slow*. Penguin Group.

Chapter 5

1. Eliot, T.S. (1950) *The Cocktail Party*. Penguin Group.

Chapter 6

1. Gladwell, M. (2008) *Outliers. The Story of Success*. Penguin.
2. Syed, M. (2010) *Bounce. The Myth of Talent and the Power of Practice*. Fourth Estate.
3. Dweck, C. (2006) *Mindset: The New Psychology of Success*. Random House.
4. Jung, C.G. (1971/1921) *Psychological Types*. London: Routledge.
5. Tichy, N., and Bennis, W. (2007) *Judgment: How Winning Leaders Make Great Calls*. Portfolio Books.
6. Clayton, M. (2010) *Smart to Wise*. Marshall Cavendish Business.

Chapter 7

1. Furnham, A. (2010) *The Elephant in the Boardroom. The Psychology of Leadership Derailment*. Bracknell: Palgrave MacMillan.
2. Furnham, A. (2014) *Bullies and Bastards*. London: Bloomsbury.
3. Owen, D. (2012) *The Hubris Syndrome*. Methven Publishing Ltd.
4. Bennis, W. (2003) *On Becoming a Leader*. Perseus Books.

Chapter 8

1. Goldsmith, M. (2005) 'Expanding the Value of Coaching'. Published in Morgan, H., Harkins, P., and Goldsmith, M. (2005) *The Art and Practice of Leadership Coaching*.

Chapter 9

1. Glenn, J., and Walker, R. (2012) *Significant Objects. Extraordinary Stories about Ordinary Things*. Fantagraphics.
2. Purkiss, J., and Royston-Lee, D. (2009) *Brand You: Turn Your Unique Talents into a Winning Formula*. Artesian Publishing.
3. Sperber, D., and Wilson, D. (2012) *Meaning and Relevance*. Cambridge University Press.
4. Oppenheimer, D. (2006) 'Problems with Using Long Words Needlessly'. *Applied Cognitive Psychology*, 20(2), 139–56.

Further Reading References

The list below is a small selection of books that may be of interest to the reader as useful guides for further exploration of some of the ideas referenced in this book.

Part 1: Reputation – Rhetoric versus Reality

Beeson, J. (2010) *The Unwritten Rules*. San Francisco: Jossey-Bass.

Goldsmith, M. (2007) *What Got You Here Won't Get You There*. Profile Books.

Kahneman, D. (2011) *Thinking Fast and Slow*. Penguin Group.

Komisarjevsky, C. (2012) *The Power of Reputation*. New York: Amacom.

Rosenzweig, P. (2008) *The Halo Effect*. Simon & Schuster UK Ltd.

Rosenzweig, P. (2007) *The Halo Effect and Eight Other Business Delusions that Deceive Managers*. New York: Free Press.

Part 2: How Reputations are Won and Lost

Bensley, D.A. (1998) *Critical Thinking in Psychology: A Unified Skills Approach*. Wadsworth Publishing Co Inc.

Carlin, J. (2012) *Nelson Mandela*. Verlag Herder.

Dweck, C. (2006) *Mindset: The New Psychology of Success*. Random House.

Goleman, D. (1996) *Emotional Intelligence: Why it can matter more than IQ*. Bloomsbury Publishing.

Thaler, D., and Sunstein, S.R. (2008) *Nudge: Improving Decisions about Health, Wealth and Happiness*. Penguin Group.

Part 3: Building and Maintaining a Personal Brand

Clark, D. (2013) *Reinventing You: Define Your Brand, Imagine Your Future*. Harvard Business Review Press.

D'Amour, C. (1997) *Networking: The Skill the Schools Forgot to Teach*. Sage Creek Press.

D'Souza, S. (2007) *Brilliant Networking: What the best networkers know, say and do.* London: Prentice Hall.

Monarth, H. (2010) *Executive Presence: The Art of Commanding respect Like a CEO.* New York: McGraw-Hill.

Purkiss, J., and Royston-Lee, D. (2009) *Brand You: Turn Your Unique Talents into a Winning Formula.* Artesian Publishing.

Watkins, M. (2003) *The First 90 Days: Critical Success Strategies for New Leaders at all Levels.* Boston: Harvard Business School Press.

Appendix: Sixty Ways to Build Reputation Capital

In most organisations, there is usually an 'official' leadership competency framework that unfortunately tends to exclude the real criteria used by senior managers to make important career and promotion decisions about promising talent in the business. Transactional successes are often transient and short lived. The following 60 'behavioural labels' are examples of informal language and soundbites often used by senior managers to make decisions about an individual's career. This information is frequently hidden or not shared with the individual, who may thus be relatively ignorant about how their career is being assessed and evaluated.

These behavioural labels are typically used in relation to four distinct areas of leadership in which all aspiring leaders need to demonstrate high levels of capability. These areas are:

- **Operational delivery and execution** to achieve business efficiency and financial success
- **Strategic, idea leadership and decision making** to grow a function or business
- **Team leadership** to optimise the contribution from the team
- **Stakeholder impact** to achieve functional alignment and cross-functional influence.

OPERATIONAL DELIVERY AND EXECUTION

1. **"Taking ownership":** Successful leaders must be prepared to take decision-making responsibility for their functional area without the need for excessive consultation with senior managers.

2. **"Personal risk taking"**: Successful leaders need to be confident in making judgements and decisions in their area of responsibility without the need for approval or reinforcement from senior managers, and they need to understand that avoiding risks is itself risky.
3. **"Managing grey"**: Successful leaders need to learn how to manage 'grey', to try to avoid the default option of wanting only tangible targets and outcomes, and to learn how to be more conceptual in their thinking.
4. **"Analysing and not just reporting"**: Successful leaders need to avoid the trap of just 'reporting and recording' on business performance, instead focussing more on analysing, evaluating and interpreting to better communicate the significance of particular results.
5. **"Leaving an intellectual footprint"**: It is important that successful leaders do not let the work of their team merely pass through them without taking the opportunity to put their own intellectual mark on it. In other words, they should have a value-add contribution to make to sharpen the offerings of their team.
6. **"Focusing on the right things"**: Successful leaders need to make choices, pick their priorities and decide where and how they should focus their thinking, time and energy.
7. **"Structure and organisation"**: Successful leaders need to be sufficiently structured and organised to demonstrate their capacity to manage a larger area of responsibility and several direct reports.
8. **"Hands-off management style"**: Successful leaders need to be sufficiently hands-off to demonstrate that they are able to manage through others and will not gravitate to their 'doing' comfort zone.
9. **"Planning for the unexpected"**: Successful leaders do not suffer from planning bias, which assumes that everything will go to plan, but instead prepare contingency plans for the unexpected.

10. **"Speed of assimilation"**: Successful leaders are good students who ask the right questions and process a lot of information rapidly in order to better understand and make a decision.
11. **"Collaborating for results"**: Successful leaders learn how to work with others for the greater good rather than self-interest.

STRATEGIC AND IDEA LEADERSHIP AND DECISION MAKING

12. **"Strategically curious about competition"**: Successful leaders need to learn to signal their interest in understanding their competition, market environment and different perspectives. This will convey a strong inquisitive curiosity and learning attitude.
13. **"Trusting their judgement":** Wisdom or sound judgement is a function of intellectual breadth and depth, so successful leaders need to demonstrate their ability to see a range of different perspectives and they need to have the ability to dig beneath the surface to understand the meaning of particular situations.
14. **"Intellectual edginess/critical thinking":** Successful leaders should have a strong capacity for critical analysis as it is indicative of a good intellectual mind to be able to identify opportunities for growth, development, improvement or change in other people and situations.
15. **"Idea/thought leadership":** Successful leaders are often seen as idea leaders, so all leaders need to learn to use networks to facilitate the emergence of new ideas. Purposeful networking provides the opportunity for issues, information, insights and ideas to be exchanged. Future leaders are frequently those individuals who can identify shared ideas from a number of colleagues and align themselves to these ideas.
16. **"Maintaining a realistic perspective"**: Successful leaders need to avoid appearing to have a skewed

judgement due to optimism bias. Credibility is often a function of the extent to which one appears to have a realistic, practical and pragmatic perspective.
17. **"Being an innovator":** Successful leaders use networks to connect with other people to explore issues, ideas, information and new insights.
18. **"Clarity of purpose":** Successful leaders need to keep a clear sense of purpose front-of-mind amidst all the everyday pressures of their work environment.
19. **"Healthy scepticism":** It is important that successful leaders have a healthy dose of scepticism to challenge the status quo and cultural norms, and to ensure that they do not fall victim to complacency.
20. **"Being opportunistic and strategic":** Successful leaders can manage the apparent contradictions between being strategic, on the one hand, and responsive and adaptable on the other, able to respond quickly to entrepreneurial opportunities.
21. **"Creating the future":** Successful leaders try to think ahead and anticipate how to stay one step ahead of the competition.
22. **"Fuelling innovation":** Successful leaders are always thinking about how to encourage others to think about how things might be done differently and try to create new and better ways of doing things.
23. **"Acting globally":** Successful leaders think about the big picture and how their actions will impact on others in different functions and areas.

TEAM LEADERSHIP

24. **"Capacity for insightful behavioural analysis":** Successful leaders must have the ability to be insightful about people in the way that they identify personal attributes to spot and recruit talent and in the way that they seek to upgrade and develop talent.
25. **"Exploring consequences of behaviours":** Successful leaders need to have the capacity and skill to move on

from describing identified behaviours and explore the positive and negative consequences of certain behaviours.

26. **"Reputational legacies":** Successful leaders will understand how the consequences of certain behaviours will enhance or diminish the reputational legacy that will drive or derail their career.
27. **"Attracting followership":** Successful leaders are able to attract followers, who will then usually have an emotional link with the leader, because they respect certain characteristics, because they feel that they want the individual to succeed or because they are emotionally inspired by the leadership actions of that individual.
28. **"Acting the part":** Successful leaders need to learn that when they transition from being a transactional operator to a producer/leader, the key focus will now be on leadership behavioural skills rather than technical transactional skills.
29. **"Setting direction":** Successful leaders will be able to communicate clearly where the team is going and how it will get there.
30. **"Creating the right climate":** Successful managers are very aware of the importance of creating the right climate for team members to give of their best.
31. **"Managing performance":** Successful leaders will have some system in place to monitor and assess performance formally. This system will focus on how tasks have been achieved as well as what tasks have been achieved.
32. **"Delegation and empowerment"**: Successful leaders need to learn the skill of successful delegation and empowerment to grow and develop people who can contribute more.
33. **"Stretching talent"**: Successful leaders need to learn to focus on what they can do to help people, up-skilling team members and helping them to be better at what they do.

34. **"Leveraging talent"**: Successful leaders seek out talented people and mentor them, providing signposts on how they need to develop from a behavioural perspective.

STAKEHOLDER IMPACT

35. **"Adopting multiple flexible influencing strategies"**: Successful leaders need to be skilful at understanding the intellectual challenge of how to influence others and need to learn how to use multiple influencing strategies.
36. **"Being a collegiate team player"**: Successful leaders need to understand that good leaders are frequently seen as altruistic in their consideration of others, and in their desire to act and behave in a way that will be of most value to their team colleagues and organisation.
37. **"Being socially intelligent"**: Successful leaders are expected to have good social skills so that they are able to build easy rapport with their colleagues, thus making themselves approachable and easy to communicate with.
38. **"Being emotionally intelligent"**: Successful leaders need to learn to read situations so that they respond appropriately in meetings and in interpersonal situations.
39. **"Having likeability"**: Successful leaders need to learn that an important factor for any leader is to be likeable. People naturally gravitate towards a likeable leader. Likeability inevitably produces a halo effect, in that a likeable leader will be seen as similarly competent in a range of different areas.
40. **"Demonstrating courageous integrity"**: Successful leaders need to be prepared to stand up and be counted for a particular point of view. They must be prepared to be assertive and opinionated if they observe that organisational values have been transgressed.

41. **"Balancing humility with confidence":** Successful leaders need to learn not to overreact or take themselves too seriously, and to communicate the importance of benefitting from the views and contribution of other colleagues in the business.
42. **"Being trustworthy":** Successful leaders are seen as authentic and trustworthy. It is important that they achieve a balance in their language as any desire to be excessively positive or negative will dilute the authenticity of their judgement.
43. **"Avoiding good news messaging":** Successful leaders try to be positive and upbeat. However, if they are seen to gloss and spin their judgement in an overly positive way, they will lose credibility as others start to correct for this, discounting their judgements.
44. **"Self-awareness":** Successful leaders must be able to assess their own abilities accurately, so that their colleagues can place more confidence in their judgement in relation to other people or situations.
45. **"Stretch appetite for personal growth"**: Successful leaders need to learn to convey an appetite for personal stretch by agreeing to seek regular feedback. They should be prepared to draft written personal-development plans to convey robustness and credibility to what they believe they have achieved.
46. **"Executive presence"**: High potentials need to learn how to create a presence by using questions to bridge between different views, by using questions to facilitate and explore differences of opinion, and by learning to summarise, hide detail and say less with more impact.
47. **"Credibility"**: Successful leaders need to learn how to act like a senior player, in that having very high volumes of personal work only emphasises a lack of delegation, a lack of good team structure or that they are staying too transactional or staying too long on tasks. It is not a good message if the 'business is managing you' rather than 'you managing the business'.

48. **"Gravitas"**: Successful leaders need to learn how to do the right things in the right situations, to follow the role model of certain senior managers, to learn how to speak with gravitas at management meetings and not to appear defensive in response to feedback.
49. **"Executive maturity"**. Successful leaders will model the core values and expect to be told if they veer away from them because they know that their reputation is based on perceptions of their character.
50. **"Sharp, short messaging"**: Successful leaders need to learn how to deliver sharp, short messages tailored to their audience. This shortness implies that they have exercised good judgement in identifying what is key and important for that audience.
51. **"Being simple but not simplistic"**: Successful leaders understand the skill in providing memorable takeaways that will resonate and grab attention.
52. **"Demonstrating passion":** Successful leaders need to learn how to convey passion in a positive, optimistic and constructive way by using appropriate language rather than 'acting out' in either positive or negative ways.
53. **"Showing respect":** Successful leaders need to learn to show that they value others' opinions and, by extension, that they value the other person.
54. **"Personal character and integrity":** As well as possessing integrity and honesty, successful leaders are warm, caring, humble and confident. They may also have the skill to tell leadership stories to demonstrate authenticity and hard-earned lessons that can include mistakes, recoveries, persistence and perseverance to reinforce desirable values.
55. **"Paradoxical thinker"**: Successful leaders are paradoxical thinkers who can hold two opposing ideas in their mind and can see possibilities and opportunities because they do not let their thinking be confined to 'either/or' decisions.

56. **"Being outgoing and sociable as well as being a good listener":** Successful leaders are socially engaging but they ask questions about the other person, actively listen and show interest in the other person's life, their job, and their views and opinions.
57. **"Insatiable curiosity":** Successful leaders want to understand why and they keep poking until they discover the essence of an issue or problem.
58. **"Stakeholder management":** Successful leaders recognise that decisions are not solo affairs and that all ideas and new approaches need to be considered and honed by all the effected parties. The refining of a potential solution or changes to a proposed idea are best done informally and face-to-face as all ideas can be improved by the input of others.
59. **"Seeing relationships as the glue and the grease":** Successful leaders recognise that relationships are the key to getting things done. As a matter of course, they will reach out, connect and create warm personal bonds to develop trust and commitment.
60. **"Differentiating a conflict of ideas from a conflict of relationships":** Successful leaders understand that an intense focus on relationships can lead to conflict avoidance. Mature leaders have learned to differentiate between a conflict of ideas and a conflict of relationships so that they can constructively address problems while maintaining positive relationships.

Milton Keynes UK
Ingram Content Group UK Ltd.
UKHW021356220823
427292UK00034B/446

9 781911 450627